Sociology Transformed

Series Editors
John Holmwood
School of Sociology and Social Policy
University of Nottingham
Nottingham, UK

Stephen Turner
Department of Philosophy
University of South Florida
Tampa, FL, USA

The field of sociology has changed rapidly over the last few decades. Sociology Transformed seeks to map these changes on a country by country basis and to contribute to the discussion of the future of the subject. The series is concerned not only with the traditional centres of the discipline, but with its many variant forms across the globe.

Naum Trajanovski

A History of
Macedonian Sociology

In Quest for Identity

Naum Trajanovski
University of Warsaw
Warsaw, Poland

ISSN 2947-5023   ISSN 2947-5031   (electronic)
Sociology Transformed
ISBN 978-3-031-48868-9   ISBN 978-3-031-48869-6   (eBook)
https://doi.org/10.1007/978-3-031-48869-6

This Palgrave Macmillan imprint is published by the registered company Springer Nature Switzerland AG.
The registered company address is: Gewerbestrasse 11, 6330 Cham, Switzerland

Paper in this product is recyclable.

I dedicate this book to my grandma, Elena, who spent her professional career administering for some of the names appearing the most in the text. Her work and commitment, as well as that of her colleagues, is most certainly embedded in the achievements of Macedonian sociology.

LIST OF MAPS

Map 1   The Balkan Peninsula in 1914

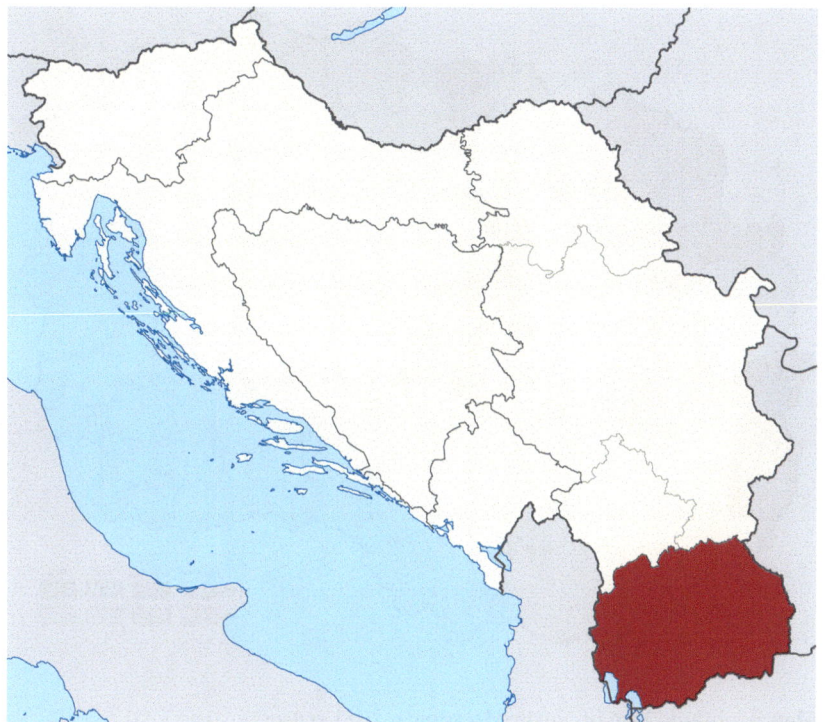

Map 2   Macedonia in socialist Yugoslavia, 1945–1991

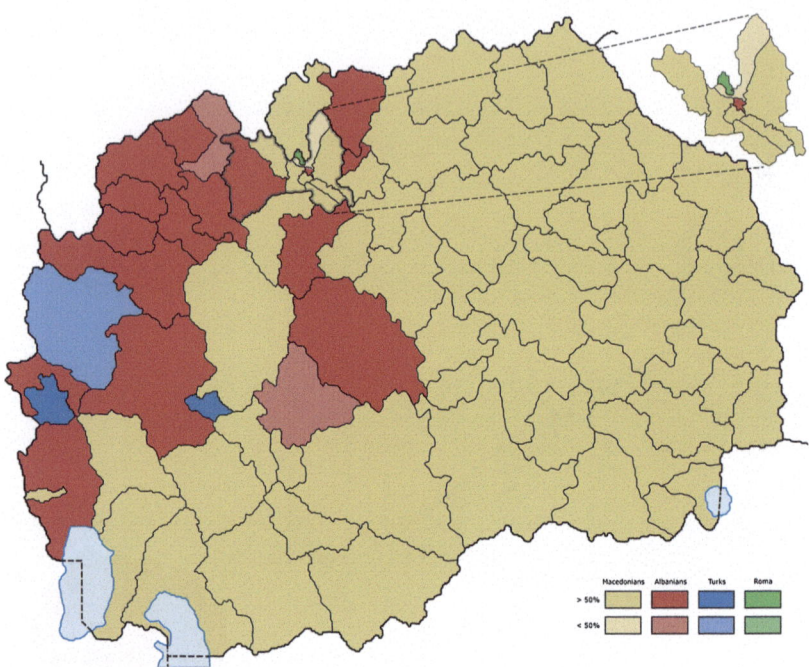

Map 3 Ethnic Map of North Macedonia, 2021 census

ACKNOWLEDGMENTS

First and foremost, I would like to thank Professor Marta Bucholc for her inspiration to write this text and her incredible support all the way to its completion. I am very much indebted to Professors Ivana Spasić, Marian Niezgoda, and Ljupčo S. Risteski who provided me with information and feedback of paramount importance. The final version would not be the same without the insights of Professors Karolina Bielenin-Lenczowska and Jolanta Sujecka, as well as the comments of Wiktor Marzec, Darko Leitner-Stojanov, and Petar Todorov. To all of them, I am beyond grateful.

I would also like to extend my sincere thanks to a number of experts and professors—Anna Engelking, Lidija Georgieva, Mirjana Maleska, Mimoza Nestorova-Tomić, Emilija Simoska, Vlado Kambovski, Konstantin Minoski, Ali Pajaziti, Ilo Trajkovski, and Stefan Troebst—from whom I learned much about various episodes of the history of the Macedonian sociology during the past several years. Indeed, as a postgraduate sociology student in Budapest and Warsaw coming from North Macedonia, I was very interested in certain episodes of Macedonian intellectual history, including sociology and sociologists, before the idea of compiling a more comprehensive review grew on me. One such episode which kept me academically busy for two years was the first large-scale social study conducted in post-earthquake Skopje in the mid-1960s by a team of Polish and Macedonian experts, for which I received a generous research grant from the Polish National Science Centre in 2019 (2019/33/N/HS3/02209).

A large portion of the materials for this text was gathered during the past few years, especially in the course of the duration of the above research grant. Here, I would like to acknowledge the help of the librarians and archivists in North Macedonia—most notably at the Skopje-based Macedonian Academy of Sciences and Arts, the Institute of Sociology, the Institute for Sociological, Political and Juridical Research, the Institute of History, the Institute of Geography, the Faculty of Law "Iustinianus Primus," and the National and University Library "St Clement of Ohrid"—the Vera and Donald Blinken Open Society Archives in Budapest, the Library of the Leibniz Institute for the History and Culture of Eastern Europe in Leipzig, the Jagiellonian Library in Kraków, the Library of the Łódź University, and Warsaw's National Library and the Archive of the Polish Academy of Sciences' Institute of Philosophy and Sociology. I am also immensely grateful to Dora Bojanovska Popovska, Elena Mujoska Trpevska, Ivana Hadžievska, Katerina Kolozova, Adela Hîncu, Kire Šarlamanov, Dejan Donev, and Goran Kitevski who helped me obtain data and materials.

I would like the express my gratitude to the organizers of the conference "Sociological perspective on contemporary post-Yugoslav societies," which took place in late May 2023 in Belgrade, for the opportunity to present a segment of this text to a very well-informed public. I also extend my thanks to the academic and ancillary staff of the Centre for Advanced Study in Sofia and Tchavdar Marinov, for agreeing to host the first discussion of the book in the late spring of 2024.

Finally, I would like to thank my family and friends for all the support needed to prepare one's first monograph in English.

All the shortcomings in the text are exclusively mine.

Author's Note

All the wording pertaining to Macedonia is used in accordance with the 2018 Prespa Agreement between Greece and the Republic of Macedonia.

The transliteration from Macedonian Cyrillic to Latin script is per the ISO/R9: 1968 system. I used the same system to transliterate from Serbian and Bulgarian Cyrillic alphabets. All the translations to English in the text are mine, if not stated otherwise.

Several other linguistic aspects bear political connotations and demand upfront clarifications. Such is the case with the surnames of some of the figures active in the interwar period when the Slavic Macedonian vernacular was not yet standardized. Many of them Macedonianized their surnames after the Second World War, usually changing the suffix -*ić* to -*ski* or -*ov*. Moreover, some of them kept the -*ić* form in its Macedonian version -*iḱ*. Others published under Serbo-Croatian transcription of their names and surnames in the early post-war period (sometimes even in Macedonian). For the sake of consistency, I decided to stick to their own articulations of their names and surnames as per the published materials in different periods, in the majority of cases in their authorship. I believe that this approach is more informative as it allows the reader to grasp both the factual situation and the individual decisions, while I certainly refrain from implying any ethnic or other sort of affiliation.

A similar situation involves the surnames of the non-Macedonians in the book. In several obvious cases, I kept the Serbo-Croatian and the other original transcriptions; nonetheless, I provided the Macedonian transcriptions of their surnames if they were published in Macedonia. Hence, some authors might appear with two versions of their surnames in the body of the text, as references, and in the list of references.

Praise for *A History of Macedonian Sociology*

"Due to their contextual closeness to the many varieties of post-1945 Marxism-Leninism—Stalinism, Maoism, Trotskyism, Titoism, etc. —social sciences under state-socialism carry with them mixed blessings: On the one hand and exactly due to this proximity, they offer ample career chances in the political realm. Yet, on the other hand, any deviation from the (currently) "correct" ideological line by scholarly arguments contains the risk of severe sanctions. This the more so when class ideology is blended with ethnic nationalism(s), as in the Macedonian case. Here, sociologists like economists, political scientists and members of the legal profession were needed by the ruling communists to prove that their ideology-based politics provided the desired results in the form of a socialist society, economy, law and culture. But at the same time critical academic theories and research-based findings were suppressed—as were their authors. A major result of Naum Trajanovski's meticulous analysis is the striking professional "universality" of Macedonian sociologists and other social scientists when it comes to the field humanities, in particular with regard to historiography and institutions of historical research. Due to their ideological corset, sociologists were obviously considered to be more reliable than historians when it came to the politically correct interpretation of Macedonian national history as the basis of Macedonian national identity. This pioneering study on the three periods of Macedonian sociology—pre-1945, state-socialism, and post-communism—amply demonstrates the critical potential of the discipline under changing political conditions as well as its fixation on what still may be called a "Macedonian Question.""

—Stefan Troebst, Professor Emeritus of East European
Cultural History, *Leipzig University, Germany*

"This meticulously crafted book invites you to explore the vicissitudes of Macedonian sociology. Delving into carefully reconstructed historical contexts and theoretical frameworks, it unveils the transformations of Macedonian social thought based on extensive original data. A unique resource for researchers and students, the book spans over a century of intellectual history in a compelling scholarly narrative."

—Marta Bucholc, *Professor of Sociology, Faculty of Sociology,*
University of Warsaw, Poland

"Synthesizing a large amount of diverse data, Trajanovski skillfully weaves the threads of history of a national sociology in the periphery of Europe. The book has something to offer to not only those working on the region of South East Europe, but also those interested in the history of ideas, especially the role of social scientific expertise in modernizing projects, as well as the contribution of intellectuals to nation-building, in the context of actually-existing socialism and postsocialist transformation."

—Ivana Spasić, *Professor of Sociology, Department of Sociology, University of Belgrade, Serbia*

"The book focuses on three issues—the history of sociological reflection (theoretical and empirical) in Macedonia, the dependence of social sciences on political climate and decisions, and how contemporary Macedonian sociology tried to become independent as a field of research and an academic discipline. It is mapping out the ways in which the University of Skopje tried to offer sociology courses to students of various faculties (geography, law, medicine) and simultaneously to create a field of sociological studies and research units. I was also reminded about my Macedonian colleagues and their efforts to go beyond Macedonia to overcome the sense of peripherality. They used the contacts within scientific organizations such as ISA and ESA, networks of francophone researchers, participation in research networks in the Balkans, and finally, organizing international sociological scientific conferences. That is why Naum Trajanovski's book is worth paying attention to and reading."

—Marian Niezgoda, Professor Emeritus of Sociology, *Institute of Sociology, Jagiellonian University, Kraków*

"The writing of a history of Macedonian sociology is far from an easy task. The historical turbulences and the (ongoing) contestations of the Macedonian nation and language make it immensely hard to map the continuities of the national sociological thought, and the selection of the relevant topics, people, and institutions which contributed to its development. As a professor in political sciences and a former senior researcher at the Institute for Sociological, Political and Juridical Research in Skopje, as well as a direct witness and participant in the democratic transition of the state and the region, I see Trajanovski's book as a unique and timely contribution to the history of Macedonian sociological ideas."

—Mirjana Maleska, *Professor of Political Sciences, School of Doctoral Studies, University of Ss. Cyril and Methodius Skopje, North Macedonia*

"Naum Trajanovski's book *A History of Macedonian Sociology: In Quest for Identity* provides a well-informed, analytical, and amazingly seamless history of Macedonian sociology. He neatly frames the Macedonian sociological developments in the 20th and the early 21st century as a continued pursuit of a disciplinary identity tightly connected with the deliberations about the groupist identities in the Macedonian society in formation."

—Ilo Trajkovski, *Professor of Sociology, Institute of Sociology, University of Ss. Cyril and Methodius Skopje, North Macedonia*

CONTENTS

ABOUT THE AUTHOR

Naum Trajanovski an adjunct at the Faculty of Sociology at the University of Warsaw, holds a PhD in Sociology from the Polish Academy of Sciences. In the past few years, he has coordinated a research project about the history of the social survey in post-earthquake Skopje (1964–65) and authored and edited books about Macedonian and Balkan sociology and politics of memory.

Abbreviations

AFŽ	Antifašistički front na ženite na Makedonija (Anti-fascist Front of the Women in Macedonia)
ANOK	Akcionen narodno-osloboditelen komitet (Action for the National-Liberation Action Committee)
ASNOM	Antifašističko sobranie za narodno osloboduvanje na Makedonija (Anti-Fascist Assembly for the National Liberation of Macedonia)
INI	Institut za nacionalna istorija (Institute of National History)
IS	Institut za sociologija (Institute of Sociology)
ISPPI	Institut za sociološki i političko-pravni istražuvanja (Institute for Sociological, Political and Juridical Research)
JUS	Jugoslovensko udruženje za sociologiju (Yugoslav Sociological Association)
KPJ	Komunistička partija na Jugoslavija (Communist Party of Yugoslavia)
KPM	Komunistička partija na Makedonija (Communist Party of Macedonia)
MANU	Makedonska akademija na naukite i umetnostite (Macedonian Academy of Sciences and Arts)
MRO	Makedonska revolucionerna organizacija (Macedonian Revolutionary Organization)
NNSG	Nastavno-naučna studiska grupa (Educational and Academic Study Group)
ORD	Ohridski ramkoven dogovor (Ohrid Framework Agreement)
PMF	Prirodno-matematički fakultet (Faculty of Natural Sciences and Mathematics)

SDSM	Socijaldemokratski sojuz na Makedonija (Social Democratic Union of Macedonia)
SKJ	Sojuz na komunistite na Jugoslavija (League of Communists of Yugoslavia)
SKM	Sojuz na komunistite na Makedonija (League of Communists of Macedonia)
SND	Skopsko naučno društvo (Skopje Scientific Society)
UKIM	Univerzitet "Sv. Kiril i Metodij" Skopje (Ss. Cyril and Methodius University in Skopje)
VMRO	Vnatrešna makedonska revolucionerna organizacija (Internal Macedonian Revolutionary Organization)
VMRO-DPMNE	Vnatrešna makedonska revolucionerna organizacija – Demokratska partija za makedonsko nacionalno edinstvo (Internal Macedonian Revolutionary Organization – Democratic Party for Macedonian National Unity)

CHAPTER 1

Introduction: In Quest for Identity

Abstract This chapter introduces the subject matter by providing a thematic and conceptual overview of the study. I commence by outlining my approach against the two prevailing modes of historicizing Macedonian sociology. The historical account starts with the late nineteenth-century proto-sociological thought pertaining to Macedonia, which was both recognized as such by Macedonian sociological scholarship and informed the sociological developments in the upcoming years. The interwar period is discussed by focusing on the Faculty of Philosophy in Skopje as an epistemic circle formatting the ways of thinking, writing, and discussing the social reality in Macedonia. The chapter ends with a brief overview of the research in and beyond Skopje before the Second World War that resorted to sociological argumentation in challenging the officialdom positions.

Keywords Macedonia • Sociology • Proto-sociology • Skopje • Epistemic circle

STUDY OVERVIEW

What constitutes a Macedonian sociology? The straightforward answer pertains to the Macedonian language, declared official by the end of the Second World War, codified and standardized in its immediate aftermath in the Democratic Federal Macedonia, and ever since being the official

© The Author(s), under exclusive license to Springer Nature Switzerland AG 2024
N. Trajanovski, *A History of Macedonian Sociology*, Sociology Transformed, https://doi.org/10.1007/978-3-031-48869-6_1

language during its Yugoslav and socialist (1945–1991) and post-Yugoslav and post-socialist history (since 1991). It was also one of the three official languages of socialist Yugoslavia since its inception in 1945 up until its violent dissolution in the early 1990s. Therefore, the corpus of works in Macedonian dealing with sociological and quasi-sociological topics from 1944 to 1945 up until the present can certainly be grasped as a methodological and idiographic whole, together with the relatively short but ardent institutional history of sociology in (North) Macedonia.

There are different interpretations as to the beginnings of Macedonian sociology, however. The earliest and most prevalent patterns of historicizing Macedonian sociological thought, starting from the 1950s, traced it back to several "proto-sociological" authors, activists, and circles from the late nineteenth century, all of them articulating the "uniqueness of the Macedonian people [and] their cultural features" (Minoski and Petkovska 2017). A few historical sociology studies found the embryonic intellectual "movement of the Macedonian national consciousness" in activists from the late eighteenth and early nineteenth centuries (e.g., Milosavlevski 1992, 74–137). This sort of reasoning about Macedonian sociology is therefore more far-ranging as it designates as Macedonian all the attempts to "sociologize" Macedonian nation- and state-building and, most frequently, the national particularities and imaginaries of its dominant group of ethnic Macedonians. From this standpoint, the qualifying criterion is the discursive content and the sociopolitical aspirations, rather than the language(s) in which they are delivered, be it in some of the regional or European ones or even the local non-standardized vernacular.

On the other hand, the first detailed chronologies of Macedonian sociology and sociological life are related to what the university professor **Petre Georgievski** (b. 1940) deems the "institutional phase" of Macedonian sociology, that is, the development of the organized forms of teaching and professionalizing sociological research in the course of the 1960s (Georgievski 1978; Josifovski and Kepevska 1978; Korubin 2000). The first such studies appeared in Serbo-Croatian, against the background of the emerging, in the 1970s, all-Yugoslav interest in the state's sociological heritage. Ever since, Georgievski established himself as the main authority in the history of Macedonian sociology: as of the 2000s, he started examining its "pre-institutional phases" (Georgievski and Gurovska 2003; Georgievski 2005), before embarking upon the task of tracing some of the earliest, pre-war sociological endeavors in Macedonia of the 1930s

(Georgievski 2011, 2012, 2021). These explorations eventually led him into locating the beginnings of Macedonian sociology back to the 1930s when the first Skopje sociological seminars were organized, in parallel to the fieldwork research of different, by and large sociological, aspects of the everyday life of the locals. In this reading, the pre-institutional phase of Macedonian sociology spans from the 1930s to the 1950s, in spite of the ideologically informed cut of sociology in its interwar configuration after the Second World War. The sociological threshold is thus the institutional and professional sociological activities and especially their venues, pinned down to Skopje and the fieldwork locations on the territory of the contemporary Republic of North Macedonia.

In this chapter, I discuss the two historicizing patterns as emic modes of reflecting upon the origins and the temporal scopes of Macedonian sociology. I start by reviewing/contextualizing the main *proto-sociological thinkers* and sketching the history of their endorsements in the national sociological scholarship. I also let myself digress beyond their methodological nationalism and map out the references of Macedonia in proto-sociologists of other national domains in this section, as the local sociological thought during the interwar period ensued both owning to and opposing them. This approach of identifying the main "conjunctures" (Roudometof 2001, 29–32), but also borrowings between the national ideologies (Marinov 2009, 2013), is in line with the intellectual *histories croisées* of the Balkans. The cross-national intertwining of sociology and sociologists reappears in the subsequent phases, as well, having in mind the academic networks and infrastructures of the First (1918–1941) and Second (1945–1992) Yugoslavias. Specifically, I do not try to decouple the Macedonian sociological developments from them, as I find such a task ahistorical and misleading: they provided not only the state-institutional backgrounds, but also the coordinates of what is to be thought, discussed, and considered a sociological classic in Macedonia in the first place.[1] The national niche, therefore, will be traced against this very backdrop.

[1] Trajkovski observes this phenomenon as "the exogenous development" of Macedonian sociology, that is, driven by foreign motives, theories, and methodologies. As an illustration for the former, he notes that the work of the Slovene sociologist **Ante Fiamengo** (1912–1979) was for the Macedonian sociologists the cornerstone study, similar to what Robert E. Perk's *Introduction to the Science of Sociology* was for the American sociologists (Trajkovski 2000, 64–65).

As of 1920 and the formation of the Faculty of Philosophy in Skopje, social scientific research was initiated in a format that supported the Serbian hegemony in Macedonia, which was not recognized at the time either as a state or as a nation. In this chapter, I offer a reading of the Faculty as an epistemic circle formatting the ways of thinking, writing, and debating social scientific issues in interwar Macedonia. Moreover, the focus on the interwar Faculty and, in the next chapter, the Skopje University after its establishment in 1946 allows for an anatomization of parts of their institutional histories, the positions of officialdom, and the corresponding discourses produced by their academic associates. It also allows for an interpretative framework that postulates them as fields of struggle between the dominant and the alternative voices, as well as the epistemological continuities and discontinuities between the pre- and the post-war social scientific life. Highly significant, in this regard, is the resorting to several forms of sociological arguments and literature in proposing different theses about the local population, that is, their identities, political loyalties, and ambitions. I trace those "controlled transgressions" (Bourdieu 1984, 326) back to several local and foreign scholars active during the late interwar period. In the immediate post-war years, the transgressions would be mostly of an ideological rather than an ethnonational nature. Finally, against the set of arguments depicting the early communist blacklisting of Yugoslav sociology as an interruption of its pre-war life (e.g., Mitrović 1974, 1982; Kostic 1983, as well as Georgievski 2012), I discuss the regime change in Macedonia as extraordinarily porous in terms of sociological and social scientific methodologies and habits of observation.

The fourth chapter deals with the eventful 1960s, the peak of Yugoslav and Macedonian sociology. In this chapter, I provide the diachrony of the main events contributing to the institutionalization, the professionalization, and the "social innovation" (Mladenovski 1997, 3) of Macedonian sociology. I also propose a reading of the above operation as a process transcending specific events, stretching back from the first attempts at empirical sociological research in late 1950s socialist Macedonia to the set of several sociological exchanges from the late 1960s and the early 1970s which helped the national sociology to assume the label of a resolute scientific discipline and an undisputed scholarly discourse. No less important, in this particular period, were the cross-national sociological exchanges between the local and regional sociologists and the other non-dogmatic national sociologies. I focus on one such episode from the Macedonian mid-1960s to illustrate the potential of sociological knowledge transfers in socialist Europe and their significance for the national sociology. The fifth chapter discusses the period of the 1970s and the 1980s, which, although challenging for Macedonian sociology, appeared to be formative in two aspects: the completion of the sociological institutionalization instigated in the 1960s and the set of initiatives aimed at showcasing the inertia of Macedonian sociology. The final chapter deals with the sociological activities in the independent Republic of Macedonia from the 1990s up until the end of the 2010s. Unlike the previous chapters, this one puts less emphasis on details and shifts from examining biographical experiences, institution-building, and discourses to a rather panoramic review of Macedonian sociology in its newest era. I do zoom in, however, on the series of domestic exchanges pertaining to the prospects of Macedonian multiculturalism, which I find the most indicative of the recently dominant trajectories of producing and instrumentalizing sociological knowledge.

Macedonian multiculturalism can even be extrapolated back in time as a dominant sociological theme in all the periods covered in this text. In other words, the plethora of questions pertaining to the (multiple) ethnic identities, cultures, and interethnic relations drove the vast majority of this text's protagonists in their often lifelong intellectual quests. Those quests were by and large coterminous with the ideological and political currents of the day, therefore being both shaped and shaping Macedonian state- and nation-building. Up until the late 1970s, I argue, the above issue was predominantly seen through the lens of what might be depicted as historical sociology, although this paradigm was not employed as such up until the 2000s. More precisely, the majority of sociological discourses, from the proto-sociologists up until the so-called ethnogenesis debate, turned to late Ottoman economic politics and agrarian histories as well as past family and professional structures to argue different points about statehood and nationhood, but also about the modernization process and class history in the aftermath of the Second World War. With the deterioration of the interethnic relations in Yugoslavia and Macedonia—as of the late 1960s, culminating in the 1980s—the leading national sociologists got involved in the pressing debate about the state prospects and their politics regarding the ethnic and religious communities. In this very context, the last of the diachronic chapters suggests that the sociological training, knowledge, and initiative of a number of Macedonian social scientists appeared to be flexible and impartial enough to provide a set of constructive solutions regarding the state's democratic future.

In the long span of changing national borders and titular nations, I offer the above aspect as a key for reading the history of Macedonian sociology in a longer perspective, highlighting its continuous pursuit of a disciplinary identity in deliberating about group identities and their prospects. Up until the 1970s, the two major social scientific struggles related to Macedonia were about its integration into the Serbian ethnonational orbit and, after the war, into the Yugoslav Marxist-Leninist canon, now as an institutionalized Macedonian state and nation. Albeit common for socialist historiographies at certain periods (see, e.g., Verdery 1991; Kopeček 2012), the prevalence of the nation-building theme in a state socialist sociology can be postulated as a distinctive feature of the Macedonian case, a point already hinted at in the 1970s (see Sicard 1973). Hence, it might come as no surprise that the formative exchanges on national sociology sought to autonomize it by expressing its distinctiveness from the cognate historiographic and ethnographic discourses. As of the 1970s, however, the major sociological struggle pertained to its adjustment and eventual delineation against the political field of power.[2] After the collapse of state socialism in Macedonia, sociological knowledge production diffused in terms of funding, personnel, and organization; yet, as noted, the "multiculturalist" prospects remained a somewhat structuring feature, arranging not only the discursive exchanges but also the institutional schemes for sociological research.

This key is exclusive nonetheless, as much as it aims at providing a comprehensive overview of the national sociological development. Its exclusiveness stems from several apparent reasons. One such reason is my limited knowledge of some of the languages of North Macedonia's minorities, such as Albanian and Turkish. I tried to compensate for this deficiency by reviewing literature in other languages I speak and by consulting

---

[2] For a general overview of the developments in socialist Europe, see Brunnbauer et al. (2011), Hîncu (2018), and Trencsényi et al. (2018a, b); for an overview of the Yugoslav context, see Duller (2018) and Flere (1994).

relevant experts. The same goes for all the peculiarities of contemporary Macedonian sociology: by focusing on maps and patterns in a longer historical perspective, I certainly missed many relevant points. To those who might find themselves left aside, I apologize in advance. This is especially the case for the many different past and present sociological developments beyond the capital city of Skopje, which I strove to include as much as I possibly could.

"Proto-Sociologists"

The late nineteenth century saw massive political turmoil in the Balkans: against the background of the demise of the Ottoman rule in its European provinces, several anti-Ottoman uprisings striving for liberation arose in the region (1875–1876). In turn, Russia seized the opportunity and declared war on the Ottomans (1877–1878), seeking to recover its losses from the Crimean War (1853–1856) and to support, in the name of the already brewing Pan-Slavism, its "Slavic siblings" in the Balkans. As an ultimate result of the series of diplomatic attempts aimed at settling the so-called Great Eastern Crisis, the territory of Macedonia remained within the Ottoman Empire after the Congress of Berlin (1878), while Romania, Serbia, and Montenegro declared independence, and principalities of Bulgaria and Eastern Rumelia were given nominal autonomy under the Empire (an overview in Roudometof 2001).

The Congress, however, despite the major geopolitical redrawing of the Balkan borders and spheres of influence, ended up further galvanizing the nationalist aspirations of the new regional states. Hence, the territory of Macedonia, although not a unified administrative or geographical unit of the late Ottoman Empire, duly became subjected to what Macedonian sociology in line with the national historiography dubs *neighboring propaganda* seeking social and historical legitimization for eventual future territorial advancements (e.g., Taševa 1997). Its Slavic-speaking, predominantly Orthodox Christian population was thus considered to be either unconscious of its ethnic affiliation (*a-national*) or halfway through its realization as ethnically Serb, Bulgarian, or Greek (*nationalized*). As neatly demonstrated by Marinov (2009, 2013), the different standpoints bore opposite political resolutions to the "Macedonian question" championed by a vast network of competing actors on the ground.

The main agent campaigning against both the neighboring impositions and the Empire came in the form of a secret Macedonian Revolutionary Organization (MRO), established in Salonica in 1893, which operated under several names upon its formation. In its early phases, the Organization strove to mobilize the local population in the name of autonomy and a Macedonian political nation. Its crescendo was the 1903 Ilinden Uprising, which eventually failed to trigger regional and international responses and was left to be brutally suppressed by the Ottomans in the same year. The MRO mobilization was backed with the several-decade-long incubation of the idea of a Macedonian liberation resonating with the work of a number of local enlighteners. This period of initial scholarly interest in the distinct character of the Macedonian vernacular and community as a shield against the impositions, lasting from the mid-nineteenth to the early twentieth century, was hence noted to be the Hrochian "phase A" of Macedonian nation-building (Troebst 2001; Boškovska 2017).

The peak of this phase was embodied in two "proto-sociological" attempts to articulate the national "structure and physiognomy" (Zografski 1966, 6) of the people populating Macedonia based on sociolinguistic, cultural, and political observations. In the early 1870s, Ǵorǵija Pulevski (1817–1893) formulated the "earliest published expression of a separate Macedonian identity" (Friedman 2000, 182). An autodidact stone mason from Western Macedonia, Pulevski's worldview was shaped by his migrant working experience, his participation in the Bulgarian and Serbian liberations, and the multilingualism of the Ottoman Empire. He turned to writing two multilingual dictionaries including his native local Slavic Macedonian vernacular as a direct reaction to the proposal of the Eastern Bulgarian dialect as a basis for the future standard language of the Bulgarian state-project including Macedonia.[3] The 1875 trilingual dictionary of Slavic Macedonian, Albanian, and Turkish, all of them written in (Serbian) Cyrillic, contained his attempt at differentiating the Slavic Macedonian peoples starting with a depiction of all the locals as inhabitants of a separate "supra-ethnic and supra-religious" community of Macedonia (Sujecka 2013, 142–150). He then derived this understanding of Macedonian

---

[3] Pulevski managed to pull this off by sending the draft in Belgrade and depicting the local vernacular as a "S. Macedonian" on the book cover, which seemed to be an abbreviation for "Serbo-Macedonian" to the Serbian authorities. In the body of the book, however, the coinage "Slavic Macedonian" appears as a depiction of one of the people-nations (more in Fridman 2011; Sujecka 2013; Sonnenhauser 2020).

from the three cases he included in the dictionary, translated as "people-nations" (*narod*) by Jolanta Sujecka, supplementing his definition with kinship relations, ethnogenesis, shared customs, and culture. The full paragraph reads:

> A people-nation is when person of the same kin who speak the same language and who live and are friends with one another, and who have the same customs and songs, and joys, these persons are called the people-nation and the place where the people-nation lives is called the homeland of that people-nation.
> Hence the Macedonians are a people-nation and their place is Macedonia.
> (Puljevski 1875, 49; translated as in Sujecka 2013, 143)

The work of the ethnographer, folklorist, and historian **Krste Petkov Misirkov** (1874–1926) is standardized in the Macedonian historiography as a scientific continuation of Pulevski in its quest for national and political emancipation.[4] He spent the turn of the century years studying and working in Russia, where he founded the St Petersburg Macedonian intellectual circle in 1902 as a platform for producing unmediated knowledge about Macedonia. In the immediate aftermath of the Ilinden Uprising, he returned to Sofia to publish his book titled *Za makedonckite raboti* (On the Macedonian Matters) (end of 1903), which argues that the struggle for political autonomy must be matched with an intellectual (read non-violent) effort toward defending the national autonomy of the Macedonian population. He hence postulated a separate Macedonian nationality, the foundations of the Macedonian language (the book is written in what he considered to be its cornerstone idiom), and an independent Macedonian Church which is to "bolster [the] project for a Macedonian nation" (Maxwell 2007, 168; more in Misirkov 2003). The book was soon banned in Bulgaria to reemerge as the most prominent manifesto of Macedonian nationalism in the late interwar period. In the wake of the Second World War, its sociological significance was primarily read in historical-political (e.g., Zografski 1966; Miljovska in Katardžiev et al. 1976; Milosavlevski 1992, 94–98; Ristovski 1995) and sociolinguistic keys (e.g., Korubin

---

[4] Misirkov was much inspired by the circle of Macedonian immigrant intellectuals around the monthly *Loza* (1892–1894), who aimed at articulating the national prospects based on the ideas for cultural affirmation of Mazzini and Renan, among the others, as well as what was labelled "psycho-voluntaristic and intellectualist theories of the nation" during the Macedonian state socialism (see, for instance, Zografski in Katardžiev et al. 1976, 229–236).

1994; Miljovska in Korubin 2000, 10), while most recently, several Macedonian sociologists have highlighted Misirkov's modernist and constructivist understanding of the phenomena pertaining to the nation (e.g., Korubin 2005; Taševa 2021; Cvetanova 2022). Misirkov was also interested in other aspects of the everyday struggles of the locals, publishing articles about their economic deprivation and fast transformations of their traditional family units and communities pressured by the emerging modes of capitalist exchanges (Miljovska 1957). Finally, in the first (and only) issue of the journal *Vardar* which he edited and printed in Odesa, he provided a list of 120 villages based on his data and observations including information about their economic status, ethnic majorities (depicting them as Macedonians in all the relevant cases), and number of households (Risteski 2022).

This over-simplistic depiction of Pulevski and Misirkov is certainly short of many conjunctures of the late Ottoman rule in Macedonia. However, it might be assumed as clear that both of them built upon the local aspirations as well as the neighboring institutional infrastructures to seek openings for the embryonic Macedonian national program, albeit in different forms and contexts and based on different educational backgrounds. The immediate reach of their work was limited, as suggested, since the upper hand in the discursive appropriation of Macedonia remained within the domains of the competing and state-sponsored nationalisms of the regional states. Those narratives pertained to radically different scenarios for the local Macedonian population, however. After 1878 and the Austro-Hungarian takeover of Bosnia and Herzegovina, Serbia shifted its attention to Macedonia and soon assumed the best position in researching its territories, including its resources but also its peoples. The Serbian geographer, ethnologist, and "proto-sociologist" (Spasić et al. 2022, 13–14) **Jovan Cvijić** (1865–1927) emerged as the leading figure in this context, while he and his work will also be formative for interwar and post-war sociology in Macedonia, discussed in the next two chapters. Cvijić, a geographer trained in Belgrade and Vienna, was among the rare scholars granted the right to conduct fieldwork research in Ottoman Macedonia (for an overview, see Duančić 2020; Atanasovski 2019). In 1898 and 1899, he conducted a Humboldtian type of exploration in the region, equipped, at every point, with a group of up to 10 people and up to five horses (Peucker 1900). His reflections about the local population were first published in the early 1900s and further in the late 1910s, culminating in his *magnum opus* on the psychic characteristics of the South Slavs.

Cvijić advanced two major theses about Macedonia and its population. Against the above background, his earliest take sought to disentangle the Macedonian knot by repositioning it on empirically derived anthropogeographical data. He ended up differentiating the "Macedonian Slavs" as a "floating mass" with an "ethnic predisposition" to become either Serbian or Bulgarian (Cvijić 1906, 9). Their hesitant but eventual choices of one of the two options, according to Cvijić, were not informed by any historical or linguistic distinctiveness but relied upon the prospects for liberation offered by the two parties.[5] Cvijić "left" Macedonia for a while to return to it with a more elaborate methodological idea about typologizing the South Slavs. His Sorbonne lectures became the book *La Péninsule Balkanique* (Cvijić 1918) and summarized his 1910s work on the several ethnopsychological types and subtypes of the South Slavs shaped by geographical as well as historical, ethnographic, and social conditions. Here, he enlisted the Macedonian Slavs among the Central Balkan type, which, for instance, is more emotional and prone to suffering in comparison to the Dinaric type of Serbian proper. Drawing upon the folk traditions, he also observed that the Central type has a more developed lyrical affinity, as opposed to the epicism of the Dinaric type. This theory informed the post-war negotiations as well as the social, cultural, and political coordinates of the new Kingdom of the Serbs, Croats, and Slovenes (SHS, Yugoslavia as of 1929): a Yugoslav nation of three South Slavic tribes, each with its spatial distribution (Baskar 2020, 13). His method was soon recognized as a precursor of sociology in interwar Yugoslavia (e.g., Tasić 1938), while his anthropogeographic school remained especially relevant in interwar Macedonia, setting the tone of the local social scientific research. In this very context, the first sociological ventures in Macedonia appeared in Skopje as responses to Cvijić's work.

INTERWAR SKOPJE

The 1919 Paris Peace Conference, following the ceasefire of the First World War, brought, among others, a new redrawing of the political map of the Balkans. Despite the few initiatives of Macedonian circles calling for its unification and autonomy, the territory of Macedonia ended up divided among neighboring Greece, the newly formed Kingdom of SHS, and

---

[5] For instance, he argued about the local usage of Bulgarian as a synonym for Slavic throughout the history, without carrying any ethnic connotation (Cvijić 1906, 28–29).

Bulgaria, without much chance of voicing such proposals on the diplomatic table (Boškovska 2017, 10–13).[6] Its northwest region became part of the Kingdom of SHS, a state formed in 1918 (and internationally recognized in Paris) on the ruins of two distinct Empires, the Habsburg in the north and the Ottoman in the south. The formation of the Kingdom as well as the general decision-making at Versailles were much informed by ethnological visions and cartographic inputs (Wilkinson 1951). Cvijić, as already hinted at, was one of the main advisors of the Yugoslav delegation and the pivotal figure behind the negotiating efforts pushing "for more, rather than less territory for Yugoslavia" (Crampton 2006, 741). Together with **Tihomir R. Đorđević** (1868–1944), another Serbian scholar, they warranted the late nineteenth-century expansionist thesis of Macedonia as Old Serbia, or a historical Serbian land, hence instrumentalizing much of his pre-war writings for concrete political goals (Halpern and Hammel 1969; also see Georgevitch 1918).

Fearing disloyalty of the local population in the claimed region (now a state province, "South Serbia," consisting of north Macedonia and Kosovo, eastern Montenegro, and Sandžak in the north), the authorities installed what the then PM rendered a "strict but just regime" (Davidović in Jovanović 2021, 273). However, it unrolled as a *de facto* colonial state in the name of the ubiquitous policy of *Serbization* of the region.[7] The latter took several forms: from a reinvigoration of the pre-war Serbian colonization of the former Ottoman peripheries to suppression of the locals' cultural particularities, while the locals were predominantly denied political equality and representation. The authorities saw education as the "best and fastest" mechanism for accomplishing the integration of the locals into the Serbian *ethnie* (Jovanović 2011, 34). The very fact that the newly claimed region was the most undereducated in the Kingdom, with poor educational infrastructure and a severe lack of cadres, was thus grasped as a chance for its conversion-cum-instruction.[8] The *Tsarist city of Skopje* was reimagined to be the "model city" (Boškovska 2017, 160–161) of this agenda: the key institutions for its dissemination were established there, such as the "Museum of

---

[6] The two Balkan Wars (1912–1913 and 1913), which preceded the First World War in the Balkans, were also formative for the political aspirations and divisions in the region.

[7] Approximately two-thirds of the Yugoslav militia and gendarmes were stationed in Macedonia at one point in the mid-1920s. Boškovska's (2017) detailed historical account of the interwar period shows that there were different phases and tonalities of these politics.

[8] In 1912, there were only 800 teachers for a quarter of a million pupils in Macedonia (Obradović in Trouton 1998, 100).

South Serbia" and the Faculty of Philosophy, while the official politics of eradicating as many urban traces of the Ottoman past aimed at setting a blueprint for the other towns in the southernmost province.[9]

The Faculty of Philosophy in Skopje, the first tertiary institution established on the territory of today's North Macedonia, is of particular importance for the history of Macedonian sociology as we will see in this and the next chapters. It was founded in 1920 as a branch of Belgrade University, whose rector at that point was Cvijić.[10] He initiated the establishment of the Faculty in response to the urgent need to have a "strong center of our civilization" in Skopje (Cvijić in Jovanović 2011, 23), while he also got personally involved in this project by providing teaching materials and resources to its associates (Jovanović 1937, 1007; Duančić 2020, 28). The language of instruction was Serbian.

The Faculty led a double life during the interwar period, however. On the one hand, its carefully selected pool of associates performed the role of intellectual torchbearers of the Serbization agenda.[11] The very first and the only sociology instructor at the interwar Faculty in Skopje, **Prvoš Slankamenac** (1892–1952), provides a great example of its scope and politics. Before he arrived in Skopje, Slankamenac was a high-school teacher in an Orthodox Christian gymnasium in Serbia and an emerging right-wing thinker equipped with a doctoral thesis in the psychology of religion from Zagreb. He made a name for himself soon after with his book *Novi humanizam* (New Humanism)—co-authored with **Vladimir Vujić** (1886–1951), a mathematician and philosopher of Serbian origins appointed as a teacher in post-war Skopje—which was published in 1923, based on their Skopje lectures from 1922 (Josifovski 1968, 105–106; Milutinović 2011, 94–97). The book appeared against the background of the looming Yugoslav criticism of Western rationalism in science, culture, and philosophy—inspirited by European irrationalism and conservative thought, but also the Russian religious philosophy and various other invocations of Far East mysticism—and the emerging all-Yugoslav debate that sought to envision the cultural politics of the new state. In their book—which provoked vehement reactions, both positive and nega-

---

[9] The reference to *Tsarist* resonated with the historical episode of the imperial coronation of the Serbian monarch Stefan Dušan in Skopje in 1346.

[10] He was twice a rector of the Belgrade University: 1906–1907 and 1919–1920.

[11] As an illustration, by 1933, not one of the employees "from the dean to the house-keeper" was born in Macedonia. By 1939, only one assistant and a trainee librarian were locals (Boškovska 2017, 236).

tive—Slankamenac and Vujić articulated a rather Bergsonian and prag-matist argument in favor of a non-rationalist culture, a *new humanism*, supportive of the communal *élan vital* as a means of fueling its artistic genius and vernacular beliefs (Vujić and Slankamenac 1923).

The opportunity to build the Skopje Pedagogical Seminar from scratch and nurture its development as a sociology instructor appeared to be an ideal fit for exploring the practical potential of Slankamenac's project.[12] Already in the mid-1920s, from a position of docent, Slankamenac set forth his pedagogical ideas about schooling in the newly claimed regions: it should integrating instead of specializing scientific knowledge and championing the *national* (read Serbian) *form* it is embedded in (e.g., Slankamenac 1926b). He outlined a more extensive theoretical account of *university pedagogics* in his programmatic text published in Skopje in 1930. Drawing upon his vitalism, anti-intellectualism, and anti-modernism, his earlier theses against specialized education, and corresponding arguments pertaining to the German educational reforms of the 1920s, he sketched higher education as a bridge translating the "irrational social impact" upon individuals with a single goal of enabling their spiritual and social life within the unified national community (Slankamenac 1930, 273). Its functionality required new institutional configurations, continued Slankamenac, ones able to transmit the synthetized knowledge to different groups and for different purposes. Hence, the university should include open-to-the-public institutes *à la* Collège de France, but also academies for political and social sciences tailored for decision-makers. Herein, he saw the sociologists' capacities as instrumental since they, alongside philosophers and historians, hold a "particular gift for syntheses" (1930, 278). In this spirit, he promoted his model beyond academia, eventually harmonizing with the emerging Serbian cleronationalism centered upon the medieval religious figure, enlightener, and patron saint of the Serbs St Sava. For instance, in a 1935 speech of his in Skopje delivered at a commemorative event dedicated to St Sava, Slankamenac portrayed the *national life* as "a figure whose body is constituted of teachers" while "at their head is the sublime and magnificent person of St. Sava" (Slankamenac in Rohdewald 2022, 581).

---

[12] The rough approximation for the start of the sociology course is the turn of the 1930s. There were several sociological courses offered in Yugoslavia already in the mid-1920s. Moreover, a royal decree from 1931 required all the law departments in Yugoslav universities to include sociological chairs and courses (more in Spasić et al. 2022, 20).

The other life of the Faculty of Philosophy in Skopje resonated with the reactions provoked by those top-down initiatives. The authorities noticed certain manifestations of discontent as early as 1921 and used them as a pretext for demanding more finances to fight the "hostile element" in Skopje, that is, the already developed "form of student life" that "was distant from and alien to" the Serbian national ideals (Boškovska 2017, 236). And, indeed, up to the late 1930s, there were several attempts to close down the Skopje Faculty, among others, also due to the lack of visible success of its Serbization agenda. The politicization of the Faculty became even more evident after the ban of the Communist Party in 1921.[13] After the ban, the Faculty became a site for displaying the local political struggles, which, according to Georgievski (2005, XIV, also see Georgievski 1987), was a "latent function" of this institution that was even more important for the local community than its "manifest" one. It also pushed the local body of leftist student activists to become more vocal within its auspices, outnumbering and openly opposing the Serbian nationalist student circles by the late 1930s (Miljovska 1971, 101). The local aspirations came in other forms, as well.[14] The main animator of the

---

[13] In 1920, in the first parliamentary elections after the war, the KPJ won 38 percent of the total votes in South Serbia, constituting a quarter of all the communist votes in the Kingdom. The good turnout was justified with the general dissatisfaction with the other parties' treatment of the Macedonian issue, as well as the VMRO's left-wingers' support of the KPJ (e.g., Willemsen 2005). The KPJ initially opted for a communist Balkan federation; however, as of the early 1920s, this line started to be internally criticized. The breakthrough came in the form of a self-determination formula proposed in the 1924 pamphlet by **Kosta Novaković** (1886–1939), a KPJ activist and representative from the Skopje constituency, where he saw the agrarian as equal to the national question in Macedonia and called for its immediate autonomy (Novaković 1966; Zografski 1990).

[14] In 1927, the authorities claimed to have uncovered an underground network of the so-called Macedonian Youth Secret Revolutionary Organization at the Faculty, which allegedly cooperated with the Bulgarian-based VMRO, and purged approximately 70 of its members (more in Trajanovski 2021). It included one of its assumed leaders, **Dimitar Guzelev** (1903–1945), a philosophy student in Skopje at that point who was helping Nedeljković in his fieldwork during the mid-1920s (Nedeljković 1926, 182), discussed below in this section. Guzelev was sentenced to 20 years, but he was eventually expelled to Vojvodina in 1931 upon reactions from the League of Nations and banned from returning and working in Macedonia. He managed to defend his doctorate about Schopenhauer as a precursor of pragmatism and intuitionism in Zagreb in 1943, which can be read as Slankamenac's influence, albeit he does not directly refer to his Skopje instructor (Guzelev 1995). Guzelev was executed immediately after the Second World War as one of the main collaborators of the wartime Bulgarian occupiers.

leftist students was the young professor **Dušan Nedeljković** (1899–1984), a philosopher of Serbian ethnic origins holding a doctorate from the Sorbonne, who came to Skopje in 1922. A Bergsonian turned Marxist, Nedeljković not only engaged the students but also the majority of Yugoslav leftist teachers relocated in the Macedonian peripheries "as in a Yugoslav Siberia" (Nedeljković 1984, 5), for whom the Faculty became a hub. They were not exclusively leftist and Serbian, however. The local discontent with the regime epitomized in the peripheral Faculty in Skopje made it attractive for several other Yugoslav scholars who did not necessarily follow the Serbian political line. Such is the case, for instance, with **Ćiro Truhelka** (1865–1942), a prominent archaeologist of Croat origins with strong anti-Serbian views, who initiated the archaeology course at the Faculty of Philosophy in Skopje in the mid-1920s.

The official responses to the above contention came in several installments during the 1920s. All of them pertained to a particular social research scheme under the Cvijićist anthropogeographical legacy, already "canonized" in and beyond Yugoslavia (Duančić 2020, 222), with a single goal of providing supportive evidence without challenging the dominant interpretative framework. As early as 1921, the management of the Faculty inaugurated the "Skopje Scientific Society" [scr. *Skopsko naučno društvo*, SND] entasked to conduct cross-institutional and multifaceted research on South Serbia.[15] After the first few uncertain years, the SND leadership reorganized its structure and budget, which was now open for donations—the King donated several times during the 1920s—and generating membership revenue. The budget was spent on research, data collection, and publishing of a biannual scientific journal (as of 1925) and a book series (as of 1926; see Grujić 1924; Radovanović 1928). In the early 1920s commenced, as well, the Ethnological Seminar at the Faculty of Philosophy, initially led by the sociologically versed Đorđević, whose students were sent to the field to "gather materials about the peoples of South Serbia"

---

[15] The SND was also designed to be a "counterweight" of the Macedonian Institute in Sofia, founded in 1923 (Boškovska 2017, 237). Other circles in Sofia produced knowledge about Macedonia and opted for different political resolutions after the First World War. One of them was the leftist circle around the newspaper *Avtonomna Makedonija* (Autonomous Macedonia), while one of its main ideologists, **Vladislav (Slavcho) Kovachev** (1875–1924), articulated "the first clear conception of the Macedonian nation," deeming it a supranational political unity that unites the Macedonians with the other minority groups in Macedonia (more in Marinov 2013, 306).

(Radovanović 1929, 309).[16] Corresponding materials were gathered by
Petar S. Jovanović (1893–1957) and his disciples as early as the early
1920s; Jovanović was a former assistant to Cvijić in Belgrade who founded
the Geographical Seminar and the Geographical Society in Skopje, the latter as a branch of the SND. Finally, in 1929, on the occasion of the second
anniversary of the death of Cvijić, a group of Skopje-based students initiated the Geographical-Ethnographical Student Society "Jovan Cvijić"
intending to work "in the spirit of the great master and scientist"
(Radovanović 1929, 310).[17] Two scholars, **Jovan Erdeljanović**
(1874–1944) and **Vojislav S. Radovanović** (1894–1957), stood out during this period, both of them best encapsulating the rationale behind those
activities of "national interest" in Skopje, conducting anthropogeographical fieldwork to "once [and] for all and with utmost priority show the
whole scientific world the real ethnic character of our people in South
Serbia" (Erdeljanović 1928, 275).[18]

This pressing need not only informed the teaching, research, and academic publishing in interwar Skopje but also tilted the state-sponsored
social scientific research in an ethnopsychological direction, one that
assumedly delivers the sharpest answers about the *real ethnic character* of
the local population. Two cases are illustrative of those developments. The
first one resonated with the all-Yugoslav debate about the Yugoslav *psyche*,
emerging in the mid-1910s and getting into full swing in the 1920s. At its
peak, several prominent scholars saw the anthropogeographical methods
as insufficient for the articulation of the Yugoslav national profile and thus
started articulating different positions inspired by German *characterology*,
the French history of mentalities, and Pan-Slavism. In turn, this endeavor

[16] Roucek depicts Đorđević as one of the rare Yugoslav scholars who was well read in
"modern English ethnology" and "showed an understanding of the most important sociological problems of his field" (Roucek 1936, 984).
[17] In 1939, a decade later, an Ethnological Society was established in Skopje which started
to issue a journal titled *Etnologija* (Ethnology) as of January 1940. The society and the journal aimed at conducting "ethnic research of the South Slavs and the other non-Slavic Balkan
peoples" (Vukanović 1940, 180).
[18] Erdeljanović, who spent his student years in Berlin, Leipzig, and Prague, was actively
arguing against authors from and beyond the region (e.g., Gustav Weigand) who problema-
tized the Serbian *character* of the local Slavic population and language (see Erdeljanović
1925, 1926). Radovanović was both a chief curator of the Ethnographic Section of the
"Museum of South Serbia" and an instructor in anthropogeography and ethnology in
Skopje, and he served as a secretary of the SND as of 1925.

resulted in several theses reducing the cultural diversity of the Yugoslav psychological types to a single unity with racial underpinnings, backed, *inter alia*, with evidence of joint oral history and folk music tradition (Nedeljković 1938; Milutinović 2011, 87–111; Baskar 2020). Slankamenac published the most ambitious Skopjan take in this regard, in an SND issue from 1926. Drawing upon van Gennep's understanding of legends and especially the folk psychology of Wundt, he outlined a structural and comparative scheme of four local hagiographies about Yugoslav anchorites, based on written and oral accounts, as a means of tracing their "utilitarian character" in creating "social solidarities" (Slankamenac 1926a). Albeit his conclusions highlighted the reasons behind the gradual dropping of ethnic (as in Slavic) elements in the legends, the text primarily aimed at articulating a methodological opening of the redressed ethnopsychology to religious history and culture. This was certainly a novel approach in the local context, albeit not necessarily new *per se*.[19]

The ethnopsychological work of the leftist Nedeljković shared a similar methodological standpoint with Slankamenac in its quest for social and psychological bonds in folk traditions. However, counterintuitively, he went one step further than both Slankamenac and all the above anthropogeographical adherents of Cvijić in Skopje in depicting the local Slavic population not as a part of the Yugoslav but rather the Serbian ethnic core. It all started with his early 1920s fieldwork across South Serbia with Cvijić's *La Péninsule Balkanique* as a "primary research guideline" (Nedeljković 1929, 1) when he observed that the "South Serbs" might not necessarily constitute a separate group (Central, as per Cvijić) but a subgroup of the Dinaric type, distinctive for Serbia proper. This argument appeared to resonate well in the new political context: even Cvijić encouraged its development by funding the research of Nedeljković. In turn, starting from the mid-1920s, Nedeljković published his first set of evidence in SND publications, which he continued to supplement up until the mid-1930s.

Nedeljković argued that the *group synergy* does not rely exclusively upon geographical and ethnopsychological features, but it is also bound

---

[19] In the early 1910s, for instance, a Polish disciple of Durkheim and a colleague of Wundt, Stefan Czarnowski, embarked upon a similar task of unveiling the "mechanisms of social cohesion in the time of modernisation" by looking at the Latin hagiographies of St Patrick and highlighting the transformations of a sacred into a national hero (more in Wawrzyniak 2019).

with what he delineated as ethical and ethological ties. Those bonds are visible if one starts considering the folk customs as social facts, a niche Nedeljković opened drawing upon British (Hollander, the Ethological Society) and French (Lévy-Bruhl, Durkheim) social psychology and moral sociology, as well as a sociological reading of Cvijić.[20] Hence, his first structured data pertained to proverbs from Skopje, which he gathered with the help of four of his students (Nedeljković 1926, 177–182). A more articulated version of his initial thesis about the *southern Dinaric type* is stipulated in his booklet *O psihičkom tipu Južnosrbijanaca* (On the psychic type of the South Serbs) published in Belgrade in 1929. Contrary to Cvijić, Nedeljković argued that the South Serbs share the same psychic characteristics with the Dinaric type despite the differences in the geographical areas they populate. We can revoke Cvijić's popularized argument about the lyricism of the Southerners to best illustrate Nedeljković's intervention: according to the latter, this feature is not exclusive to this group *per se* as it can be observed among other Dinaric subtypes (somewhat supported by the Yugoslav characterological scholarship at the time). The specific nuances of the *southern Dinaric type*, he continued, can be grasped with a more precise ethnopsychological methodology which he evolved from rather descriptive accounts of proverbs in the mid-1920s to quantitative surveys and psychotechnical measurements of the aesthetical sensitivities and the mnemonic capacities of the locals in the 1930s (e.g., Nedeljković 1930, 1934). He used this methodological apparatus to solve some of the "Macedonian issues" puzzling Cvijić and promoted his results in and beyond Skopje and Yugoslavia.[21]

---

[20] A neat summary of this interpretation is provided in his text published in the festschrift in honor of Cvijić published by the Serbian Academy of Sciences and Arts in 1968 (Nedeljković in Ćulibrk 1971; also see Tasić 1938).

[21] The case of the two neighboring western Macedonian villages that developed two different reactions to the Albanian migrations during the Ottoman times is immensely telling (the first one adopted the Albanian language but kept the Orthodox Christian faith, while the other one kept the Slavic vernacular but converted into Islam). Cvijić looked at the geographical features of the villages for possible answers; Nedeljković, however, claimed this was a misleading approach and opted for a solution based on a "more exact experimental ethnopsychological method" (1934, 127). In conclusion, he argued that the first group of villagers is characterized with a higher degree of *mnemic functions*, including the capacity to learn new languages. Nedeljković published his findings in a monograph and several texts, and presented them on several occasions, such as the 1938 International Psychotechnical Congress which took place in Budapest (Nedeljković 1938, 190).

The curious intellectual alliance of Slankamenac and Nedeljković exposes the best of the academic culture in the interwar Skopje of the 1920s up until the mid-1930s, embodied in the Faculty and the SND: it permitted different ideological convictions, research methodologies, and considerations about the Yugoslav *psyche* as long as the dominant manner of thinking about the Serbian *character* of the province was not questioned. Several other public coalitions were formed with the single goal of popularizing this "missionary" culture in Skopje (Grgić 2020, 237). A neat example is the Cultural Society "Jefimija" established in Skopje in 1930 (more in Jovanović 1937, 1021): it hosted exhibitions, lectures, and other high society events promoting Serbian identity and heritage, having both Slankamenac and Nedeljković associated with its management (Vardar 1936; more in Kačeva et al. 2002).

Another telling case is the leftist judge in South Serbia and a lawyer in interwar Skopje, **Aleksandar Krušković**. Krušković supported the SND (Radovanović 1928, 34) while being actively engaged in socialist-agrarian politics on local and national levels (e.g., Buchenau 2018; Petrović 2019). Importantly, he authored one of the first Yugoslav books aimed at introducing the scientific scope of sociology, published in 1933 in Skopje under the title *Problemi sociologije* (Sociological Problems). Besides being the first sociological monograph ever published in Skopje, the book illuminates several other aspects significant both for the local and the state context. To start with, it hints at the circulation of sociological literature and ideas in interwar Skopje: Krušković's synthetic take on sociology as a meta-science that determines the study objects of all the specific and analytical sciences was built upon Worms and Spencer, directly, and indirectly, upon the earlier and local corresponding arguments of Slankamenac (who predominantly read German and French authors). Additionally, in line with this epistemological position, Krušković stripped away all the activist potentials of sociology, a point he promoted in different formats and beyond Skopje up until the early 1940s, albeit with references to Engels in his later work (see Krušković 1940). This position of his might have contributed to the sidelining of his work as "marginal" during the debate in late socialist Yugoslavia about the state's sociological legacies (e.g., Mitrović 1974, 1982, 151–153). However, the more recent historical accounts applaud Krušković for being among the first Yugoslavs to discuss the sociological scientific coordinates when only a handful of sociologists and sociological handbooks (Palante, Sorokin) were available in Serbo-Croatian (e.g., Antonić 2018, 9; Spasić et al. 2022, 21).[22]

The introduction of dictatorship in Yugoslavia in 1929 centralized more political power into the hands of the King and recalibrated the state's politics, now aimed at policing a unified Yugoslav nation. Following this, the Kingdom's name changed to Yugoslavia, and the names of the now integrated territorial units of *Banovinas* changed as well; South Serbia hence became Vardar Banovina, after the largest river in the region. All those reforms had limited success, however, ultimately failing to mitigate the political mobilization for ethnic federal units. In Macedonia, the Serbization of the locals was insignificantly decelerated. This notwithstanding, the new political constellation opened up a limited set of opportunities ranging from open calls for Macedonian independence (mostly Macedonian leftist student circles across Yugoslavia; e.g., see Apostolov 1976) to more toned-down discourses circulating in Skopje, which primarily saw Yugoslavism as a certain buffer against Serbian hegemony. The Skopjan agenda-setters were several outlets such as the biweekly *Vardar* in the beginning (issued from 1932 to 1936) and especially the monthly *Luč* and the group of so-called *Lučists* preparing the journal (published from June 1937 until May 1938). The latter best reflects the local entanglements with the state politics of the late 1930s. Assembling a "very mixed group" of politically aligned and unaligned intellectuals and autonomists of different provenance, *Luč* soon became a platform calling for a better political representation of the locals and mainstreaming the term Macedonia and the Macedonian idiom without adhering to a specific ideology (Boškovska 2017, 88–91).[23] This inclusivity of *Luč* was challenged by the political left and right at the time, both portraying it as a regime's tool for controlling the imminent Macedonian independence movement (e.g., Miljovski in Fidanova 1971, 123; Guzelev in Boškovska 2017, 91). Indeed, *Luč* was initiated with Ban's decree and

---

[22] **Rastko Purić** (1903–1981), a Serbian official and "sociologist" (Petkovski in Stardelov et al. 2000, 128), another member of the "Jefimija" circle, held several high administrative posts in welfare institutions in interwar Skopje and used his insights to author several texts reviewing the situation of the local workers (Hadjievska 2021). Slankamenac reviewed his work on the migrant workers from South Serbia as a pioneering "sociological-economical" contribution (Slankamenac 1940, 181–182).

[23] *Luč* translates as light. The journal's subtitle was a *monthly for cultural, economic, and social issues—Skopje*, with the motto of the *Lučists—Light in the dark social hours*. Interestingly enough, only Nedeljković, as an ethnic Serb, was allowed to publish a single, philosophical text in *Luč*. The rest of the authors were locals.

it refrained from challenging unified Yugoslavia in its editorials; however, the monthly was also banned in less than a year due to apparent anti-Serbian and pro-independence stances.[24]

Its co-editor and one of the most prominent *Lučists* was **Boris Arsov** (1906–1954), born in Kriva Palanka, who studied law and philosophy in Marseille in the mid-1920s and defended his doctoral thesis about economic life in nineteenth-century Macedonia at the Sorbonne in 1936. Arsov's direct exposure to French sociology and psychology provided him the scientific apparatus to question the prevailing modes of deliberating about the society in his homeland. Hence, as of the late 1920s, he criticized both the *geographism* of Cvijić and his school and the *metaphysicism* of ethnopsychology.[25] In turn, he embarked on an investigation of the local society sketched upon the Durkheimian *représentations collectives*, aimed at discovering both its centripetal forces and political ambitions. The economic history appeared to be the most fitting optics for this endeavor, as it allowed for different emphases of the local developments against the macro-historical background and, to a certain extent, for a mirror reflection of the interwar politics he was witnessing.[26]

This research agenda hence resulted in two major projects of his during the late interwar period. The first one was his doctorate, published in 1936 in French, in Paris, immediately upon his defense. It presents a detailed account of the history of economic relations in Ottoman Macedonia and unveils several of Arsov's underpinning sociological and political standpoints. The first and the most obvious one refers to the very

---

[24] For the post-war Macedonian historiography, it was most common to paint *Luč* in an escapist light of a liberal circle and outlet, giving its board a credit, however, for the courage to engage with "topics from the domain of the Macedonian history" without confronting the dominant ideology (e.g., Zografski 1981, 22).

[25] MANU Archive "Haralampie Polenakoviḱ" in Skopje, Boris Arsov Fund, Sociološki studii: *Sociologija i psihologija* (1929); *Savremeni problemi sociologije*. The latter text was prepared as a response to the Serbian historian and an instructor in Russian and Western Slavic history in Skopje, **Aleksej Jelačić** (1892–1941), published in *Vardar* in 1936. Arsov also reviewed Krušković's book for *Vardar* in 1933, immediately upon its publication (in Vojinović 2016).

[26] Corresponding research of the regional economic history with clear political undertones was done by **Todor Mirovski** (1904–1959), another *Lučist* holding a doctoral degree in economics from Zagreb, in around the same time period. **Borislav Blagoev** (1912–2009), born in Skopje, was another legal scholar who, similar to Arsov, specialized in Paris and Geneva in the interwar period and published on the social and economic issues of the Macedonian villages in the late 1930s (Blagoev 1979, 5).

name of the region in focus. Although his thesis contained *South Serbia*, he published the book switching the title to *Macedonia*, thus making a clear statement backed in the introductory chapter: he considered South Serbia a politically charged and a mere administrative name (Arsov 2000, 23). His methodological treatment of economic history—including political history and social morphology (as yet another inclination to Durkheim in lieu of Cvijić)—further signals his line of thought: he saw the failed mid-nineteenth-century reforms for modernizing the Ottoman Empire as nonetheless formative for the local Slavic population, as they empowered certain "economic initiatives" (Arsov 2000, 46) and social mobility, culminating in the formation of the *esnafs* (guilds) as nuclei of the emerging local bourgeoisie. In a leftist manner, he saw the esnafs and their positioning and behavior within the emerging market relations as determining for national cohesion, more important than the Church in this regard.

His second project was about publishing an agrarian sociology of the Povardarie region (or the Vardar river valley). It remained unpublished in this format, however, although certain parts of it were issued as articles in *Luč* and several chapters are still available as archived manuscripts. Drawing upon a similar theoretical and methodological position as in his doctorate, Arsov expanded his analysis to the twentieth century to argue that the agrarian reform in the southernmost province of the Kingdom failed due to the neglect of the social and psychological needs of the local population. He then continued with mapping the social formations in the region and their historical development, ascribing them the agency of drivers of the national society.[27] This argument might be read as yet another of his responses to the anthropogeographical takes on Macedonia in all their nuances, as they predominantly saw the local population as intact and static. Arsov promoted his theses in *Luč*, as well, openly criticizing the tribal nationalisms (without the Macedonian) in Yugoslavia as atavist, while claiming that the lack of such a nationalist experience in the South makes this community a fit for a bearer of the idea of an integral Yugoslavism (Boškovska 2017, 285). His writings eventually hit a nerve since he was imprisoned after the ban of *Luč*, so he spent several years in the Novi Sad prison. Arsov managed to get out of jail, join the wartime Macedonian partisans, and emerge as one of the architects of the post-war legal system in socialist Macedonia, an episode discussed in the next chapter. His inter-

[27] MANU Archive "Haralampie Polenakoviḱ" in Skopje, Boris Arsov Fund, Sociološki studii: *Agrarna sociologija Povardarja*.

war work, however, remained sidelined for a particular reason, discussed in the next chapter, despite being a leftist effort to place the Macedonian nation-building within the historical materialist understanding of history. His doctorate was translated into Macedonian and published by the MANU only in 2000, while it would be Petre Georgievski who engaged the most with his work in the 2000s and started portraying him as the first Macedonian sociologist (e.g., 2005, 2012).

BEYOND SKOPJE

The Great Depression hit Yugoslavia in the early 1930s, shattering the state's delicate progress and social cohesion from its first decade. The rural population, comprising more than two-thirds of the total Yugoslav inter-war population, was especially vulnerable to the slump in agricultural prices that in certain regions pushed it to the brink of economic survival (Boškovska 2017, 77). Such was the situation in the southernmost Banovina, which remained the most underdeveloped region of the Kingdom in the 1930s despite the initial interest of the royal dictatorship in its betterment. The political tensions rose while the brewing separatism culminated in a Macedonian-Croat conspiracy for the assassination of the King, which eventually took place in Marseille in October 1934.

In neighboring Bulgaria, the economic crisis led to a military *coup d'état* that soon after criminalized the VMRO and stripped away its *de facto* hegemony in South-East Bulgaria (part of the geographical Macedonian territory). This allowed for more unobstructed activism of the leftist pro-Macedonian circles and activists in Bulgaria, such as the group around the Sofia newspaper *Makedonski vesti*, published in 1935 and 1936. The group started developing a Marxist-Leninist discourse about the "Macedonian Revival" as a historical backing of the idea of the Macedonian Slavs as ethnically distinct group, aimed not as much at the intelligentsia but at revoking the *Macedonian consciousness* of the Macedonians in and beyond Macedonia (Sujecka 2013, 178–187; Vezenkov and Marinov 2013, 448–451). One of its most prominent activists was **Kosta Veselinov** (1908–1942), who was jeopardized by the so-called mihajlovist VMRO so he moved to study law in Belgrade in the early 1930s before returning to Bulgaria after the coup (Ristovski 1990, 458–490). His booklet *Natsionalno-porobeni narodi i natsionalni* *maltsinstva: nauchno-sotsiologichena etyuda* (Nationally-suppressed peoples and national minorities: a scientific-sociological study), published in Sofia in 1938, paved the way for a "historiographic codification" of the distinction between the Bulgarian and the Macedonian Revivals, the former frequently appropriating Macedonia as its "cradle" (Vezenkov and Marinov 2013, 449).[28]

The 1930s saw a renewed and even popular interest in what is nowadays deemed the *Balkan extended/joint family.* Gaining attention as yet another Slavic extended family under a male leadership and with a common economic life, a number of experts and activists, including sociologists, started to project different sociopolitical visions upon this agrarian society as of the early nineteenth century. The first wave of those understandings in Yugoslavia emerged a bit later as *zadruga* studies, that is, under its South Slavic name, pioneered by a number of local enlighteners and "Yugoslav aspirants for doctorates at foreign universities" (Roucek 1936, 983).[29] Equally telling is the case of some of the earliest leftist activists and their usage of zadrugas' egalitarianism and collectivism as tokens for domesticating Marxist-Leninist ideology and Soviet practice (McClellan in Halpern and Hammel 1969). Back in Skopje, and in a similar vein, Nedeljković considered the local zadrugas he encountered during the 1920s as "proto-communist" forms of economy and socialization; however, he provided this observation only *en passant,* failing to inform his

---

[28] His next publication, *The Revival in Macedonia and the Ilinden Uprising* (1939), summarized the circle's attempts at positioning the armed anti-Ottoman struggle of the Macedonian Revolutionary Organization as distinctly Macedonian. It became the first history textbook in Macedonia in 1944–1945 (Vezenkov and Marinov 2013, 451). A similar pattern followed the 1934 booklet *Zošto nie Makedoncite sme oddelna nacija* (Why we the Macedonians are a separate nation) authored by **Vasil Ivanovski** (1906–1991), another member of the *Makedonski vesti* circle, which he expanded in 1942, during his prison term near Skopje, to become the "first professional history of the Macedonian nation written by a Macedonian" (Sujecka 2013, 198). Ivanovski served as the first editor-in-chief of *Nova Makedonija,* the first daily newspaper published in Macedonian.

[29] In brief, zadruga is "a household composed of two or more biological or small families, closely related by blood or adoption, owning its means of livelihood jointly and regulating the control of its property, labor, and livelihood communally" (Mosely in Todorova 2023, 3). Recent scholarship points to several differences between the Balkan joint family, including zadruga, and the other Eastern European joint families pertaining to their distinctive geneses and social histories (overview in Kaser 1994).

main ethnopsychological argument (Nedeljković 1929, 4).[30] The zadruga was also appropriated and instrumentalized by the Serbian right and radical right in the early Yugoslav interwar period as a conveyor of anti-capitalist, anti-Western, and anti-modernizing messages (Stojanović 2020). As of the 1930s, the first Western scholars (e.g., Mosely) arrived in the region to conduct fieldwork research about the local zadrugas, eventually contributing to what in the recent historical accounts of zadruga studies is considered to be its "demystification" as an object of ideological and nationalist romanticizing (Todorova 2023; also see Hammel 1980; Kaser 1994).

In the first chapter of his agrarian sociology of Povardarie, Arsov provides a theoretical discussion of zadrugas from a position much aligned with the *demystified* mode of reasoning, albeit coming from a different position and most probably unaware of the existence of the above research. Again, in a Durkheimian spirit, he saw the "internal cohesion of zadrugas" as driven not only by kinship relations but also by the "collective representations [and] psychological and economic moments" as well as other social institutions such as religion and tradition.[31] The focus on collective representations allowed for a historicizing and cross-cultural comparison of its phenomenon, which Arsov extended to Irish and Normans drawing upon French sources (Maunier). His other argument pertained to the economic history of the region: he highlighted zadrugas' gradual adjustment to the major political and economic shifts as a result, to a certain extent, of the preservation of the South Slavic oral law and the development of certain proto-democratic forms of rural governance. Neither of the arguments was particularly new; however, their novelty lies in their resonance with the local political developments in the 1920s.[32] For instance, even Weber

---

[30] In what might be considered a Marxist contribution, Nedeljković praised the "labor heroism" of the local population but only as a feature comparable to some other *Dinaric subtypes* (1929, 43–50), noticed even by Cvijić. Eventually, due to his "wrong opinions" about the Macedonian national question, he and "his group" were expelled from the communist party in Macedonia in the early phases of the Second World War (Gigov 1973, 149–151).

[31] MANU Archive "Haralampie Polenakoviḱ" in Skopje, Boris Arsov Fund, Sociološki studii: *Agrarna sociologija Povardarja*, 6.

[32] The question about the origins of zadruga is still discussed, with the present consensus being put on the recognition that they evolved "through an ongoing process of emergence, fission, and reconstruction" since their first documentation in the fourteenth century. The theories that saw their formation as an Old Slavonic institution and a result of the Byzantine tax collection system are nowadays considered to be "obsolete" (overview in Kaser 1994, 251).

in the late 1910s argued against the Russian anarchists' appropriations of *mir*, that is, the Russian form of zadruga, as a model of a society without a legal compulsion. The members of mir executed coercive power over its communities, albeit in a stateless form (Weber 1961; for context, see Honigsheim 1949). Arsov's intervention was thus directly opposing Cvijić's argument about the patriarchal history of the South Slavic families and collectives, and juxtaposing this understanding to his argument claiming the lack of so powerful a *pater familias* in the local zadrugas. At another instance, he argued that this pseudo-democratic culture of the local zadrugas was in direct opposition to the dominant Byzantine feudal culture, championed by "firstly by the Bulgarians and then by the Serbs."[33]

The late 1930s also saw the most ambitious Yugoslav attempt at gathering first-hand evidence about the changes in family life, coordinated by **Vera Stein Erlich** (1897–1980), a leftist Croat Jewish anthropologist and pedagogist. In 1937, encouraged by the local Bosnian community where she led a women's emancipatory action, she started mailing a questionnaire containing 134 questions about family relations all around Yugoslavia. The survey provoked mass interest: a number of teachers and other local volunteers, including Macedonian, mailed back their responses in the course of the late 1930s, while it also became popular among experts who eagerly used their networks in forwarding the questionnaires. The wartime turmoil further contributed to the "legendary" (Erlich 1971, 160) status of this survey, since she managed to protect herself and her chest with the survey's responses from the bombings of Split and South Italy up to the safe haven in the USA. The materials served as a basis for her major project: the book *Family in Transition: A Study of 300 Yugoslav Villages*, published in Serbo-Croatian in 1964 and translated into English in 1966. The book, as well as her return as a social anthropology instructor in Zagreb in the 1960s, equipped with knowledge in American anthropology and sociology (Supek-Zupan 1984), set the tone for the Yugoslav, including the Macedonian, family sociology, discussed in more detail in the next chapter.

Erlich's book about the transformations of family and family life in Yugoslavia had the Yugoslav villages grouped into seven separate regions, all of them shaped by different historical experiences, with Macedonia consisting of two regions: Albanian (Muslim) and Christian villages. The

---

[33] MANU Archive "Haralampie Polenakoviḱ" in Skopje, Boris Arsov Fund, Sociološki studii: *Agrarna sociologija Povardarja*, 8.

focus on the socio-psychological features of family life, such as authority, conflicts, love and hate, rank and transformation,, led to the conclusion that the southern (Macedonian) regions which were no longer under Ottoman rule retained more indices of conservatism than those liberated earlier. Supportive of this claim was the argument that the two Macedonian regions preserved the most zadrugas and pre-individualistic forms of communal life. Erlich's study can also be read as an account of the state of the Macedonian society of the 1930s. She observed that the political transformations, as well as the introduction of "modern state administration" and "progressive economy" in Macedonia (although resulting in a regression during the crisis), failed to shake the old patriarchal roles which were eventually "softened" by other, "human" approaches related to the above set of socio-psychological features. As an illustration, she colored Macedonia as a region with an "Oriental tinge, without a belligerent note" (1966, 363–364). The other important takeaway is her rather ontogenetic argument about the "historical sequence" of the Yugoslav regions, where the stage of the less developed region "left one with the incapable impression" of witnessing "the past of family life in other regions" (1966, 26). From this perspective, Macedonia was the last in the diachronic row, the ultimate *Volksmuseum* of Yugoslavia and the Balkans in general.

Just a few years before Erlich, another scholar of anthropology and the South Slavs, the Pole **Józef Obrębski** (1905–1967), was dreaming of finding his own *terra incognita* the same way his teacher and close collaborator **Bronisław Malinowski** (1884–1942) discovered in the Trobriands. This dream came true after an immensely interesting chain of biographical events stretching from Kraków to interwar London: Obrębski ended up living in a zadruga among the allegedly isolated highlanders of Western Macedonia's Upper Poreče, where he conducted the first-ever European functionalist fieldwork research from August 1932 to March 1933 (more in Bielenin-Lenczowska and Engelking 2015; Engelking 2018, 2022). His state-of-the-art training, vast knowledge about the South Slavs and their languages, and motivation stemming from his success in unveiling a community "further than the peripheries of the civilization" (Obrębski in Engelking 2018, 187) granted him the opportunity to note many emic nuances related to the folklore and especially the social reality of the locals. Indeed, he would emphasize the sociological and social anthropological aspects in the first of the several monographs he intended to write about Poreče, with a "sociological account" in its title.[34] Unfortunately, this work was destroyed in the Second World War, unlike his 1500 pages of notes and 500 negatives from Macedonia that miraculously survived the wartime years buried under the obliterated Warsaw (published in three volumes from 2020 to 2023). His stay in Macedonia somewhat set the ground for his further research pertaining to the dynamics and the effects of nationalizing processes, which he first pursued in the Polish Polesie in the course of the late interwar period and among the post-slavery communities of Jamaica during the late 1940s.

The functionalist perspective of Obrębski also allowed for a more nuanced understanding of the interwar modernizing of Poreče in particular and Macedonia in general. Unlike Erlich, whose historicism of the region was noted as a trace of "imperial legacies" in her research (also habitual for Cvijić, in Baskar 2020, 25–26), Obrębski did not turn to history looking for "surrogate time machines" (as Gellner noted for Malinowski in Gellner 2004, 133) when discussing the simpler societies. He tended to see the indeterminate ethnicity at Polesie, for instance, as a certain signal of the surplus of the local identity and not a lack of it. This understanding was hence above the radars of not only the local stakeholders in Yugoslavia but also the Polish social sciences at the time (Lubaś 2019; Engelking 2022). It took some time for the Macedonian ethnologists and anthropologists to note the significance of the "Macedonian phase" of Obrębski, which was observed as the first pioneering fieldwork research in Macedonia providing unmediated insights into the local community of Poreče (e.g., Vražinovski et al. 2003; Vražinovski 2006, 2009; Risteski 2011).[35] The Macedonian sociologists built upon this interpretation and further highlighted the methodological breakthrough in Obrębski's fieldwork research in Macedonia (e.g., Taševa 2004; Georgievski 2021). The shared ethnological-sociological legacy of Obrębski is frequently nostri-

---

[34]Obrębski was very observant of the sociological scholarship, deeming the "sociological turn" in ethnology a "renaissance" (Obrębski 1939). His usage of *ethnosociology* was a conceptual translation of the English *social anthropology* (Engelking 2001).

[35]The major event, in this regard, was the commemoration of the 70th anniversary of the start of his research, which was marked with a scientific conference followed by a placement of his monument in the village of Samokov in Upper Poreče. Obrębski himself showed initiative to revisit Macedonia in the mid-1960s, which remained unfulfiled due to his death in 1967 (Vražinovski in Vražinovski et al. 2003, 52–53).

fied in the recent Macedonian scholarship, drawing upon his treatment of the locals as a separate cultural and linguistic group (e.g., Georgievski 2012), clear from the influence of the "Balkan ideologies" (Vražinovski 2009, 356).

REFERENCES

Antonić, Slobodan Č. 2018. Osnivanje Sociološkog pregleda 1938. godine. *Sociološki pregled* 52 (1): 7–23.

Apostolov, Aleksandar. 1976. Od aktivnosta na naprednite studenti na Belgradskiot univerzitet vo 1936. *Istorija* 12 (1–2): 28–63.

Arsov, Boris. 2000. *Ekonomskiot život na Makedonija vo XIX vek.* Skopje: MANU.

Atanasovski, Srđan. 2019. Producing Old Serbia: In the Footsteps of Travel Writers, on the Path of Folklore. In *Rethinking Serbian-Albanian Relations: Figuring Out the Enemy*, ed. Aleksandar Pavlović, Gazela Pudar Draško, and Rigels Halili, 22–38. London and New York: Routledge.

Baskar, Bojan. 2020. Vera Stein Erlich and the Conundrum of Yugoslav Cultural Diversity. In *Diversities. Theories & Practices: Festschrift for Reinhard Johler*, ed. Jan Hinrichsen, Jan Lange, and Raphael Reichel, 11–34. Tübingen: EKW-Verlag.

Bielenin-Lenczowska, Karolina, and Anna Engelking. 2015. Poreče: An Ethnographic Revisit. In *Anthropology of Continuity and Change: Macedonian Porece 80 Years After Józef Obrębski's Research*, ed. Karolina Bielenin-Lenczowska, 9–30. Warszawa: Instytut Slawistyki PAN.

Blagoev, Borislav. 1979. *Monografski materijali za raǵanjeto i razvitokot na industrijata vo Makedonija.* Skopje: MANU.

Boškovska, Nada. 2017. *Yugoslavia and Macedonia Before Tito: Between Repression and Integration.* London and New York: I.B. Tauris.

Bourdieu, Pierre. 1984. *Distinction: A Social Critique of the Judgement of Taste.* Cambridge: Harvard University Press.

Brunnbauer, Ulf, Claudia Kraft, and Martin Schulze Wessel. 2011. Introduction: Sociology and Ethnography in East-Central and South-East Europe Under State Socialism. In *Sociology and Ethnography in East-Central and South-East Europe*, ed. Ulf Brunnbauer, Claudia Kraft, and Martin Schulze Wessel, 1–29. München: Oldenbourg Verlag.

Buchenau, Klaus. 2018. What Is Justice? Complaints About Courts in Interwar Yugoslavia. *Südost-Forschungen* 77: 121–136.

Crampton, Jeremy W. 2006. The Cartographic Calculation of Space: Race Mapping and the Balkans at the Paris Peace Conference of 1919. *Social & Cultural Geography* 7 (5): 731–752.

Ćulibrk, Svetozar. 1971. Cvijić's Sociological Research into Society in the Balkans. *The British Journal of Sociology* 22 (4): 423–440.

Cvetanova, Ganka. 2022. Reflections on Krste Misirkov's Theory: From Ethnocultural Entity to Politically Legitimate Nation. *Slavia Meridionalis* 22: 1–24.

Cvijić, Jovan. 1906. *Promatranja o etnografiji makedonskih Slovena*. Beograd: Knjižara Gece Kona.

———. 1918. *La Péninsule Balkanique: Geographie Humaine*. Paris: Librarie Armand Colin.

Duančić, Vedran. 2020. *Geography and Nationalist Visions of Interwar Yugoslavia*. Basingstoke: Palgrave Macmillan.

Duller, Matthias. 2018. Yugoslav Sociology: Political Autonomy Under a Single-Party Regime. In *Social Sciences in the "Other Europe" Since 1945*, ed. Adela Hîncu and Victor Karady, 159–184. Budapest and New York: Central European University Press.

Engelking, Anna. 2001. The Ethno-sociological Expedition of Jozef Obrebski to Polesie, 1934-37: Organization, Research Methods, Problems, Participants. *Etnografia Polska* 45 (1-2): 23–45.

———. 2018. Macedońskie Trobriandy. Józef Obrębski i pierwsze badania wsi europejskiej w paradygmacie funkcjonalizmu. *Lud* 102: 185–210.

———. 2022. From Archaic to Colonial Peasantries: An Intellectual Biography of Józef Obrębski, the (Forgotten) Polish Disciple of Malinowski. *History of Anthropology Review* 46: 1–44.

Erdeljanović, Jovan. 1925. *Makedonski Srbi*. Beograd: Državna Štamparija.

———. 1926. Profesor Vajgand o "makedonskim" Srbima. *Glasnik Skopskog Naučnog Društva* I: 275–285.

———. 1928. Predlog za proučavanje naroda u Južnoj Srbiji. *Glasnik Skopskog Naučnog Društva* III: 275–276.

Erlich, Vera St. 1966. *Family in Transition: A Study of 300 Yugoslav Villages*. Princeton: Princeton University Press.

———. 1971. Trideset i tri godine transformiranja porodice (Istraživanja, odjeci, perspektive). *Sociologija i prostor* 31–32: 159–168.

Fidanova, Slavka. 1971. *Ulogata na KPJ vo povrzuvanjeto na borbata na rabotničkata klasa so nacionalnooslobodilnoto dviženje na makedonskiot narod od 1935-1941*. Skopje: Filozofski fakultet na Univerzitetot vo Skopje.

Flere, Sergej. 1994. The Development of Sociology as a Contested Science in Post-World War II Yugoslavia. In *Eastern Europe in Transformation: The Impact on Sociology*, ed. Mike Forrest Keen and Janusz Mucha, 113–124. Westport and London: Greenwood Press.

Fridman, Viktor. 2011. *Makedonistički studii*. Skopje: MANU.

Friedman, Victor A. 2000. The Modern Macedonian Standard Language and Its Relation to Modern Macedonian Identity. In *The Macedonian Question: Culture, Historiography, Politics*, ed. Victor Roudometof, 173–201. New York: Columbia University Press.

Gellner, Ernest. 2004. *Language and Solitude: Wittgenstein, Malinowski and the Habsburg Dilemma*. Cambridge: Cambridge University Press.

Georgevitch, Tihomir R. 1918. *Macedonia*. London and New York: George Allen & Unwin Ltd. and The Macmillan Company.

Georgievski, Petre. 1978. Razvoj sociologije na Filozofskom fakultetu u Skopju. *Revija za sociologiju* 8 (3–4): 100–108.

———. 1987. 40 godini na Filozofskiot fakultet – Prvata visokoškolska institucija vo SR Makedonija. *Godišen zbornik na Filozofskiot fakultet* 40: 31–41.

———. 2005. Osumdeset i pet godini dejnost na Filozofskiot fakultet vo Skopje. *Godišen zbornik na Filozofskiot fakultet* 58: XIII–XXVII.

———. 2011. Sociologijata kako kritika na opštestvenata promena. In *Sociologijata i opštestvenite promeni: 30 godini studii po sociologija na Filozofskiot fakultet vo Skopje*, ed. Petre Georgievski et al., 17–40. Skopje: Filozofski fakultet.

———. 2012. *Sociologijata kako kritika na opštestvenata, obrazovnata i kulturnata promena*. Skopje: Matica makedonska.

———. 2021. *Prilozi za istorijata na sociološkata metodologija*. Skopje: Matica.

Georgievski, Petre, and Mileva Gurovska. 2003. Macedonian Sociology in the 1990s: Between the Old Conceptions and New Challenges. In *Sociology in Central and Eastern Europe: Transformation at the Dawn of a New Millenium*, ed. Mike Forrest Keen and Janusz L. Mucha, 107–116. London: Praeger.

Gigov, Strahil. 1973. *Seḱavanja*. Skopje: Naša kniga.

Grgić, Stipica. 2020. The Kingdom of Diversity and Paternalism: The Kingdom of Serbs, Croats, and Slovenes/Yugoslavia, 1918–1941. In *Interwar East Central Europe, 1918–1941: The Failure of Democracy-Building, the Fate of Minorities*, ed. Sabrina P. Ramet, 213–248. London and New York: Routledge.

Grujić, Radoslav. 1924. Skopsko Naučno Društvo. *Narodna starina* 3 (7): 75.

Ǵuzelev, Dimitar. 1995. *Šopenhauerovata pragmatistička kritika na umot*. Skopje: Semejstvo Ǵuzelovi.

Hadjievska, Ivana. 2021. "The workshops are seedbeds for degeneration": Forms of Exposure and Protection of Workers' Bodies in Vardar Macedonia. *TRAFO – Blog for Transregional Research*, 14 July 2021.

Halpern, Joel M., and Eugene A. Hammel. 1969. Observations on the Intellectual History of Ethnology and Other Social Sciences in Yugoslavia. *Comparative Studies in Society and History* 11 (1): 17–26.

Hammel, Eugene A. 1980. Household Structure in Fourteenth-Century Macedonia. *Journal of Family History* 5 (3): 242–273.

Hîncu, Adela. 2018. Introduction: "Peripheral Observations" and Their Observers. In *Social Sciences in the "Other Europe" Since 1945*, ed. Adela Hîncu and Victor Karady, 1–25. Budapest and New York: Central European University Press.

Honigsheim, Paul. 1949. Max Weber as Historian of Agriculture and Rural Life. *Agricultural History* 23 (3): 179–213.

Josifovski, Jonče. 1968. Teorijata na poznanieto i formalnata logika kaj Srbite od početokot na XX vek do početokot na II svetovna vojna. *Godišen zbornik na Filozofskiot fakultet* 20: 49–112.

Josifovski, Ilija, and Jovanka Kepevska. 1978. Empirijska sociološka istraživanja u SR Makedoniji. *Revija za sociologiju* 8 (3–4): 93–99.

Jovanović, Mirko, ed. 1937. Društva i ustanove. *Glasnik Skopskog Naučnog Društva* I: 1007–1050.

Jovanović, Vladan. 2011. "Prosveta – najbrži tvorac nacije": Filozofski fakultet u Skoplju 1920-1941. *Tokovi istorije* 2: 23–41.

———. 2021. Serbia, Kosovo, and Macedonia from Revolt to Resettlement to Repression. In *The Routledge Handbook of Balkan and Southeast European History*, ed. John R. Lampe and Ulf Brunnbauer, 272–279. London and New York: Routledge.

Kačeva, Alla, et al. 2002. *Životot vo Skopje: 1918-1941*. Skopje: Muzej na grad Skopje.

Kaser, Karl. 1994. The Balkan Joint Family: Redefining a Problem. *Social Science History* 18 (2): 243–269.

Katardžiev, Ivan et al. (eds.). 1976. *Krste P. Misirkov i nacionalno-kulturniot razvoj na makedonskiot narod do osloboduvanjeto*. Skopje: Institut za makedonski jazik "Krste Misirkov" Skopje.

Kopeček, Michal. 2012. Historical Studies of Nation-Building and the Concept of Socialist Patriotism in East-Central Europe 1956–1970. In *Historische Nationsforschung im geteilten Europa 1945-1989*, ed. Pavel Kolář and Miloš Řezník, 135–150. Köln: SH-Verlag.

Korubin, Blagoja. 1994. *Makedonski istorio-sociolingvistički temi*. Skopje: Matica makedonska.

Korubin, Jovan, ed. 2000. *Institut za sociologija: 25 godini*. Skopje: UKIM.

———. 2005. Misirkoviot sociološki diskurs. In *Deloto na Krste Misirkov*, ed. Blaže Ristovski, 285–292. Skopje: MANU.

Kostic, Cvetko. 1983. Sociology in Yugoslavia 1960–1970. *International Review of Modern Sociology* 13 (1–2): 375–395.

Krušković, Aleksandar. 1940. Pojedinac i društvo. *Arhiv za pravne i društvene nauke* 58 (2): 291–300.

Lubaś, Marcin. 2019. Dokument myśli otwartej. Studia poleskie Józefa Obrębskiego a rozwiązania o grupach etnicznych i stosunkach narodowościowych w polskiej etnologii i socjologii. *Sprawy Narodowościowe* 51: 1–20.

Marinov, Tchavdar. 2009. We, the Macedonians: The Paths of Macedonian Supra-Nationalism (1878–1912). In *We, the People: Politics of National Peculiarity in*

Southeastern Europe, ed. Diana Mishkova, 107–138. Budapest and New York: Central European Press.

———. 2013. *Famous Macedonia, the Land of Alexander.* Macedonian Identity at the Crossroads of Greek, Bulgarian and Serbian Nationalism. In *Entangled Histories of the Balkans: National Ideologies and Language Policies*, ed. Roumen Daskalov and Tchavdar Marinov, 273–332. Leiden and Boston: Brill.

Maxwell, Alexander. 2007. Krsté Misirkov's 1903 Call for Macedonian Autocephaly: Religious Nationalism as Instrumental Political Tactic. *Studia Theologica* 5 (3): 147–176.

Miljovska, Desanka. 1957. Eden interesen napis na Misirkov za ekonomskata sostojba na makedonskoto selo vo krajot na minatiot vek. *Glasnik na INI* 1 (1): 253–270.

———. 1971. Za studentskoto progresivno dviženje na Filozofskiot fakultet vo Skopje. *Istorija* 7 (2): 97–109.

Milosavlevski, Slavko. 1992. *Sociologija na makedonskata nacionalna svest.* Skopje: Kultura.

Milutinović, Zoran. 2011. *Getting over Europe: The Construction of Europe in Serbian Culture.* Leiden and Boston: Brill.

Minoski, Konstantin, and Antoanela Petkovska. 2017. Sociology in Dialogue: Macedonian Sociology in-Between Surviving and Internalization. In *Forth ISA Council of National Association Conference.* Taipei, Taiwan.

Misirkov, Krste Petkov. 2003. *On Macedonian Matters.* Skopje: MANU.

Mitrović, Milovan. 1974. O potrebi preispitivanja našeg sociološkog nasleđa. *Sociološki pregled* 8 (2–3): 351–361.

———. 1982. *Jugoslovenska predratna sociologija.* Beograd: Istraživačko-izdavački centar SSO Srbije.

Mladenovski, Ǵorǵe. 1997. Blaga Petroska – portret za istorijata na makedonskata sociologija. *Sociološka revija* 3 (1–2): I-VIII.

Nedeljković, Dušan. 1926. Osnovne etografsko-etološke karakteristike skopskog narodnog života. *Glasnik Skopskog Naučnog Društva* I: 177–204.

———. 1929. O psihičkom tipu Južnosrbijanaca. Beograd: Državna štamparija Kraljevine Srba, Hrvata i Slovenaca.

———. 1930. Mavrovska psihička grupa. *Glasnik Skopskog Naučnog Društva* VII–VIII: 237–266.

———. 1934. Gornjorekanska etnopsihološka grupa. *Glasnik Skopskog Naučnog Društva* XIII: 83–130.

———. 1938. Razvoj naše etnopsihologije za poslednje dve decenije. *Učitelj* 19 (3–4): 181–191.

Nedeljkoviḱ, Dušan. 1984. *Istorija na filozofijata: Skopski predavanja.* Skopje: Makedonska kniga.

Novaković, Kosta. 1966. *Makedonija Makedoncima! Zemlja zemljoradnicima!* Čačak: Istorijski arhiv.

Obrębski, Józef. 1939. Etnologia i socjologia. *Wiedza i Życie* 14 (3): 151–156.

Petrović, Dragan. 2019. *Kraljevina Jugoslavija i SSSR 1929-1935*. Beograd: IMPP.

Peucker, K. 1900. Dr. Jovan Cvijić's Researches in Macedonia and Southern Albania. *The Geographical Journal* 16 (2): 215–219.

Puljevski, Đorđe. 1875. *Rečnik od tri jezika*. Beograd: Tab Olunmiš.

Radovanović, Vojislav S. 1928. *Godišnjak 1921–1928*. Skoplje: Stara Srbija.

———. 1929. Radovi etnološkog seminara skopskog fakulteta na proučavanju naroda Južne Srbije. *Glasnik Skopskog Naučnog Društva* V: 309–310.

Risteski, Ljupčo S. 2011. Josef Obrebski's Anthropological Research on Macedonia. *Etnoantropološki problemi* 6 (4): 837–858.

———. 2022. Mesečnikot "Vardar" vo uredništvo na Krste Petkov Misirkov od 1905 godina i makedonskoto prašanje. *EtnoAntropoZum* 22: 196–266.

Ristovski, Blaže. 1990. *Portreti i procesi od makedonskata literaturna i nacionalna istorija*. Vol. III. Skopje: Kultura.

———. 1995. *Makedonija i makedonskata nacija*. Skopje: Detska radost.

Rohdewald, Stefan. 2022. *Sacralizing the Nation Through Remembrance of Medieval Religious Figures in Serbia, Bulgaria and Macedonia*. Leiden and Boston: Brill.

Roucek, Joseph S. 1936. The Development of Sociology in Yugoslavia. *American Sociological Review* 1 (6): 981–988.

Roudometof, Victor. 2001. *Nationalism, Globalization, and Orthodoxy: The Social Origins of Ethnic Conflict in the Balkans*. Westport and London: Greenwood Press.

Sicard, Emile. 1973. Travaux et recherches sociologiques en Yougoslavie. *L'Année sociologique* 24: 149–174.

Slankamenac, Prvoš. 1926a. Legende o južnoslovenskim anahoretima. *Glasnik Skopskog Naučnog Društva* I: 215–234.

———. 1926b. Škole u Južnoj Srbiji. *Letopis Matice srpske* 307: 267–277.

———. 1930. Pedagogika na universitetu. *Glasnik Skopskog Naučnog Društva* VII–VIII: 267–292.

———. 1940. Pregled literature: Rasto Purić i Dr. Borislav Iv. Blagojević. *Glasnik Skopskog Naučnog Društva* XXI: 181–185.

Sonnenhauser, Barbara. 2020. The Virtue of Imperfection. Gjorgji Pulevski's Macedonian-Albanian-Turkish Dictionary (1875) as a Window into Historical Multilingualism in the Ottoman Balkans. *Journal of Historical Sociolinguistics* 6 (1): 1–29.

Spasić, Ivana, Jelena Pešić, and Marija Babović. 2022. *Sociology in Serbia: A Fragile Discipline*. Basingstoke: Palgrave Macmillan.

Stardelov, Georgi, et al., eds. 2000. *Istorijata na ideite na počvata na Makedonija*. Skopje: MANU.

Stojanović, Dubravka. 2020. Imagining the *Zadruga: Zadruga* as a Political Inspiration to the Left and to the Right in Serbia, 1870–1945. *Revue des études slaves* 91 (3): 333–353.

Sujecka, Jolanta, ed. 2013. *Macedonia: Land, Region, Borderland*. Warsaw: Faculty of "Artes Liberales" University of Warsaw.

Supek-Zupan, Olga. 1984. Utjecaj američke antropologije na rad Vere Stein Erlich. *Revija za sociologiju* 14 (3-4): 319–326.

Taševa, Marija. 1997. *Etničkite grupi vo Makedonija: Istoriski kontekst*. Skopje: Filozofski fakultet.

———. 2004. Makedonskite istražuvanja na Jozef Obrembski. *Sociološka revija* 1–2: 5–14.

———. 2021. Rereading Misirkov: The Nation as a Factor of Unification. In *Science and Society: Contributions of Humanities and Social Sciences*, ed. Ratko Duev, 407–418. Skopje: Faculty of Philosophy.

Tasić, Đorđe. 1938. Opšti pregled naše sociologije i naših društvenih nauka. *Sociološki pregled* 1 (1): 230–271.

Todorova, Maria. 2023. Introduction: The History of the "Balkan Family". *Genealogy* 7 (1): 1–18.

Trajanovski, Naum. 2021. "A Patriotic Act for Macedonia": The Mnemohistory of Commemorations of Mara Buneva in Skopje (2001–2018). *Contemporary Southeastern Europe* 8 (2): 83–104.

Trajkovski, Ilo. 2000. *Sociologija: Što e i kako se praktikuva?* Skopje and Melbourne: Matica makedonska.

Trencsényi, Balázs, et al. 2018a. *A History of Modern Political Thought in East Central Europe. Volume II: Negotiating Modernity in the "Short Twentieth Century" and Beyond. Part I: 1918–1968*. Oxford: Oxford University Press.

———. 2018b. *A History of Modern Political Thought in East Central Europe. Volume II: Negotiating Modernity in the "Short Twentieth Century" and Beyond. Part II: 1968–2018*. Oxford: Oxford University Press.

Troebst, Stefan. 2001. IMRO + 100 = FYROM? The Politics of Macedonian Historiography. In *The New Macedonian Question*, ed. James Pettifer, 60–78. Basingstoke: Palgrave Macmillan.

Trouton, Ruth. 1998. *Peasant Renaissance in Yugoslavia 1900-1950: A Study of the Development of Yugoslav Peasant Society as Affected by Education*. London and New York: Routledge.

Vardar. 1936. Nova uprava Društva prijatelja umetnosti "Jefimija" u Skoplju. Vardar, December 4.

Verdery, Katherine. 1991. *National Ideology under Socialism: Identity and Cultural Politics in Ceausescu's Romania*. Berkeley: University of California Press.

Vezenkov, Alexander, and Tchavdar Marinov. 2013. The Concept of National Revival in Balkan Historiography. In *Entangled Histories of the Balkans: Shared Pasts, Disputed Legacies*, ed. Roumen Daskalov and Alexander Vezenkov, 406–460. Leiden and Boston: Brill.

Vojinović, Staniša. 2016. Skopski list Vardar (1932-1934): Književnost, kultura, istorija. *Vardarski zbornik* 11: 289–374.

Vražinovski, Tanas. 2006. Józef Obrębski i macedońska etnografia. *Sprawy Narodowościowe. Seria nowa* 29: 53–62.

———. 2009. Kako Jozef Obrembski gi doživeal Makedonija i Makedoncite vo 1932/1933 godina. In *Otkrivanjeto i proučuvanjeto na Makedonija vo evrop-skata nauka do formiranjeto na makedonskite državni institucii*, ed. Cvetan Grozdanov et al., 343–358. Skopje: MANU.

Vražinovski, Tanas, Ana Engelking, and Džoel M. Halpern, eds. 2003. *Jozef Obrembski: Poreče 1932-1933*. Prilep: Institut za Staroslovenska Kultura.

Vujić, Vladimir, and Prvoš Slankamenac. 1923. *Novi humanizam*. Beograd: Geca Kon.

Vukanović, Tatomir. 1940. Pregled literature: Etnologija. *Glasnik Skopskog Naučnog Društva* XXI: 179–180.

Wawrzyniak, Joanna. 2019. From Durkheim to Czarnowski: Sociological Universalism and Polish Politics in the Interwar Period. *Contemporary European History* 28 (2): 172–187.

Weber, Max. 1961. *General Economic History*. New York: Collier Books.

Wilkinson, Henry R. 1951. *Maps and Politics: A Review of the Ethnographic Cartography of Macedonia*. Liverpool: Liverpool University Press.

Willemsen, Heinz. 2005. The Labour Movement and the National Question: The Communist Party of Yugoslavia in Macedonia and the Inter-War Period. *Moving the Social: Journal of Social History and the History of Social Movements* 33: 99–121.

Zografski, Dančo. 1966. Krste Misirkov za nacionalnosta na Makedoncite. *Glasnik na INI* 10 (1): 5–18.

———. 1981. Dostiganja i karakteristiki na makedonskata istoriografija. In *Za ponovite proučuvanja na Jugoistočna Evropa*, ed. Dančo Zografski and Orde Ivanoski, 17–30. Skopje: INI and Društvo za izučuvanje i istražuvanje na Jugoistočna Evropa.

———. 1990. *Za makedonskoto prašanje*. Skopje: Misla.

CHAPTER 2

Walking a Fine Line: The Skopje University in the Early Post-War Period (1945–1950s)

Abstract The end of the Second World War and the establishment of the Second Yugoslavia paved the way for the formation of a Macedonian state—for the first time in history. The immediate post-war national institution-building including the scientific, educational, and publishing politics in Macedonia created a peculiar context where academic workers were expected to navigate a fine line between the national and class criteria in research and teaching. In this chapter, I focus on the early post-war Skopje University to discuss the epistemological ruptures and continuities between the pre- and post-war habits of observation, methodologies, and social research themes. Despite the official prohibition of sociology in its pre-war form, this period is extremely instructive for the framework of the early post-war articulation of social phenomena in Macedonia and, especially, the context for institutionalizing sociology in Macedonia in the 1960s.

Keywords Socialist Macedonia • Yugoslavia • Skopje University • Ruptures • Continuities

The Second World War and its official end brought a new era in the Balkans. Drawing upon the victorious Yugoslav partisans' struggle led by the KPJ and its head **Josip Broz Tito** (1892–1980), which already laid the foundations of a multinational socialist federation in the final stages of the war, the Federal People's Republic of Yugoslavia was constituted with

N. Trajanovski, *A History of Macedonian Sociology*, Sociology
Transformed, https://doi.org/10.1007/978-3-031-48869-6_2

a series of political and legal moves in late 1945 and early 1946. The post-war Federation (mostly) shared the territorial borders with the Kingdom of Yugoslavia and became its legal successor; however, the supranational all-Yugoslav wartime mobilization as well as the KPJ agenda of self-determination and national/socialist liberation translated into a radically different political arrangement after the war. The so-called Second Yugoslavia now consisted of six federal People's Republics, molded upon the Soviets, with Belgrade remaining a federal capital city. It did not take long for the state to face a new set of security challenges, now coming from its ideological torchbearer and former wartime ally the Soviet Union. The quarrel with the Soviets and the 1948 Tito-Stalin split resulted in a shift in Yugoslav foreign politics: a break from the idea of Yugoslav-Bulgarian unification, official policy just a year before; and a decline and an eventual halt of the Yugoslav support of the Greek communists in the Greek Civil War (1946–1949), redefining the state's relations with the West, and, as of the 1960s, spearheading the non-aligned movement. It also triggered a political purge of anticommunists and especially (alleged) Stalinists in Yugoslavia in the late 1940s. Henceforth, "by pursuing a stra-tegic search for a new legitimacy to distance itself from Moscow" (Cosovschi 2015, 47–48), the KPJ terminated the post-war collectiviza-tion agenda and conducted a series of reforms granting greater political and economic decentralization, encapsulating the best in the development of the Yugoslav self-management system in the 1950s.

The Democratic Federal Republic of Macedonia—as of 1946: People's Republic of Macedonia—occupying a large chunk of the territory of pre-war Vardar Banovina, was now the southernmost Yugoslav federal state. The window of opportunity for establishing a Macedonian nation-state created by wartime mobilization and gains prompted a number of autono-mist activists of various backgrounds to unite in an anti-fascist state-building platform. Most notably, they took part in constituting—on 2 August 1944, the day of the Ilinden Uprising—the provisional wartime government and a supreme legislative body which set forth the legal provi-sions for the future Macedonian state: the Anti-fascist Assembly for the National Liberation of Macedonia [mk. *Antifašističko sobranie za narodno osloboduvanje na Makedonija*, ASNOM]. The ASNOM paved the way for instituting national identity markers, such as the codification of the stan-dard Macedonian language (1944–1945), and establishing the key national institutions in the aftermath of the war, among them the Macedonian national library, theater, and opera (all in 1945; more in

Troebst 1997), and, especially important for this study, the Skopje University in 1946.[1] The first Macedonian University was conceived with an ambitious goal to not only provide a platform for educating the local population, still below the Yugoslav average at that point, but also to deliver an intellectual backbone in research and provide cadres for the new Macedonian state. For these reasons, its leadership perceived its creation as a radical juncture in Macedonian history—matched only by the medieval school of St Clement of Ohrid—as it empowered the local population to study, in Macedonian, "our past, our present, and our future as a single unity" and "overcome the centuries-long backwardness" (Kantardžiev et al. 1976, 9). The faculty members recruited predominantly from the ranks of the partisans, who were therefore expected to be academic curators of the above agenda.

The Macedonian post-war nation-building under communist state ideology was a polyvalent process, however. With a multicultural, multiethnic, and multiconfessional population of approximately 1,150,000 after the war, Macedonia comprised 7 percent of the total Yugoslav population. Alongside the dominant group of ethnic Macedonians, which amounted to approximately 67 percent of the total Macedonian population, and following the federal line, the state recognized the political and cultural rights of its minorities, as well as their rights related to language use, education, and freedom of assembly, again, for the first time in history. The recognition drew upon the wartime political slogan turned to guide interethnic relations principle—*brotherhood and unity*—while it was further legitimized with the local histories of joint anti-Ottoman and anti-fascist struggles in Macedonia. The political turmoil of the late 1940s and the deterioration of relations with Bulgaria and Greece impacted Macedonia, calling forth responses from the Macedonian side. They eventually came from the associates of Skopje University, the core of post-war Macedonian scientific life. In this chapter, I note several such endeavors. Firstly, I map the attempts of the first Macedonian generation of Marxist instructors at Skopje University to situate the Macedonian case within a class theory of history. I then proceed with the associates of the Natural Sciences and

---

[1] Instigated during the ASNOM, it took less than a year for the Macedonian government to prepare the inauguration of the five initial faculties of the Skopje University: the Faculty of Philosophy started its work in December 1946, followed by the Medical and Agriculture-Forestry Faculties in 1947, the Technical Faculty in 1948, and the Faculty of Economics in 1950, which soon afterwards was restructured as the Faculty of Law and Economics (1951).

Mathematics Department whose research, to a great degree, aimed at drawing the frontiers of the Macedonian *ethnie* in the post-war Balkans. Against the background of the national vulgate, best epitomized in the work of **Dimitar Vlahov** (1878–1953)—one of the leading early post-war intellectuals and a member of the Presidium of ASNOM—after 1948, the dominant sociopolitical view about the post-war state borders was that they did not match the geographical ones delineating a Macedonian national entity sharing a common language and a historical consciousness (Livanios 2008, 198–208; also see Voss 2006).[2] Finally, I look at the academic attempts to assign the ethnic Macedonians the titular role in socialist Macedonia. I postulate that all three cases, dubbed the *main road*, showcase the structuring properties of the nation in articulating social phenomena in early post-war Macedonia.

On the other hand, similar to the Soviet Union, Yugoslav state officials rushed to eradicate any traces of the pre-war "bourgeois" sociological activities in the immediate post-war years, a process well covered in the literature (e.g., Lukić 1959; Kostic 1983). The cutting of the Yugoslav-Soviet ties in 1948 and the pursuit of a different path to communism of the former with, *inter alia*, less dogmatic interpretations of Marxism, loosened the grip over social scientific research, debates, and assembling in Yugoslavia already in 1953 and 1954, leading, for instance, to the formation of the Yugoslav Sociological Association in 1954, the first in socialist Europe, as well as the Institute of Social Sciences in Belgrade in 1957. As early as 1948, Nedeljković, now one of the leading KPJ intellectuals and a rector of the Belgrade University in the early post-war years, was among the first to claim that "there is no place for forced uniformity of thought in Marxism-Leninism" (Duančić 2019, 70). However, it was not until the late 1950s and early 1960s that sociology assumed the contours of an autonomous scientific discipline in Yugoslavia and Macedonia, a process discussed in the next chapter. Here, I argue that the ideological opening presented in 1948 evolved in a set

[2] A group of Macedonian intellectuals associated with the partisans saw the Second World War as an opportunity for a unification of all the Macedonians. They initiated an informal group Action for the National-Liberation Action Committee [mk. *Akcionen narodno-osloboditelen komitet*, ANOK] and attempted to shift the course of the KPJ. Albeit such provisions are also stipulated in the main ASNOM documents, the group failed to alter the federal politics and it was sidelined in different ways.

of interesting developments in Macedonia during the late 1940s and early 1950s. More precisely, in the last section of this chapter, I postulate that in several individual cases the proper combination of certain pre-war scholarly capital, wartime engagement, and political leverage allowed for *controlled transgressions* in exploring some non-dogmatic and even reactionary sociological discourses. In other variations, however, those very factors informed the decisions of restraining what was to be researched and taught, and by whom. Finally, I turn to the popular science book series of *Kultura*, published in Skopje in the course of the 1950s and early 1960s, as yet another platform for exploring dogmatic and non-dogmatic theories and disciplines by (predominantly) the associates of the Skopje University.

THE MAIN ROAD

The first professor of the "Marxist subjects"—including dialectical and historical materialism and political economy (Kantardžiev et al. 1976, 19)—at the Faculty of Philosophy's Philosophy Group was **Dragan Taškovski** (1917–1980). A pre-war municipal official in Katlanovo in the near vicinity of Skopje, he was caught agitating socialist ideas among the local miners and was interned by the Bulgarian authorities during the war. Taškovski had a rapid promotion to the academic and political elite after the war based on his wartime support of the partisans, his mobilization in the later stages of the war, and especially his 1945 tract on dialectics which was well received by some of the leading Bulgarian and Yugoslav Marxists of the day.[3] He lectured at the Faculty of Philosophy for only two years, from 1946 to 1948, leaving the academy for the position of instructor at the training center of the KPM/SKM, where he also served as a director from 1953 to 1970. He continued his education in Belgrade specializing in political sciences during the early 1960s, before returning to Skopje and taking the position of sociology professor at the Agriculture-Forestry and the Medical Faculties.

Taškovski best reflects the two prevailing patterns in the biographical experiences of the first generation of Macedonian Marxist instructors: they all spent a certain period of their lives studying or living in the federal

---

[3] MANU Archive "Haralampie Polenakovik̂" in Skopje, Dragan Taškovski Fund, *Avtobiografija*.

capital city of Belgrade, while on the other hand, they all showed a strong inclination toward national Macedonian history and historiography. Furthermore, a common denominator of their scholarly work is their attempts to frame the Macedonian case within the dominant Yugoslav intellectual and policy approaches to the so-called national question, including the interethnic and interstate relations as well as the power plays over the federal states' entitlements. As will be suggested in this section, this turned out to be a delicate task for the Macedonians, since they also had to adjust to the political, regional, and bilateral dynamics of the day. Ultimately, the group of first Marxist instructors setting out the *main road* in Macedonia assumed enough power in the immediate aftermath of the war to act as official ideologists, determining the right and wrong ways of deliberating about the state ideology and the nation.

Taškovski's work is extremely interesting as it hints at the Macedonian officialdom's positions about the nation during the different phases of early Macedonian socialism. In the late 1940s and early 1950s, for instance, Taškovski's dialectical and historical materialism course materials illuminate his strong emphasis on the *national question* seen in classic Marxist terms.[4] His orthodox views were apparent up until the late 1950s: for instance, in a 1959 booklet published in the *Kultura* series, which I discuss in the next section, he argued against the Marxists' borrowings of Freud. He remained observant of the dogmatic and non-dogmatic theories of the nation, dedicating almost half of his sociology course in the 1960s to different questions related to the nation.[5] His shifting interests and positionings are also visible when looking at his rich publishing career which started only after he left his first academic post. In 1949, for instance, soon after the straining of the Yugoslav-Bulgarian relations, he issued a booklet on the Bogomils, a medieval Christian dualist movement on the Macedonian territory (Taškovski 1949; also see Taškovski 1951).[6]

The Bogomils as an anti-feudal formation was an already established pseudo-Marxist trope in the Bulgarian leftist publications at the turn of the century (e.g., Dimitar Blagoev in Szwat-Gyłybowa 2005, 89–97).

---

[4] MANU Archive "Haralampie Polenakoviḱ" in Skopje, Dragan Taškovski Fund, *Predavanja za marksizmot* (file 179).

[5] MANU Archive "Haralampie Polenakoviḱ" in Skopje, Dragan Taškovski Fund, *Programa za predavanje po predmetot sociologija* (file 163).

[6] The Bogomils are considered to be founded by the priest Bogomil in the tenth century as a Gnostic sect that rejected both the ecclesiastical hierarchy and state authorities.

Moreover, several Macedonian authors, such as Arsov, Guzelev, and **Kosta Solev Racin** (1908–1943)—a Macedonian poet and anti-fascist fighter, considered to be one of the founders of Macedonian literature—wrote sociographies with political undertones about the Bogomils during the interwar period.[7] The novelty Taškovski proposed built upon the new political constellation which legitimized not only a class but also a national reading of the history of the Bogomils: he claimed, for instance, that they "acquired not only [an] anti-feudal character, but also the stamp of a national liberation movement" of the "Macedonian Slavs" against the "Bulgarian invaders" (Taškovski 1975, 79–80). In a more elaborate attempt and in a different political context of the early 1980s, he elucidated his thesis about the national "enhancement" of the social conflict in the First Bulgarian Empire and its exploitation and violence over the Macedonian Slavs (Taškovski 1982, 51).

Back to the early post-war years, after his first texts about the Bogomils, Taškovski continued to popularize different episodes of Macedonian history, writing historical books and film scenarios. In 1961, for instance, he wrote the first booklet on the medieval Samuel's state in the Macedonian historiography, deeming it a result of the rejection of the "Bulgarian yoke" by the "Macedonian Slavs" (more in Panov 2019, 352–353). Finally, in the late 1960s, he established himself as one of the leading Macedonian intellectuals with the development of his rather sociological theory of the ethnogenesis of the Macedonian people—an episode which will be discussed in more detail in the next chapter.

Taškovski's departure from the Faculty of Philosophy left ample room which, due to the lack of domestic cadres, had to be filled by relocating professors from other Yugoslav republics in the late 1940s. He was first substituted with Nedeljković himself, who, at that point still a rector of the Belgrade University, finished his cooperation with the Yugoslav State Commission for the Investigation of Crimes Committed by the Occupiers and their Collaborators and the Yugoslav delegation to the Nuremberg trials.[8] Nedeljković was soon replaced by **Desanka (Desa) Miljovska** (1918–2013), née Mirić, in 1950, when she took over the place of an

---

[7] Racin's poetic work will eventually inspire his acquaintance Nedeljković during the 1960s, an episode discussed in the next section.

[8] It was not uncommon for scholars from all over the Federation to end up filling empty positions in post-war Skopje; among them **Bogdan Šešić** (1909–1999), who stayed at the Skopje University from 1950 to 1954, a logician trained in interwar Berlin and Prague and the author of the textbook-introduction to dialectical logic in the late 1950s.

instructor in historical materialism. Miljovska turned out to be a pivotal figure for Macedonian sociology as she co-initiated the Sociology Chair at the Skopje University in 1973 and constituted, alongside **Blaga Petroska** (1939–2021), the "first generation" of two female Macedonian sociologists (Trajkovski 2000). Born in Prizren, the war struck Miljovska in Skopje where she was finishing her pedagogical studies. She then took an important part in the anti-fascist struggle with her activities also being of an intellectual and political nature, as she co-edited the bulletin of the Third Macedonian Assault Brigade, *Ogin* (1944–1945), and the AFŽ's organ *Makedonka* (1944–1952), the critical outlet promoting women's emancipation in Macedonia (Hadžievska and Kocevska 2022). After the war, Miljovska assumed several important positions, becoming the first female dean of the Faculty of Philosophy (1963–1965), a Minister of Culture of socialist Macedonia (1971–1974), and a President of the JUS (1978–1981). She and her husband **Kiril (Kiro) Miljovski** (1912–1983), another high-profile member of the movement—part of the ASNOM and its Presidium as well as the first rector of the Skopje University (from 1949 to 1954)—constituted the core of the Macedonian Marxist intelligentsia.[9] Petroska, on the other hand, did not have direct experience in the anti-fascist struggle since she was born in Bucharest where she started studying philosophy before moving to the post-war Skopje. She was appointed an assistant in historical materialism after she finished her studies in 1956 (Mladenovski 1997). However, similar to Miljovska, she was also interested in women's emancipation and structured both her popular and scientific work upon this premise from the late 1950s and especially during the 1960s, as we will see in the next chapter.

The novel political reality, with the Macedonian state and nation recognized as part of a socialist federation, calibrated the intellectual horizons of the leading Marxists in post-war Macedonia. They stood up in front of another challenge as they were expected to legitimize the formation of a Macedonian socialist state from a Marxist-Leninist standpoint. In other

---

[9] Miljovski was also a professor of the *Marxist subjects* at the Agriculture-Forestry Faculty as of 1949, where he taught political economy and history of political economy, and at the Faculty of Law, where he was a visiting professor. He is considered to be the founder of economics in Macedonia, while his academic interests also extended to economic and sociological interpretations of demographics and migrations (Dimitrov 1984; Uzunov and Stojkov 1993). In 1951, for instance, he opened the annual art exhibition of Macedonian painters, setting the ground for future Macedonian artisanship as not only an engaged enterprise but also one inspired by the national forms (Petkovski 1989, 223–224).

words, classic Marxism, now an official state ideology, saw the national bourgeoisie as a *condition sine qua non* not only for the proletarian revolution but also for the establishment of nation-states in the first place. This, in turn, called for an adjustment of certain standpoints of Macedonian historiography.

Miljovska articulated two key points in this context, developed in the 1950s and based on her archival research in France (Korubin 2000, 9), as well as her doctoral thesis defended in Belgrade in 1962 (Miljovska 1962) and reprinted as a longer article in the Faculty of Philosophy's *Annuiare* (Miljovska 1963a).[10] The first one pertains to the various traces of Macedonian petite bourgeoisie from the eighteenth up until the late nineteenth century. She mapped several structural and organizational modalities of what she dubbed a "national homogeneous" group (1963, 59) across the territories of geographical Macedonia, deeming it a precursor for the armed Macedonian resistance in the coming years. This standpoint entitled her to draw information from the nationally "contaminated" pre-war literature about Macedonia—authored, *inter alia*, by ethnic Serbs, such as Cvijić, and ethnic Bulgarians, such as **Vasil Kanchov** (1862–1902)— which was considered a resource now ready to be reread in a different class/national key. On the other hand, it also allowed for a new and more structured Marxist interpretation of the late Ottoman economic relations than the interwar authors such as Arsov and Mirovski, which Miljovska omitted in her analysis, especially relevant for her second intervention.

Her second intervention thus relates to the arrested development of the process of industrialization of Macedonia, a novel approach to Macedonian nation-building that eventually became paradigmatic in the course of the 1950s. Namely, Miljovska traced the halt in the full development of the Macedonian bourgeoisie back to several key economic and political events from the late Ottoman Empire. As for the economic ones, she saw the introduction of the *chiflik* land management system as a certain breakthrough toward private ownership, yet insufficient for a more profound transformation to a capitalist economy.[11] This system allowed for the Turkish landowners to retain ownership of the arable land in Macedonia, while the local

---

[10] Miljovska was on a research stay at the University of Boston from November 1962 to April 1963 (Korubin 2000, 9).

[11] Chifliks were hereditary estates outside government regulation which allowed for greater freedom of the owners in their treatment of peasant workers. This occurred in spite of the fact that the Ottoman Empire formally prohibited feudal relations in the mid-nineteenth century.

population had few options other than working on those properties with almost no chance of establishing ownership (an overview in Dimeski 1979). As an illustration, almost 70 percent of the locals at the turn of the century did not own any arable land, while the rural population of more than 80 percent lived in chifliks. The situation was further complicated by the fact that the majority of non-chiflik villages were populated by Turkish and Muslim inhabitants, while the tiny segment of non-chiflik non-Turkish villages occupied less fertile locations, usually in the highlands (Miljovska 1957, 254). This interpretation soon gained prominence, setting the ground for the pioneering historical and sociological research in socialist Macedonia (for an overview of the historiography, see Stojanov et al. 1982, 65–67). One of the first ever Macedonian empirical studies thus aimed at gathering first-hand evidence about the chifliks in late Ottoman Macedonia (touched upon in the next chapter). As for the political events, Miljovska depicted the 1870s—and the series of diplomatic events dating back to this decade hinted at in the first chapter—as detrimental to the political hesitation of the Macedonians regarding a more rigorous liberation agenda. She also saw the above process as a reason for the decline of the *esnafs* (or craft guilds) in Macedonia, whose members became more and more prone to emigration over time (Miljovska 1963b). In the coming decades, she focused on the Macedonian armed struggle and provided, for instance, a Marxist interpretation of the Ilinden Uprising: she claimed that albeit the rising has certain merit in triggering the national liberation struggle "in different historical conditions" (Miljovska 1986, 329), that is, the Second World War, she saw its failure in 1903 as yet another suppressed opportunity for the development of a Macedonian bourgeoisie.

Kiril Miljovski's close collaborator from the Agriculture-Forestry Faculty, **Dančo Zografski** (1920–1997), another professor of economics (at the Faculty of Law and Economics, as of 1951), embarked on a corresponding mission to Miljovska's of tracing the earliest forms of the Macedonian bourgeoisie as assets for legitimizing the historicity of the Macedonian nation. Zografski, a Germanophone, studied law, social sciences, and economics in Belgrade and did archival research across Germany and Austria. He held several high-level positions in the late 1940s as, for instance, an associate editor of the first (and the most important in state socialism) Macedonian daily newspaper *Nova Makedonija* and a Minister-President of the Foreign Trade Committee. His main research interest lay at the intersection of "economic history, the workers' and communist movement in Macedonia, and the complex of the Macedonian national question" (Georgievski 1997, 31). And, indeed, up until the late 1950s, Zografski almost exclusively published about the history of the Macedonian national movement; he is also considered to be part of the first generation of Macedonian historiographers (Petreska 2006; also see Stojanov et al. 1982). Zografski followed, as well, the development of the Yugoslav Marxist thought about the national question (e.g., Zografski 1962), an interest of his which culminated in his monograph about the history of the Marxist deliberations on the Macedonian nation titled *Za makedonskoto prašanje* (On the Macedonian Question) (Zografski 1990). His theses about the *capitalist elements* in Macedonia started appearing in the late 1950s and culminated in his almost 600-page monograph, published in 1967 by *Kultura*. In brief, Zografski embarked on mapping out various economic developments in eighteenth- and nineteenth-century Macedonia to explain the "different forms of exploitation" of the Macedonian people, with the late nineteenth-century chiflik system as a *de facto* reintroduction of feudalism in Macedonia. In line with Miljovska, he also explained the lack of a fully developed Macedonian bourgeoisie as an outcome of the sudden jump from the semi-feudal Ottoman social structure to the aggressive, already non-progressive and non-Macedonian, capitalist relations of production (Zografski 1967).

Another early post-war intellectual lineage with Cvijić, albeit reading him in a different key and with a different scientific goal in mind, is **Jovan F. Trifunoski** (1914–2002), one of the first four employees of the Natural Sciences and Mathematics Department.[12] Trifunoski, born in the village of Vrutok in Western Macedonia, was a graduate of the interwar Faculty of Philosophy in Skopje and the Ethnographic Institute of the Serbian Academy of Sciences and Arts in 1950. A staunch Cvijićist before the war, Trifunoski took part in the fieldwork research of the Albanian population in Yugoslavia in 1940–1941 under Jovanović (he published the results only in the 1980s, in Trifunovski 2019), and kept procuring data on Macedonia even during his wartime stay in Belgrade.[13] By invitation of the

---

[12] The department and its Chair in Geography with Ethnology [mk. *Katedra po geografija so etnologija*] was part of the Faculty of Philosophy until 1958, when the then Institute of Geography (formed in 1955) joined the newly founded Faculty of Natural Sciences and Mathematics (PMF) in Skopje (Gorgoski 2016, 239–263; Markoski 2019).

[13] Trifunoski's anthropogeographical monograph about the Ohrid-Struga region, based upon fieldwork which he did in the region during the late 1970s that was eventually published in Belgrade in 1992, opens with an editorial note which announces him as a researcher who "strictly" follows Cvijić's research guidelines (in Trifunoski 1992, XI).

post-war Macedonian authorities, Trifunoski returned to Skopje to take part in the formation of the Faculty of Philosophy and to continue pursuing his anthropogeographic research. Trifunovski's post-war work was a continuation of that of his master Cvijić and his anthropogeographical school in Skopje, a *no-stone-unturned* approach aimed at gathering data about, *inter alia*, the economic history, migration, family structures, and different communities living within the imagined national borders, now with a changed national affiliation of the dominant ethnic group, Macedonians, and all the subsequent adjectives suggesting national affiliation such as in *Macedonian urban settlements* (in Trifunoski 1947), instead of Serbs/Serbian or South Serbs/Serbian. He also changed, or *Macedonianized*, his surname from Trifunović to Trifunoski after the war. Up to the end of the 1950s, Trifunoski alone gathered a vast amount of demographic data on the geographical region of Macedonia, South Serbia, and Albania (see, e.g., Trifunoski 1947, 1948, 1952, 1954).

His work is illustrative of three other important points, all of them illuminating the academic positioning toward the political imaginaries of the nation and the state in early socialist Macedonia. Trifunoski's life-long focus on regional migration and interethnic contiguity, especially between (Albanian) Muslims and non-Muslims in Macedonia, was initially designed to provide meat for Cvijić's chief argument about the ethnic implications of the *metanastatic* (Cvijić's term for migration, locating their origins in the Ottoman conquests) Albanian relocations on Serbian territories. After the war, Trifunoski, drawing upon his vast collection of oral histories and information about toponymy and locations of (often destroyed) Christian churches and graveyards, resorted to seemingly sociological and historical interpretations to elevate his findings: the past interethnic encounters tended to result in the assimilation of the Slavic population, while the family memories of kin groups in Albania proper, and the resemblance of rituals, hint at the spatial beginnings of their migration histories (Trifunovski 2019; see, as well, Mežnarić 1989). Up until his last years spent in 1990s Belgrade, Trifunoski magnified his views to argue that more than three-fourths of the Albanians in Macedonia are newcomers, something that has recently been rejected as factually misleading (more in Ilievski 2021).[14] The political implications of such a claim resonate with the process of

---

[14] His last intellectual project was an attempt to back the past politics about the formative character of the South Serbian legacy for the Serbian state that was "inexplicably" aborted after 1945 (more in Trifunoski 1995).

"nationalizing nationalism" observed by Rogers Brubaker (2009): certain state-building contexts facilitate a peculiar type of self-entitlement of the dominant ethnocultural group to mobilize the institutional capacities for compensating the past discrimination against it, often targeting other (minority) groups on the way. So, in the context of the proclaimed *brotherhood and unity*, Trifunoski's research fed the idea of the entitlement of the dominant ethnocultural group which was well received by the political and academic elite in the late 1940s and during the 1950s.

The anthropogeographic orientation and methodology of Trifunoski came in handy anew as a scholarly legitimization of the thesis about the geographical borders of the nation understood in ethnic terms. Already in 1946, for instance, Trifunoski published a booklet in Belgrade about the Macedonians in Aegean Macedonia (present-day Greece), supporting this worldview. Hence, if his work on migration can principally be read in the key of ascribing the ethnic Macedonians the dominant role, then his 1946 study of the Macedonians that "remained in Greece" (Trifunoski 1954; also see Wilkinson 1952) can be seen as a token for nurturing the spatial frontiers of the *ethnie* in the novel geopolitical constellation. This idea entertained a wider network of social scientists as of 1948; for instance, Zografski himself co-led a team of historians for research titled "Aegean Macedonia in our history" which culminated in an approximately 400-page publication issued in 1951.

The final context where the pre-war anthropogeography appeared to be fruitful was the one pertaining to the elite-driven *soft-nation-building* project of Yugoslavism [scr. *Jugoslovenstvo*] which, as of the early 1950s, promoted a supranational mode of identification complementary to the ethno-national identities (more in Haug 2012; Cosovschi 2015; Ivešić 2023). Drawing upon the Leninist argument for the eventual but voluntary merging of the nations into a supernational community, localized by **Edvard Kardelj** (1910–1979), one of the leading Yugoslav intellectuals of Slovene ethnic origins and an ideological architect of self-management, the KPJ undertook a series of attempts to foster such an identification in the course of the 1950s, starting with the change of the sovereigns in the 1953 federal Constitution, from the nations to the working people, the introduction of the category *Yugoslav-undefined* in the 1953 population census, to the 1954 Agreement about the Serbo-Croatian language. The proponents of this project sought further legitimization in the "early sociological and anthropological research" conducted in the 1950s (Ivešić 2023, 184). For instance, representatives of the first generation of post-war Yugoslav sociologists, such as another Slovene **Boris Ziherl** (1910–1976), backed this project by invoking the notion of supranational Yugoslav socialist patriotism, a "higher synthesis of the national homeland of individual nations" (Ivešić 2021, 146). On a different note, the *anthropological research* across Yugoslavia, especially in ethnically mixed areas such as Vojvodina, was recognized as real-time evidence for the inevitable merger into Yugoslavism. Most notable for this study is the research about the Macedonian *colonists* to Serbia conducted separately by Trifunoski and **Branislav Rusić** (1912–1971), the other of the first four employees of the Natural Sciences and Mathematics Department in Skopje, and published in Novi Sad by *Matica srpska*. Both the authors came to similar conclusions about the ethnically mixed marriages between the colonists and the natives: they would eventually result in a diminishing of the national particularities and customs (Trifunoski 1958; Rusić 1958), a conclusion similar to that of the Montenegrin researchers (Ivešić 2023, 184).[15]

THE DETOURS

The academic fate of Rusić is illustrative of the porosity of the thin line between desired and undesired scholarship in early post-war Macedonia. More precisely, it suggests that the peculiar entitlement to organizing research operated upon a very subtle ability to maneuver between the mainstream political, national, social, and educational currents of the day, and it was hence possible only in specific formats. Born, like Trifunoski, in Western Macedonia, Rusić started researching in mid-1930s Skopje, before graduating in ethnology in Belgrade where he stayed to work in Belgrade's Ethnographic Museum in 1945 and 1946. Rusić also held a brief post at the post-war Yugoslav Ministry of Foreign Affairs advising Vlahov, who was then a Yugoslav representative at the Paris Peace Conference (Ilievski 2015, 67). He returned to Skopje to assist in the formation of the University by leading the Ethnological Group up to 1952 when it was shut down due to "political and mundane" reasons despite its popularity among students (Risteski and Dimova 2013, 276). The high-level backlash against Rusić, including Miljovski from a position of a rector, had much to do both with his research and teaching activities. Trained in a Cvijićist spirit by his supervisors Đorđević and Erdeljanović,

---

[15] A brief summary and a comparison of both the studies was published in the first issue of *Sociologija*, the first Yugoslav sociological journal (Kostić 1959, 170–170).

Rusić, as already suggested, conducted several fieldwork studies in and beyond the geographical territory of Macedonia in the late 1940s and early 1950s. Besides his major anthropogeographic interest in migration, he was also an observer of social rituals, local customs, family memories, cultural artifacts, and models of contacts between different groups (e.g., see Rusić 1950a, b), all of them below the radar of the anthropogeographical assimilationist take on migration and interactions across cultures (e.g., Baskar 2020, 26). He eventually ended up unveiling some of the downsides of the short but fateful collectivization agenda in Macedonia, especially regarding the rural areas (Ilievski 2015, 68).

Rusić's seminars thereby mirrored his research agenda and presented platforms for discussing his often-non-dogmatic positions. He was, for instance, persistent in the usage of *ethnology*, as he understood the science dealing with the ethnogenesis of the peoples, in spite of the top-down directives for its refurbishment into a Soviet-like *ethnography* in the early post-war years (Risteski and Dimova 2013, 275–276). Even on the record, the ministerial decision-making board hinted at the inability of the former approach to equip the future graduates with "operative" skills as a rationale behind the shutting down of his seminar (Risteski 1997, 2020). Operative, in this regard, was the attested anthropogeographic method—"a bit of geography, a bit of ethnography, and a bit of history" (Svetieva in Aštalkovska Gajtanoska 2021, 96)—as it provided data (and rarely engaged in its explanation) for the dialectic interpretations of the nation, the only desirable framework for articulating the national history in early post-war Macedonia. Ultimately, the drawbacks of this decision appeared to be far-reaching. They predominantly concerned the Group, which was eventually moved away from the Faculty of Philosophy together with the natural sciences (Rusić was apparently against this decision, as he considered ethnology to be closer to the social sciences and humanities, in Lafazanovski 2009). Rusić himself was also relocated to the Institute of Folklore "Marko Cepenkov" established in Skopje just two years earlier, in 1950. He led several unsuccessful initiatives aimed at reenvisioning the institution by widening its research scope; however, it remained by and large focused on folklore and cultural heritage, while approaching the ethnonational culture in a rather "static" sense, as something to be "preserved" (Aštalkovska Gajtanoska 2021, 28). Nonetheless, it took approximately four decades for the return of ethnology as a separate university program, predominantly as a consequence of the surplus of geographers at the PMF (Risteski and Dimova 2013, 281).

Folklore studies as an outpost for undesired social research and research-ers was a recurring theme of the Yugoslav 1950s and 1960s. Nedeljković's case is also telling, as he resorted to such research after the tirade on his positions in the early 1950s, which will be discussed at the end of this chapter. In brief, in response to the criticism depicting him as a dogmatic Marxist, he rediscovered his interwar interest in folk psychology as an opportunity for dodging the attacks and an eventual reinvention of him-self and his work. However, unlike Rusić, Nedeljković was more successful in getting his research agenda approved by the official gatekeepers. More precisely, alongside the circle around the Belgrade-based journal *Folklor* (1964–1968), he started portraying the vernacular folklorist forms as pre-cursors for the socialist revolution in Yugoslavia against the "rusticaliza-tion" of the study field (Stojković 1980, 105–106; also see Nazor 1967). More sensitive to the Macedonian national particularities after his wartime conflict with the Macedonian communists, Nedeljković researched and published, *inter alia*, about the workers' and revolutionaries' songs in Yugoslavia and got especially interested in the work of his pre-war acquain-tance in Skopje, Kočo Racin (Oinas 1966, 413; Nedeljkoviḱ 1973). Racin was especially appropriate to this agenda, as he mostly explored and relied on the pre-revolutionary Macedonian folklorist motifs for his politically engaged and socialist poetry. Nedeljković was admitted as a member of the Macedonian Academy of Sciences and Arts in 1974 and he was well received anew as a Marxist theoretician in the Macedonia of the 1970s, a point which will be contextualized in the fourth chapter. He is nowadays considered to be among the key figures for the establishment of philo-sophical studies (see, e.g., the introduction to his "Skopje lectures" in Nedeljkoviḱ 1984), while his interwar work in ethnopsychology is by and large undiscovered (e.g., Penušliski 1981, 48).

A revealing Macedonian case for the ethnological research agenda in the times of hindered ethnological studies is the one of **Galaba Palikruševa-Nazim** (1928–2009). Initially a history student, she gradu-ated in ethnology under Rusić in 1954 just before the closure of the pro-gram. After her graduation, she took up several high positions at museums across Macedonia before assuming research and teaching posts at the INI and the Skopje University as of the 1960s. Palikruševa-Nazim is nowadays considered to be the formative figure behind the reactivation of ethnology studies in Macedonia, with the inauguration of the Ethnology Chair at the PMF in the mid-1980s being her "unbelievable" success (Svetieva 2009, 272). Her appointment at the Skopje University overlapped with the major political shift at federal level and especially the consequences it bore for the interethnic relations in the state, which will be discussed in more detail in the next chapter. In brief, the defeat of the centralist camp allowed for a general reconsideration of the party's approach to the so-called question of the nationalities, now acknowledging, for instance, Yugoslav Muslims as a separate entity, "a sixth Yugoslav nationality" (Ramet 1984, 145–155). This decision, however, was differently received in Bosnia and Herzegovina, where the Bosniak Muslims were finally able to promote their identity vis-à-vis the tendencies of Serb and Croat appropriations, and in Macedonia, where the vast majority of Orthodox Christian Macedonians understood the above developments pertaining to the small group of Macedonian Muslims as a threat to their selfhood. What followed was a series of top-down deliberations about the ethnic belonging of the Macedonian-speaking Macedonians of Islamic faith (an overview in Bielenin-Lenczowska 2008).[16] In this very context, Palikruševa-Nazim, unlike Nedeljković who had a more careful approach to the heated topics, stepped forward in 1965 with a doctoral thesis about the contrasts between the Macedonian Muslims and the Orthodox Christian Macedonians populating their immediate surroundings.[17] Drawing upon Ottoman sources and ethnographic observations, she claimed that the formation of the ethnic boundaries occurred in spite of the shared language and due to the different religious socialization and the past political decisions of the community (in Gorgiev 2018). Her argument and especially her early 1970s feuilleton aimed at popularizing her thesis provoked a massive set of reactions which will be touched upon in the next chapter.

The Faculty of Law in Skopje opened up another possibility for a sociological scholarly detour during the early post-war period. It involved Boris Arsov, whose pre-war work and instrumentalization of sociology were discussed in the previous chapter. After his imprisonment, he joined the antifascist struggle and fought his way up to taking part in ASNOM and the

---

[16] Palikruševa-Nazim was among the initiators of the research about the ethnogenesis of the Yuruks in the 1950s, a Turkoman ethnic group populating Macedonia and especially the region of Štip where she led the city museum at that point (Tomovski et al. 1986; for context, see Stojanov et al. 1982, 29).

[17] Interestingly enough, Nedeljković worked on this very topic in the interwar period, as discussed in the previous chapter, arguing in favor of an ethnic unity of the different groups populating the area and supporting his argument with ethnopsychological methods.

committee that drafted the first Macedonian constitution.[18] In the wake of the war, he took the post of Deputy Minister of Justice, which allowed him to develop a set of studies of the Soviet legal apparatus as a blueprint for developing the Macedonian one. His archive in the Macedonian Academy of Sciences and Arts consists of published and mostly unpublished studies of Soviet jurisprudence, legal institutes, and criminal law procedures, as well as draft projects for the Macedonian laws on peoples' committees and administration. In 1952, he joined the newly formed Faculty of Law and Economics as an instructor in international private law and he is nowadays considered to be part of the first Macedonian generation of law professors (Dokmanoviḱ 2007). Besides his workbook in international private law, he continued exploring Marxist philosophy and political economy in the late 1940s and early 1950s but also reverted to some earlier research interests of his, such as comparative law, sociology, and psychology. Among these files is his study titled *Pregled na nekoji psihološki koncepcii vo francuskata buržoazna nauka* (A Review of Some Psychological Concepts in French Bourgeois Science), which could easily be the first sociological text ever written in Macedonian had it been published at that point in time.[19]

Authored in or shortly after 1948—as per the archival note; the typescript is unfortunately not dated—Arsov provides two reasons for picking up such a seemingly non-Marxist topic. The first one is ethical and political: he postulates that the working class, the "only legal successor of the positive benefits of the bourgeois culture and civilization" (pp. 1–2), holds every right to instrumentalize those very benefits in its struggle against everything idealist and reactionary. The second one is rather

[18] The Macedonian communists were not enthusiastically welcoming of intellectuals in the resistance movement and the Macedonian branch of the KPJ in the early phases of the war and occupation. **Vladimir Poležinoski** (1912–1980), another Sorbonne graduate in law of ethnic Macedonian origins, joined the party after a heated discussion over his admission. His legal training, similar to Arsov, facilitated his way up to the team preparing ASNOM, while he was also a member and a second secretary of its Presidium. In the aftermath of the war, the Yugoslav military mission recruited Poležinoski to France, because of his knowledge of legal French, and then to West Germany. In the midst of the Yugoslav-Soviet quarrel, he paid a civil visit to a Soviet counterpart of his in Frankfurt; he was dismissed shortly afterward and accused of treason and spreading enemy propaganda. He served three years in the infamous political prison and labor camp Goli Otok from 1951 to 1954, but he gradually rehabilitated his career, first in Belgrade and then in Skopje (more in Čepreganov et al. 2013).

[19] MANU Archive "Haralampie Polenakoviḱ" in Skopje, Boris Arsov Fund, Psihološki studii: *Pregled na nekoji psihološki koncepcii vo francuskata buržoazna nauka*, 1–23.

epistemological and gnoseological: the early positivist assumptions about the human mind triggered a century-long French consideration over the operation of a domain which, albeit inferior to dialectical logic, might inform certain materialistic interpretations. This resonates with the Yugoslav zeitgeist, epitomized in Nedeljković's call mentioned earlier. Arsov traced the intellectual genesis of this domain, mapping the main protagonists, arguments, and debates from the nineteenth century to the First World War (Comte, Durkheim, Tarde, Le Bon) to the post-First World War period (among others, Lévy-Bruhl, Bergson, Halbwachs, and De Roberti—from his Paris days). Despite his diachronic review methodology, his text is not Leninist *per se* as he rather traces their inherent discursive continuities and discontinuities. He concludes with a very limited takeaway: positively evaluating Durkheim and the Durkheimians in line with his earlier work, especially regarding their understanding of the collective consciousness and the primitive societies. The acknowledgment of Durkheim, moreover, helps unveil another underlying tone of the study which pertains to the emphasis on the history of ideas about decoupling the scientific scope of the social and the psychological.

As already mentioned, the study was never published, although well edited and seemingly ready (and most possibly awaiting a more welcoming political climate); however, Arsov died in 1954 at the age of only 48, leaving not only this and another set of unpublished studies behind him, but also the academic scene in Macedonia with no one so directly exposed to and versed in the history of French sociology and sociologists. In Belgrade, for instance, another Sorbonne law graduate, **Radomir D. Lukić** (1914–1999), had the corresponding and necessary cultural and political capital to become a formative figure in the establishment of the first sociological institutions in 1950s Yugoslavia. However, it is also possible that Arsov used the text as teaching material, even though there is no hard evidence supporting this claim. If one can further expand this scenario, he managed to interact with the first generation of law students— such as **Slavko Milosavlevski** (1928–2012), whose work will be discussed in detail in the next chapters—which grew to be instrumental in establishing the sociological courses at the Faculty of Law in the early 1960s and sociology in Macedonia in general.

The early post-war period saw another set of invocations of sociological references in Macedonia. Unlike in the interwar period, when the Yugoslav Marxists attempted to combine the popular understanding of Marxism with neopositivism, psychoanalysis, and contemporary physics, after 1945, the dominant Yugoslav model of disseminating scientific knowledge was much like the Soviet one: guarding the dialectical materialist principles from idealism via widely printed "ersatz textbooks" (Duančić 2019, 56–58). As per the catalogue of the national and university library in Skopje, the earliest publications in Macedonian containing the keyword "sociology" can be traced back to such a textbook from 1949: the translated *stenogram* of **Fyodor V. Konstantinov**'s (1901–1999) Moscow lecture about the role of progressive ideas for social development (see Konstantinov 1949). His booklet was already available in Serbian, in a similar format; however, it took several more months for it to appear in Macedonian, interestingly enough, despite the major geopolitical reshuffling of the day. After several translations of Soviet literature, the next set of articles containing the keyword "sociology" is linked to the name of **Emanuel (Mane) Čučkov** (1901–1967), an ethnologist-musicologist, another member of the ASNOM and the ANOK, whose wartime political agenda was ultimately defeated but who nonetheless held several high positions in Macedonia during the early post-war decade—a parliamentary deputy (1946–1950), the first director of the National Library, and the founder of the Folklore Institute and the national musical ensemble *Tanec*—before assuming the position of a docent in economic geography at the Faculty of Economics in Skopje in 1954 (Ristovski 2005). Čučkov later published several articles during the mid- and late 1950s, combining his pre-war interest in anthropogeography with the prevailing themes of the 1950s: industrialization, migrations, and demographics (an overview in Mileski 1967).

The publishing politics of the Skopje-based major publishing house *Kultura* unveils several modes of domestication/discussion not only of Marxist themes as of the late 1950s but also Western social scientific approaches and studies in humanities. Most notable, in this regard, is the booklet series titled *Popularna biblioteka* (Popular Library) and initially subtitled *Filozofski problemi* (Philosophical issues), shifting to "Philosophy" and "Sociology" in the early 1960s (for context, see Radičeski 2023). Two of the earliest booklets, both published in 1959, best reflect the two doctrinaire yet diverging paths of theoretical Marxism claimed by Macedonian scholars. Taškovski's *Freudianism and Marxism*, to start with, is illustrative for the first path.[20] He criticized Freud's "sociological"—and not

[20] Taškovski studied Marxist and non-Marxist scholars, such as Diderot and Halbwachs, during the interwar period as per his autobiographical account. In MANU Archive "Haralampie Polenakoviḱ" in Skopje, Dragan Taškovski Fund, *Kratka biografija.*

"clinical"—theory from a Marxist-Leninist perspective by reviewing Freudian writings about the "sociologist" Marx, and, in turn, juxtaposing them with Marx's paragraphs about biologism, culture, labor, and social development, deeming the two authors irreconcilable despite the then emerging attempts otherwise by Western Marxists (Taškovski 1959). His discursive operation of attributing *sociology* to Marx and Marxism can be hence read as an attempt at "sociologizing historical materialism" (Voříšek 2012, 132–133), already occurring in mid-1950s Czechoslovakia and Poland. It was certainly not aimed at widening the scope of dogmatic historical materialism; rather, it was a metonymic way of engaging with emerging and critical work while defending dogmatic positions.

The other path was trailed by **Jonče Josifovski** (1920–2009), a Macedonian philosopher and logician, who studied in Belgrade, Moscow, and Leningrad before graduating in Skopje in 1951 as the first graduate student of philosophy. In the meantime, he co-authored the first post-war Macedonian primer in 1945 (Leitner-Stojanov 2019), while after his graduation, he established himself as the leading figure of philosophical education in Skopje, being, as such, a teacher of philosophy and logic to the vast majority of Macedonian sociologists. Josifovski's 1959 booklet titled *Neopozitivizmot* (Neopositivism) is a detailed overview of its predecessors, key points, and the relation between neopositivism and dialectics. Similar to Taškovski, Josifovski maps out the Western neopositivist references of sociology as proofs for their authors' anti-dialectical stances. However, contrary to him, he was attentive to certain neopositivist arguments about "the clarity and the determinacy of the thought" (2004, 432), criticizing Soviet and Polish dogmatic philosophers who remained dogmatic in this regard.

The booklet series of *Kultura* also included titles authored by other associates of the Skopje University, such as Petroska (1962), as well as Yugoslav scholars whose fate brought them to teach in Skopje—such as Šešić, **Zagorka Mićić** (1903–1982), and **Abdulah Šarčević** (1929–2021)—or to be connected with the city in other ways—such as **Andrija B. Stojković** (1924–2007), who was a disciple of Nedeljković. It would be some of these authors who introduced different understandings of sociology in the Macedonian context and hence fostered its development and institutionalization in the 1960s.

The work of Mićić is very instructive in this regard. A scholar of Serbian origins, she studied psychology in Berlin and wrote her doctoral thesis in philosophy in Freiburg im Breisgau under Husserl and Fink on the eve of the war.[21] She came to Skopje in 1954, after rejecting the position of chair of the Belgrade Philosophy Department, and stayed in the Macedonian capital city until 1972, where she helped develop the philosophical program in Skopje.[22] Already in the early 1950s, she was among the first to criticize Nedeljković's public lectures series for inconsistencies in what would emerge as the key philosophical debate of the decade. Thenceforth, starting from her first article published in Skopje (Mićić 1955), her booklet for *Kultura* in 1961, titled *Sovremenite graǵanski filozofi za marksizmot* (The Contemporary Bourgeois Philosophers on Marxism), as well as other articles published in Skopje during this period (Mićić 1962, 1966), Mićić opted for a more open, contemporary, and humanistic understanding of Marxism. The humanistic virtues in Marxism have both theoretical and political implications, she argued, as they enable pluralism of thought and a common ground for a wider and "lively" debate between Marxists and non-Marxists (Mikik 1961, 60–61). To demonstrate this position, Mićić mapped out the contemporary traces of non-Marxist interpretations of Marxism in existentialists (Sartre, Merleau-Ponty) and phenomenologists (Löwith, Landgrebe), but also explored the possible meeting points between Marxism and the emerging scientific discourses of sociology and psychology.[23] Mićić's arguments helped embed "the 1960s turn towards the categories of existentialism and phenomenology" in Yugoslavia, while

---

[21] It took her some time to face her "long internal conflict" and acquaint herself with the Marxist literature (Mićić in Marić 2016, 88).

[22] Together with **Pavao Vuk-Pavlović** (1894–1976), an aesthetician of Croat Jewish origins, critical of the dogmatic Marxism, who stayed at the Skopje University from 1958 to 1971, and several other Macedonian philosophers. The program had a blast during this period, which overlapped with the liberal communist turn in the early 1960s and the room for public deliberations it tolerated (discussed in the next chapter). The philosophy program developed an atypical, for the Yugoslav context, aesthetic laboratory and participated in organizing theater and youth festivals (e.g., Temkov 2003).

[23] Another such publication of *Kultura* is **Zagorka (Zaga) Pešić-Golubović's** (1930–2019), "one of the most prominent Serbian social scientists" (Spasić et al. 2022, 44), 1963 booklet titled *The issues of the contemporary man*. The booklet's structure is twofold: the first part deals with *philosophical* and the second one with *sociological* issues. In the second part, she discusses the social character of the individual focusing on, *inter alia*, the issues of alienation in the Frankfurt School, but also reverting to Freud and Wright Mills. The main takeaway of Pešić-Golubović's booklet pertains to her view of the sociological studies as evaluators of the development of the Marxist theory in practice, as well as the challenges which the population is facing in the course of this process (Pešik-Golubovik 1963, 41–57), an agenda which she adhered to during the coming decades.

Nedeljković was "dethroned" as a Stalinist by 1953 by the sociologists and philosophers around the journal *Praxis* (Blagojević 2022). The outer borders of scientific Marxism were the main themes of the two booklets authored by Andrija B. Stojković, a post-war professor of Marxism in the 1950s and 1960s, who turned to exploring sociology and the history of social thought in Serbia in the 1970s. In his 1962 booklet published by *Kultura*, Stojković outlined the scope of sociology against the background of the epistemological potentials of praxis; however, he also hints at its corrective function pertaining to older theories, such as the theory of reflection, rejected as Stalinist by the non-dogmatic Yugoslav intellectuals. In his typology of sciences, sociology is seen in a rather "histmat" light (Stojkovik 1962). For instance, he differentiates between the *immature* and the *mature* consciousnesses concerning the relations of production: the first one attributed to the social utopians, such as Fourier and Saint-Simon, and the second to the Marxist thinkers. Stojković expresses a more attentive view of sociology in his second booklet published the very next year under the title *Klasifikacija na naukite* (Classification of the Sciences). Building upon both **Jože Goričar** (1907–1985) and Lukić, in spite of their different views (see, e.g., Lukić 1957, 54–59), Stojković defined sociology as a meta-science, a scientific synthesis of the other, not exclusively social, sciences (Stojkovik 1963, 61–62).

REFERENCES

Aštalkovska Gajtanoska, Ana. 2021. *Od etnocentrizam kon humanizam: Dominantnite izrazi na makedonskata folkloristika, etnologija i antropologija niz istorijata*. Skopje: Studentski servis.

Baskar, Bojan. 2020. Vera Stein Erlich and the Conundrum of Yugoslav Cultural Diversity. In *Diversities. Theories & Practices: Festschrift for Reinhard Johler*, eds. Jan Hinrichsen, Jan Lange and Raphael Reichel, 11–34. Tübingen: EKW-Verlag.

Bielenin-Lenczowska, Karolina. 2008. The Construction of Identity in a Multiethnic Community: A Case Study on the Torbeši of Centar Župa Commune, Western Macedonia. *Ethnologia Balkanica* 12: 167–181.

Blagojević, Una. 2022. Phenomenology and Existentialism in Dialogue with Marxist Humanism in Yugoslavia in the 1950s and 1960s. *Studies in East European Thought* 75: 417–435.

Brubaker, Rogers. 2009. *Nationalism Reframed: Nationhood and the National Question in the New Europe*. Cambridge and New York: Cambridge University Press.

Čepreganov, Todor, et al. 2013. *D-r Vladimir Poležinoski – život i delo.* Skopje and Kičevo: Institut za nacionalna istorija and Sovet na Opština Kičevo.

Cosovschi, Agustin. 2015. Between the Nation and Socialism in Yugoslavia. The Debate Between Dobrica Ćosić and Dušan Prijevec in the 1960s. *Slovanský přehled* 101 (2): 293–317.

Dimeski, Dimitar. 1979. Opštestveno-ekonomskite priliki vo Makedonija (1878-1903). *Istorija* 15 (2): 81–103.

Dimitrov, Evgeni, ed. 1984. *Spomenica: Kiril Miljovski.* Skopje: MANU.

Dokmanoviḱ, Mišo. 2007. Istoriskiot razvoj na Pravniot fakultet. In *Praven fakultet "Justinijan Prvi" – Istoriski razvoj 1951-2006,* ed. Vlado Popovski et al., 21–85. Skopje: Praven Fakultet "Justinijan Prvi".

Duančić, Vedran. 2019. Learning About Politics Through Science: Popular Science in Early Socialist Yugoslavia, 1945–1950. *Historyka: Studia Metodologiczne* 49: 55–76.

Georgievski, Taško, ed. 1997. *Dančo Zografski: 1920-1997.* Skopje: MANU.

Ǵorgiev, Dragi. 2018. Galaba Palikruševa, Islamizacijata na Torbešite i formiranjeto na torbeškata subgrupa. *Glasnik na INI* 62 (1–2): 263–266.

Ǵorgoski, Icko, ed. 2016. *70 godini Prirodno-matematički fakultet – Skopje.* Skopje: PMF.

Hadžievska, Ivana, and Jana Kocevska. 2022. *Arhivi na nevidlivite: Makedonka – Organ na AFŽ (1944-1952), istoriski iskustva i kulturna memorija.* Skopje: CINIK.

Haug, Hilde Katrine. 2012. *Creating a Socialist Yugoslavia: Tito, Communist Leadership and the National Question.* London and New York: I.B. Tauris.

Ilievski, Borče. 2015. Semejnite i ličnite fondovi – značaen izvor za istoriski istražuvanja. *Godišen zbornik na Filozofskiot fakultet* 68: 63–76.

———. 2021. Migraciite vo Skopskata Kotlina vo XIX vek – pomeǵu antropogeografskite istražuvanja na Jovan F. Trifunoski i istoriskite izvori. *EtnoAntropoZum* 21: 258–276.

Ivešić, Tomaž. 2021. The Yugoslav National Idea Under Socialism: What Happens When a Soft Nation-Building Project Is Abandoned? *Nationalities Papers* 49 (1): 142–161.

———. 2023. Yugoslav Experts, Yugoslavism and the National Question in the 1960s. *European Review of History* 30 (2): 180–203.

Josifovski, Jonče. 2004. *Filozofski tekstovi.* Skopje: Az-Buki.

Kantardžiev, Risto, et al. 1976. *Filozofskiot fakultet vo Skopje 1946-1976.* Skopje: Filozofski fakultet na Univerzitetot "Kiril i Metodij" vo Skopje.

Konstantinov, Fedor V. 1949. *Roljata na naprednite idei vo opštestveniot razvitok.* Skopje: Kultura.

Korubin, Jovan, ed. 2000. *Institut za sociologija: 25 godini.* Skopje: UKIM.

Kostić, Dara. 1959. Dve studije o makedonskim kolonistima u Vojvodini. *Sociologija* 1 (1): 170–171.

Kostic, Cvetko. 1983. Sociology in Yugoslavia 1960–1970. *International Review of Modern Sociology* 13 (1): 375–395.

Lafazanovski, Ermis. 2009. Državata i folklorot: Institucionalizacijata na folklorot i etnologijata vo procesot na nacionalnata izgradba vo Makedonija posle 1945. In *Ehoto na nacijata*, ed. Žarko Trajanoski et al., 38–55. Skopje: Templum.

Leitner-Stojanov, Darko. 2019. Militarization via Education: A 1945 Primer from Socialist Macedonia. *Journal of Educational Media, Memory and Society* 11 (1): 35–52.

Livanios, Dimitris. 2008. *The Macedonian Question: Britain and the Southern Balkans 1939–1949*. Oxford: Oxford University Press.

Lukić, Radomir. 1957. *Uvod u sociologiju*. Beograd: Savez Udruženja pravnika Jugoslavije.

———. 1959. Društveni uslovi razvoja sociologije u Jugoslaviji. *Sociologija* 1 (2–3): 97–113.

Marić, Ilija. 2016. Prva naša posleratna kritika klasika marksizma: O ciklusu predavanja Dušana Nedeljkovića na Kolarčevom narodnom univerzitetu početkom 1952. *Glas Sprske akademije nauka i umetnosti* 32: 71–98.

Markoski, Blagoja. 2019. *Makedonskata geografska misla po povod 70 godini Makedonsko geografsko društvo*. Skopje: MGD.

Mežnarić, Silva. 1989. Jovan Trifunoski: Albansko stanovništvo u Makedoniji. *Migracijske teme* 5 (2-3): 241–250.

Mićić, Zagorka. 1955. Istorija filozofije kao nauka. *Godišen zbornik na Filozofskiot fakultet* 8: 59–84.

———. 1962. Idejno teorijsko jedinstvo nauka i filozofija. *Godišen zbornik na Filozofskiot fakultet* 14: 29–52.

———. 1966. Kontakti između savremene filozofije i psihijatrije. *Godišen zbornik na Filozofskiot fakultet* 17–18: 15–30.

Mikić, Zagorka. 1961. *Sovremenite građanski filozofi za marksizmot*. Skopje: Kultura.

Mileski, Gigo. 1967. Vo sekjavanje na prof. d-r Mane Čučkov: Život i dejnost. *Geografski razgledi* 5: 167–171.

Miljovska, Desanka. 1957. Eden interesen napis na Misirkov za ekonomskata sostojba na makedonskoto selo vo krajot na minatiot vek. *Glasnik na INI* 1 (1): 253–270.

———. 1962. *Klasne snage nacionalno-oslobodilačkog pokreta makedonskog naroda u drugoj polovini XIX veka*. Skopje: Filozofski fakultet.

———. 1963a. Ekonomski uslovi društvene strukture makedonskih gradova u drugoj polovini XIX veka. *Godišen zbornik na Filozofskiot fakultet* 15: 51–120.

———. 1963b. Dve razvojni etapi vo ekonomsko-opštestveniot razvitok na Makedonija vo XIX vek. *Glasnik na INI* 7 (2): 35–79.

———. 1986. Ušte ednaš za opštestveno-ekonomskite uslovi i karakterot na Ilindenskoto vostanie. *Godišen zbornik na Filozofskiot fakultet* 39: 316–331.

Mladenovski, Ǵorǵe. 1997. Blaga Petroska – portret za istorijata na makedonskata sociologija. *Sociološka revija* 3 (1–2): I–VIII.

Nazor, Ante. 1967. Narodno stvaralaštvo – Folklor. Organ Saveza udruženja folklorista Jugoslavije. *Narodna umjetnost* 5-6 (1): 654–657.

Nedeljkoviḱ, Dušan. 1973. *Kosta Racin: Poet na revolucijata*. Skopje: Makedonska kniga.

———. 1984. *Istorija na filozofijata: Skopski predavanja*. Skopje: Makedonska kniga.

Oinas, Felix J. 1966. The Study of Folklore in Yugoslavia. *Journal of the Folklore Institute* 3 (3): 398–418.

Panov, Mitko. 2019. *The Blinded State: Historiographic Debates About Samuel Cometopoulos and His State (10th–11th Century)*. Leiden and Boston: Brill.

Penušliski, Kiril. 1981. *Makedonskiot folklor*. Skopje: Misla.

Pešiḱ-Goluboviḱ, Zaga. 1963. *Problemite na sovremeniot čovek*. Skopje: Kultura.

Petkovski, Boris. 1989. *Za makedonskata umetnost (odbrani trudovi)*. Skopje: Naša kniga.

Petreska, Darinka. 2006. Politikata, ideologijata i makedonskata istoriografija 1944-1953 g. *Godišen zbornik na Filozofskiot fakultet* 59: 197–220.

Petroska, Blaga. 1962. *Klasicite na marksizmot za brakot i semejstvoto*. Skopje: Kultura.

Radičeski, Neven. 2023. Izdavačata politika vo NR Makedonija vo vtorata polovina na 50-tite godini od XX vek. *Glasnik na INI* 67 (1–2): 135–146.

Ramet, Pedro. 1984. *Nationalism and Federalism in Yugoslavia, 1963–1983*. Bloomington and London: Indiana University Press.

Risteski, Ljupčo S. 1997. *Rakopisnata zaostavština na Branislav Rusiḱ: Prilog kon istorijata na etnološkata misla vo Makedonija*. Bitola: Misirkov.

———. 2020. "Samo što izlegovme od opinci, etnolozite sakaat povtorno da nè vratat vo niv". Statusot na etnologijata vo Makedonija vo periodot na socijalizmot (1946-1953). *EtnoAntropoZum* 20: 28–60.

Risteski, Ljupčo S., and Rozita Dimova. 2013. Between Folklore, Geography, and Ethno-nationalism: Ethnology in Macedonia During and After Socialism. In *The Anthropological Field on the Margins of Europe, 1945–1991*, ed. Aleksandar Bošković and Chris Hann, 273–292. Zürich and Berlin: LIT.

Ristovski, Blaže. 2005. Profesorot i državnik Mane Čučkov pred i po ASNOM. *Sovremenost* 5: 37–69.

Rusić, Branislav. 1950a. Pitanje Zakamena. *Godišen zbornik na Istorisko-filološki oddel* 3 (7): 3–22.

———. 1950b. Saidžije u Makedoniji. *Godišen zbornik na Istorisko-filološki oddel* 3 (8): 3–10.

———. 1958. *Beleške o najnovijim naseljenicima iz Makedonije u sedam sela vršačkog dela Banata*. Novi Sad: Matica srpska.

Spasić, Ivana, Jelena Pešić, and Marija Babović. 2022. *Sociology in Serbia: A Fragile Discipline*. Basingstoke: Palgrave Macmillan.

Stojanov, Petar, et al., eds. 1982. *Istoriografijata na Makedonija 1965-1975*. Skopje: Studentski zbor.

Stojković, Andrija B. 1980. *Ideologija srpske revolucije 1804-1830: U celini razvitka filozofske i društvene misli u Srba*. Beograd: SANU and Istorisjki institut u Beogradu.

Stojkoviḱ, Andrija. 1962. *Što e praktika?* Skopje: Kultura.

———. 1963. *Klasifikacija na naukite*. Skopje: Kultura.

Svetieva, Aneta. 2009. D-r Galaba Palikruševa-Nazim (1928-2009). *EtnoAntropoZum* 6: 268–274.

Szwat-Gyłybowa, Grażyna. 2005. *Haeresis Bulgarica w bułgarskiej świadomości kulturowej XIX i XX wieku*. Warszawa: Instytut Slawistyki Polskiej Akademii Nauk and Fundacja Slawistyczna.

Taškovski, Dragan. 1949. *Bogomilskoto dviženje*. Skopje: Naučen institut za nacionalnata istorija na makedonskiot narod.

———. 1951. *Bogomilstvoto i negovoto istorisko znacenje*. Skopje: Državno knigoizdatelstvo na NR Makedonija.

———. 1959. *Frojdizmot i marksizmot*. Skopje: Kultura.

———. 1975. *Bogomilism in Macedonia*. Skopje: Macedonian Review Editions.

———. 1982. Klasniot i socijalniot karakter na bogomilstvoto. In *Bogomilstvoto na Balkanot vo svetlinata na najnovite istražuvanja*, ed. Ljuben Lape et al., 41–54. Skopje: MANU.

Temkov, Kiril. 2003. Etičkite i aksiološkite idei vo filosofskata poezija na Pavao Vuk-Pavloviḱ. *Godišen zbornik na Filozofskiot fakultet* 56: 75–98.

Tomovski, Krum, et al., eds. 1986. *Etnogeneza na Jurucite i nivnoto naseluvanje na Balkanot*. Skopje: MANU.

Trajkovski, Ilo. 2000. *Sociologija: Što e i kako se praktikuva?* Skopje and Melbourne: Matica makedonska.

Trifunoski, Jovan F. 1947. *Makedonska gradska naselja*. Beograd: Štamparija Davidović.

———. 1948. Moravica. *Godišen zbornik na Prirodno-matematički oddel* 1: 223–256.

———. 1952. Makedonski rodovi vo Polog so poteklo od Albanija. *Godišen zbornik na Istorisko-filološki oddel* 1: 223–256.

———. 1954. Novija preseljavanja stanovništva u Makedoniji. *Hrvatski geografski glasnik* 16–17 (1): 97–98.

———. 1958. O posleratnom naseljavanju stanovništva iz NR Makedonije u tri banatska naselja. Novi Sad: Matica srpska.

———. 1992. *Ohridsko-struška oblast: Antropogeografska proučavanja*. Beograd: Srpska akademija nauka i umetnosti.

———. 1995. *Makedoniziranje Južne Srbije*. Beograd: Cicero.

Trifunovski, Jovan F. 2019. *Albanskoto naselenie vo Socijalistička Republika Makedonija: Antropološki i etnografski istražuvanja*. Skopje: Magor.

Troebst, Stefan. 1997. Yugoslav Macedonia, 1943–1953: Building the Party, the State, and the Nation. In *State-Society Relations in Yugoslavia, 1945–1992*, ed.

Melissa K. Bokovoy, Jill A. Irvine, and Carol S. Lilly, 243–266. New York: St. Martin's Press.

Uzunov, Nikola, and Metodija Stojkov. 1993. Pridonesot na Kiril Miljovski za ekonomskata nauka vo Makedonija. In *Ekonomskata nauka i stopanskiot razvoj na Republika Makedonija*, ed. Nikola Uzunov et al., 7–24. Skopje: MANU.

Voříšek, Michael. 2012. *The Reform Generation: 1960s Czechoslovak Sociology from a Comparative Perspective*. Kalich: Kalich Publishers.

Voss, Christian. 2006. The Macedonian Standard Language: Tito-Yugoslav Experiment or Symbol of 'Great Macedonian' Ethnic Inclusion. In *Language Ideologies, Policies and Practices: Language and the Future of Europe*, ed. Clare Mar-Molinero and Patrick Stevenson, 118–132. Basingstoke: Palgrave Macmillan.

Wilkinson, Henry R. 1952. Jugoslav Macedonia in Transition. *The Geographical Journal* 118 (4): 389–405.

Zografski, Dančo. 1962. *Jugoslovenskite socijalisti za makedonskoto prašanje*. Skopje: Kultura.

———. 1967. *Razvitokot na kapitalističkite elementi vo Makedonija za vreme na turskoto vladeenje*. Skopje: Kultura.

———. 1990. *Za makedonskoto prašanje*. Skopje: Misla.

CHAPTER 3

The Leap Forward: The Benefits and Challenges of the Institutionalization of Macedonian Sociology (1960s–Early 1970s)

Abstract The processes of professionalizing and institutionalizing Macedonian sociology progressed from the earliest such initiatives in the mid-1950s, the first sociological courses and empirical research in the late 1950s and the early 1960s, to the establishment of the first sociological research institute in Skopje in 1965. It took a bit more time, however, for Macedonian sociology to acquire the label of a resolute discipline and situate itself as an undisputed scientific discourse. In this chapter, I map all the major events against the background of the emerging anti-dogmatic sociology in and beyond Yugoslavia. I also highlight the episodes of cross-national sociological knowledge transfers in the 1960s and finish up with the formative sociological exchanges in Macedonia from the late 1960s and the early 1970s.

Keywords Institutionalization • Professionalization • Sociology • Empirical sociology • Socialist Republic of Macedonia

The 1960s saw a tidal wave in Yugoslav and Macedonian politics. The prevailing KPJ/SKJ's course toward economic and political decentralization calibrated during the 1950s culminated in the drafting of the new Yugoslav Constitution in the early 1960s (adopted in 1963). Apart from

N. Trajanovski, *A History of Macedonian Sociology*, Sociology
Transformed, https://doi.org/10.1007/978-3-031-48869-6_3

67

the Constitution, the 1964 Party Congress made official the break with the state-sponsored support of the Yugoslavism concept, thus facilitating a shift toward a model of a Federation-shelter of the separate ethnocultural and national identities (Rusinow 1977; Ramet 1984). However, equally, if not more important, were the outcomes of the political power plays of the day. The opposition to decentralization was rallied behind **Aleksandar Ranković** (1909–1983), a former Minister of Interior and an erstwhile First Vice President of Yugoslavia, who pushed for centralization of decision-making via, *inter alia*, campaigning against and bashing the national minorities and non-Slavic groups, most notably the Albanians in the autonomous province of Kosovo.[1] He and his group were faced with a cohort of so-called liberal politicians in all the republics, principally in those where they managed to assume the leading political positions: in Slovenia and Croatia, where they opted for a better economic redistribution and autonomy, and in Macedonia, where they predominantly aimed at safeguarding against the centralist (understood as Serbian hegemonic) tendencies. In one of the critical events of the decade, the liberals found the struggle for national interests, albeit with their local particularities, as a political common ground. Preeminently, the Macedonian group led by **Krste Crvenkovski** (1921–2001) and backed by Skopje's Faculty of Law sociology circle, which assumed power in Macedonia already in 1963, emerged as a frontrunner of this agenda at a federal level due to the leverage of the history of affirmative Yugoslav treatment of the *Macedonian national interests* (Trebst 1997, 74). As an illustration, the final nail in the coffin of the centralist and so-called conservative politics in the 1960s was set by Crvenkovski himself, who chaired the Commission investigating the tapping affair involving Ranković, who allegedly masterminded a blackmailing scheme and bugged Tito's bedroom, that ended with his dismissal in 1966.

Despite the nominal improvement of Yugoslav–Bulgarian relations in the 1960s under the framework of tightening the Yugoslav-Soviet bonds, the bilateral issue over Macedonian history, identity, and language reemerged as early as 1963. Hence, the first half of the 1960s was marked by the Bulgarian inclination to securitize everything "Macedonian"—that is, zero-sum-game diplomacy over the above issues and an eventual *re-Bulgarization* of Yugoslav Macedonia—while the second half of the

---

[1] The altercation built upon a far more complex prehistory and unfolded in a series of political and legal maneuvers in the 1960s (a brief overview in Bešlin 2021).

decade saw several (unsuccessful) Yugoslav/Macedonian-Bulgarian high-level attempts at reconciliation (Trebst 1997; Marinov 2020). The liberal Macedonian leadership showed readiness for certain compromises, however. Unlike their Croat counterparts, whose economic nationalism led to a mass "national euphoria" (Rusinow 1977, 298) in the late 1960s and early 1970s, Crvenkovski and his inner circle had a different vision for the state and the nation. The main rationale behind their project of *modernizing* the nation was the further development of institutions that would ultimately secure the much-needed protection from both inter-federal and regional claims over the Macedonian national attributes.[2] Such was the rationale behind the formation of the Macedonian Academy of Sciences and Arts and the proclamation of the autocephality of the Macedonian Orthodox Church, both in 1967. Most ambitious, in this regard, was the sociological proposal, suggested "by our intellectuals" (Crvenkovski 1989, 17), pertaining to the "delayed" development of the Macedonian nation as a token for solving the bilateral dispute, discussed in the last section. The modernizing politics also had an effect on the interethnic relations in the state: during the 1960s, the Macedonian authorities granted the equal status of the minority languages, the usage of minority flags in several municipalities, and better representation of the minorities in the state institutions (Trajanovski 2021a). As will be argued at the end of this chapter, these politics were backed with political sociological arguments in favor of more inclusive political participation.

Both Yugoslavia and Macedonia faced another set of critical social challenges in the 1960s. Rural-to-urban migration accelerated to 170 percent between 1953 and 1961 (Ginić 1964), leaving the industry and the urban infrastructure unable to absorb the influx. The further south one looked, the more those disparities were visible. Moreover, the urbanization process in Macedonia was immensely accelerated with the calamitous earthquake that struck Skopje on 26 July 1963, killing 1070 people and destroying two-thirds of the urban fabric, and the post-earthquake urban reconstruction of the city. In 1973, for instance, the population of Skopje was 10 times that before the war, despite the ongoing reconstruction (Trajanovski 2021a, 22). In this very context, sociological research in

---

[2] Crvenkovski assumed high-profile positions in the wartime anti-fascist movement and was awarded an Order of People's Hero in 1953. In the 1950s, he was a federal Minister of education and culture, while in 1963, he rose to the top of the Macedonian communists, serving as a Secretary of the Party from 1963 to 1969 (for an overview, see Radičeski 2013).

Yugoslavia adopted a "new role to play" (Spasić et al. 2022, 37), one that legitimizes the Yugoslav state socialism as a political system interested in the actual societal developments that can be grasped, measured, and discussed with the help of non-dogmatic thinking and jargon (see, e.g., Supek 1959). In turn, the Yugoslav political and academic authorities granted the "imprimatur" (Mladenovski 1997, 4) for the establishment of sociological organizations, their networks, and cooperation across the Federation (Bogdanović et al. 1990; Spasić et al. 2022). The sociological opening followed the Yugoslav political opening to the West, which translated, among others, into transfers of knowledge and methodological know-how. Hence, the 1960s are also perceived as a period of "Westernization" of the Yugoslav social scientific theories (adoption of functionalism) and methodologies (turn to positivism, in Lazić 2011, 87). Corresponding breakthroughs took place in Poland and Czechoslovakia as a result of the exposure to Western academia during the windows of "liberalization" of the socialist political regimes (Denitch 1971; Voříšek 2012; Bucholc 2016; Skovajsa and Balon 2017; Kilias 2017). The three "revisionist" national sociologies (Voříšek 2008) developed a series of critical cross-national exchanges in the name of shared anti-dogmatism. The Yugoslav journal *Praxis* (1964–1974), for instance, emerged as one of the key anchors of the theoretical deliberations about Marxist humanism, breaking the East–West division (Sher 1977; Satterwhite 1992). The post-earthquake reconstruction of Skopje under the baton of the United Nations (UN) authorized yet another such sociological exchange in the mid-1960s, this time Polish-Macedonian, which albeit instructive from many different aspects, remained underresearched for a long time. I discuss this episode in a separate section in this chapter.

Finally, in this chapter, I argue that the professionalization and institutionalization of sociology in Macedonia unfolded as a lengthy process taking place from the late 1950s up to the early 1970s. Despite the slower tempo in establishing the initial set of sociological institutions, Skopje was not lagging behind the other Yugoslav centers in terms of initiative and what Bogdanović observes for the Serbian context as the "élan and enthusiasm" of the first generation of sociologists (Bogdanović et al. 1990, 307). For instance, the earliest attempts to form a separate sociology group at the Faculty of Philosophy in Skopje are traced back to the late 1950s (Mladenovski 1997; Georgievski 2012). As of the early 1960s, sociology was offered as a separate course not only at the Faculty of Philosophy, Economics, and the PMF but also at the Macedonian equivalent of

Polytechnics, while the first textbooks in Macedonian were already written (Taneski 1962; Jordanovski 1962) or translated (e.g., Popoviќ 1963) by 1963. In 1962, a group of Macedonian scholars initiated the Macedonian Association of Philosophy and Sociology [mk. *Društvo za filozofija i sociologija*], three years earlier than the Slovene one and six years before the Montenegrin (Bogdanović et al. 1990, 161). Moreover, empirical research loomed in late 1950s Macedonia, conducted as part of all-Yugoslav surveys (e.g., Ilić 1960, 139), but also by individual Macedonian researchers and institutes, such as the one about the "participation and integration" of Albanians in Macedonia done by the Skopje-based Institute of National History [mk. *Institut za nacionalna istorija*, INI] in the late 1950s (Sinadinovski 1961b). The other way around, Macedonians were also actively participating in the federal sociological developments: Miljovska, for instance, was part of the editorial board of *Sociologija* in the 1960s; **Kiro Gligorov** (1917–2012), a high-profile Macedonian economist and politician in Belgrade, who would become the first president of the post-socialist Republic of Macedonia, was part of the board of Belgrade's Institute of Social Sciences in the mid-1960s; while several Macedonian authors published their works in the first organ of the JUS, the sociological journal *Sociologija* (e.g., Sinadinovski 1959; Bošale 1962).[3] The peak of the above developments was the inauguration of the Institute for Sociological, Political and Juridical Research [mk. *Institut za sociološki i političko-pravni istražuvanja*, ISPPI] in Skopje in 1965. Despite its modest start, in a matter of years the ISPPI expanded its workforce and fields of expertise and established itself as a major Macedonian partner institution for the Yugoslav cross-national sociological research. Lastly, the end of the 1960s saw several domestic discursive exchanges which mark a threshold for Macedonian sociology. There is a critical difference between the quest for sociological autonomy in the Macedonian 1960s and later 1970s, a point which will be discussed in the next chapter.

THE FIRST ATTEMPTS

The very first attempts to execute empirical sociological research in Macedonia can be traced back to several academic circles. At the PMF, it was centered upon the duo of **Jakim Sinadinovski** (1924–2000) and

---

[3] An all-Yugoslav sociological conference was held in Ohrid in May 1965, hosting more than 100 participants (Tomović 1968, 164–165).

Mitko Panov (1927–2000). Soon after their employment in the mid-1950s, both of them expressed interest in applying slightly different research methodologies than their supervisors: as put by Panov later on, exploring the *applicative* rather than the *descriptive* scientific potentials (1969). Interestingly enough, this shift appeared in the course of the institutional separation of the PMF and the Faculty of Philosophy, finalized in 1958. Panov, for instance, wrote a doctoral thesis in anthropogeography, but in 1958 argued for a disciplinary opening to empirical sociology in urban planning, citing Western sources and experiences (1958, 121–123). He eventually moved toward researching and teaching social geography and demographics and established the postgraduate (interdisciplinary) program in spatial planning (e.g., see Panov 1976a, b, 1978).

The case of Sinadinovski is even more revealing bearing in mind his biographical experience and drive for research innovations. After joining the partisans in Western Macedonia as a high school student, he was caught and spent some time in the Tirana prison in 1943. He managed to escape and join the Albanian partisans just in time for the liberation of his homeland across the border (more in his autobiographical accounts in Sinadinovski 1974, 1985). In the aftermath of the war, he carried on propaganda activities as a political commissar of the Macedonian 6th assault brigade. He then dropped his army career to finish the philosophy program in Skopje where he graduated as the only student of his generation in 1953. After graduation, Sinadinovski took the position of associate editor of *Nova Makedonija*, while he was also the founder and the first director of the workers' university in Skopje in the mid-1950s. During the late 1950s, he taught political economy, Marxism, and philosophy at the PMF, and sociology as of the early 1960s.

In the late 1950s and early 1960s, Sinadinovski demonstrated his vast scope of scholarly interests by engaging, as one of the rare Macedonian scholars, in Yugoslav debates about theoretical Marxism, arguing, for instance, against the turn to the *Young Marx* across the globe and, especially, in Yugoslavia (see Sinadinovski 1962a; for context, see Tomović 1969). He was, however, equally if not more observant of the empirical sociological research both in and beyond Yugoslavia, reviewing and critically evaluating the initial undertakings commissioned by industrial and labor organizations (1959, 1968). In all his reviews, Sinadonovski praised empirical research as an instrument for labor rationalization and improvement of workers' human relations, calling for a more systematic approach and professionalization of research (1959) and criticizing certain interpretative aspects (1962b). He also drew inspiration from Polish empirical and theoretical sociology: he authored a very detailed overview of the Polish sociological state of the art (1961a) and reviewed the first post-war Polish textbook in sociology (1960) authored by **Jan Szczepański** (1913–2004), one of the leading Polish sociologists at the time (more in Bucholc 2016). The relaunching of the Polish–Yugoslav sociological cooperation was triggered by the *normalization* of the diplomatic relations between the two countries after 1956 (Wawryszuk 2018). It resulted in a number of exchanges of personnel, ideas, and periodicals in the late 1950s and early 1960s (Trajanovski 2021a, 15–16; also see Kilias 2017), while Szczepański himself took part in the development of the first sociological curriculum for Belgrade University in the late 1950s (Bogdanović et al. 1990, 25; Spasić et al. 2022, 39–40). Sinadinovski also paid a short research visit to Poland in the 1970s, the outcomes of which will be discussed in more detail in the next chapter.

Building upon this momentum, Sinadinovski started pitching empirical study ideas in Macedonia already in 1962. However, the processes of securing research funding, teaming up, and organizing fieldwork took some time. For instance, the republican science fund approved his 1962 proposal, in its final form as a PMF application, for a study of the "structural changes, phenomena, and processes in the post-war period of development of the villages in the municipality of Titov Veles" only in 1965, while it took two more years to conduct the fieldwork and an additional two to publish the report. Once out in the field, Sinadinovski and his colleagues were cordially supported by the municipal and labor organizations, as well as local schoolteachers in handing over approximately 2400 questionnaires and interviewing 175 locals. Their bottom-line interpretation pertaining to the impact of industrialization on the villages in the foci was "negative rather than positive" (more in Sinadinovski, Ivanovski, and Panov 1969, 553–560). In the following years, Sinadinovski proceeded to develop this thesis by discussing the side effects of *deagrarization* (1971), as well as its impact on families and unemployment in Macedonia (1970). In parallel, he and his colleagues started offering *socio-economic* empirical research projects to the industrial sector. One such endeavor, drafted by Sinadinovski in the early 1960s, was molded upon a participant observation methodology and it eventually took place in 1965–1966 among the workers of several labor units of the Macedonian railways. Sinadinovski's pioneering approach to the local context required persuading—**Stoilko Ivanovski**, one of the co-heads and a frequent research collaborator of his during this period, noted Sinadinovski's assistance in the team's acknowledgment of the "benefits of observation in sociological research" (Ivanovski 1966, 4)—but the results were eventually more than satisfying: the team proudly announced, for instance, their job-shadowing of workers for approximately 12 hours in certain cases.

As of the early 1950s, **Dime Bojanovski-Dize** (1909–2002) started developing research about the economic history of Macedonia, involving qualitative methods such as biographical interviews in its early phases. Bojanovski-Dize was a notable pre-war communist imprisoned for several years in the 1930s due to his political activities. He managed to return to Prilep during the wartime period, translate, and give lessons in Marxism to leftist groupings (Gigov 1973, 150–151), and reassume a high position in the Macedonian partisan *Generalstab*. After the war, he finished law and served as a Minister of Justice up until the late 1950s, while he held, in parallel, the positions of an instructor in political economy at the Faculty of Law and Economics in Skopje and a first director of the newly established Economic Institute in Skopje (in 1952). In the course of 1952 and 1953, Bojanovski-Dize coordinated a team of 50 students and associates of the above two institutions which interviewed 1462 citizens from 727 villages about the turn of the century chifliks on the Macedonian territory, their specificities, and structures.[4] According to this pioneering research of this type, the chiflik families were 2.1 percent of the total population of Macedonia during late Ottoman Macedonia, yet their influence over the society was detrimental; for instance, he observed that they owned approximately 36.5 percent of all the arable land, while the general attitude toward the local contractors was "exploitative" (Bojanovski 1954, 491; also see Bojanovski-Dize 1974; Kartalov 1982). He co-developed other research methodologies with the associates of the Economic Institute, among them **Ana Pemovska** (1925-?), **Kiril Džonov** (1916-?), **Lazar Sokolov** (1914-?), and **Kosta Sidovski** (1910-?), which allowed them to examine the economic histories of the agrarian, industrial, and demographic developments in the country (see, e.g., Bojanovski et al. 1955; Adži-Mitreski et al. 1960; for context, see Janevski 2022).

---

[4] Bojanovski-Dize signaled that he himself conducted similar surveys "during the previous years" (Bojanovski 1954, 467). Those exploratory attempts were formative for the research methodology of collective fieldwork in the course of 1952 and 1953: the major rationale was to allow the informants to speak uninterruptedly, while the interviewers were provided strict guidelines on when and how to intervene during the conversations, mostly concerning information related to quantitative data.

The early 1960s also saw the first signs of empirically informed *policy sociology* in Macedonia. Sponsored by political institutions and party organizations, the initial research of this type was predominantly related to studying the various forms of social, political, and economic participation of Macedonian citizens. One of the earliest such endeavors was published in 1964 by Ivanovski, alongside the group of sociologists from the Faculty of Law, Milosavlevski and **Tomislav Čokrevski** (1934–2017) (Milosavlevski et al. 1964). The predominant focus of this research agenda pertained to the SKM (renamed as of 1952; see, e.g., Čokrevski et al. 1965) and it was initially done by the group of associates of the Faculty of Law in Skopje, including Milosavlevski, Čokrevski, and **Milan Nedkov** (1931–2018), in cooperation with party associates. Soon afterwards, this research agenda was dubbed as a Marxist critical "sociology of the party" (Čokrevski 1973), that is, a perspective which allows for a closer look at the party's social function, program, and the reception of its activities, the latter in a format which will be discussed in a bit more detail in the next chapter. It was mainly transported to the ISPPI immediately upon its formation together with the researchers (both Milosavlevski and Nedkov served as its directors in the late 1960s, while Čokrevski was appointed a researcher), while the above group started articulating theoretical aspects of political sociology which will be discussed in the last section of this chapter. The sociological circle at the Faculty of Law in Skopje also authored several sociological textbooks.

As already hinted, the industrial sector was another important agency sponsoring and promoting empirical (sociological) research in 1960s Macedonia. For instance, from 1965 to 1982, this sector funded approximately a third of the empirical studies in the state (Bošale et al. 1987, 9). Before the formation of the ISPPI, two Skopje-based institutions, the Faculty of Economics Research Department and the Economic Institute, were the most likely scientific partners of this sector. The Faculty of Economics uncoupled from the Faculty of Law in 1956, while some of its associates continued pursuing their interest in both theoretical and empirical sociology. In 1964, for instance, **Vladimir Taneski** (b. 1921-?) issued another volume in his series of sociological textbooks aimed at helping his students who "had a hard time overcoming the study material" in the past (1964, 5).[5] Miljovski and Zografski were also cooperating with the Faculty

---

[5] Taneski held degrees in philosophy and law from the Skopje University and was a journalist and an editor of the post-war Radio Skopje. He joined the Faculty of Economics in 1960 as a sociology instructor.

of Economics at this point. However, its institutional capacities for empirical research were developed by **Nikola Uzunov** (1930–2010) and his team; Uzunov, a professor of economics with a doctorate from Belgrade, had an impressive history of research stays in the late 1950s and during the 1960s, for example, Oxford University (1957), Vanderbilt University (1959–1960), the University of Chicago (1960), and the London School of Economics (1965–1966). His major research focus in the 1960s was on comparative industrialization, while he also aimed at popularizing economics by publishing his work in the *Kultura* edition discussed in the previous chapter (e.g., Uzunov 1961). An example of his empirical research is a study of rural-to-urban migration conducted in the early 1970s and published in 1975. The study's goal was more than statistical, as it aimed at revealing the *causes* of such migrations: drawing upon a survey of 700 people who migrated from 1968 to 1972, Uzunov and his team argued in favor of a political and economic *rationalization* of the irrevocable migration movement which was not necessarily a product of economic deprivation (Uzunov 1975).

THE SKOPJE SOCIAL SURVEY (1964–1965)

The early morning of 26 July 1963 in Skopje saw a calamitous earthquake that killed 1070 people and destroyed more than two-thirds of its urban fabric. What followed was a prompt reaction by the federal and national authorities, succeeded by the international community: more than 80 states and a number of international organizations provided help to Skopje and Skopjans in the immediate aftermath of the catastrophe. Moreover, at the peak of the Cold War after the Cuban Missile Crisis, the United Nations believed that the earthquake in the third-largest city of the non-aligned Yugoslavia might present an extraordinary opportunity for promoting ideological reconciliation/cooperation in the name of basic human solidarity. Hence, the UN took the lead in coordinating the international support for the city and endorsed the Yugoslav political decision to reconstruct the Macedonian capital city already in October 1963, creating an unprecedented special fund for this purpose. The urban reconstruction was thus envisioned as a collaborative endeavor of domestic and international experts under the baton of the UN, a decision well received in the post-catastrophe city of Skopje, which prepared itself for hosting the international workers under its new byname: the *City of Solidarity* (Trajanovski

2021b). In addition, the Macedonian authorities and crisis managers declared Skopje an *open city* after the disaster, seeking to increase the population influx to the city as a means of securing the much-needed workforce for its reconstruction. They even coupled the post-earthquake demographic politics with the above-discussed agenda of interethnic cooperation in Yugoslavia: Crvenkovski, for instance, viewed the population influx to Skopje of Macedonians and other Yugoslav citizens, mostly Kosovars, as a "positive instrument for the rapprochement of the peoples" (in Trajanovski 2021a, 6).

For one particular reason, Macedonian scholars interested in empirical sociology saw the UN urban reconstruction project as a gift from the gods: among other things, it also outlined an all-embracing social survey of the local population for urban planning purposes. So not only would the research funding be secured and the study coordinators equipped with the required instruments, assistants, and support, but also the benefactors guaranteed that the findings would be taken into consideration and eventually implemented. This was certainly a novelty even in the wider Yugoslav context: despite the emerging empirical sociological research and the opening to urban sociology in the early 1960s, the Yugoslav urban planners and architects were distrustful of implementing such findings, sticking to their narrower understanding of urban planning methods and practice (Padgett 1973; Le Normand 2008). Internationally, however, social surveying for urban planning purposes was gaining traction as the criticism of the dominant modernist urbanism—and its lack of sensitivity to cultural particularities, for instance—was increasing in both ideological camps (for an overview, see Mumford 1992). Hence, it came as no surprise that Sinadinovski and Ivanovski drafted a detailed blueprint for such a social study and published it as an article by the end of 1963 in Belgrade's *Sociologija*. In the text, which was observed to be the first Macedonian empirical sociological study ever written (Josifovski and Kepevska 1978, 93), the authors envisioned two main roles for the sociologists on top of the social study in post-earthquake Skopje, both of them hinting at the practical, empirically driven goals. The first role was one of the *social engineers* or experts who participated in the urban design by reality-checking it with sociological data, while the second one was *house doctors*, indicating their tasks of monitoring the (novel) social interactions developing in the urgency and looking for their "healthy and bearable" flow (Sinadinovski and Ivanovski 1963, 78; also see Sinadinovski 1964). The authors concluded by arguing that such a study was needed yesterday rather than today and called for trans-Yugoslav sociological support for the Macedonian sociologists.

However, a series of events in 1963 and 1964 forged another path for the Skopje social survey. Starting from the earliest visits of international experts to Skopje, both the UN and, especially, the Yugoslav government carefully maintained the "parts and counterparts" balance between the "conflicting political line-ups" (Tolic 2019, 45). As an illustration, one of the earliest such delegations to post-earthquake Skopje consisted of a Frenchman, a Briton, a Czechoslovak, and a Soviet Russian. In a similar manner, "Western concepts and idioms" were localized or countered with corresponding achievements of socialist scientists (Spaskovska 2020, 139). In brief, the story of the social survey unfolded in this fashion: in February 1964, a board of UN and Yugoslav experts entrusted the Greek Doxiadis Associates studio with the preparation of the Skopje outline project. The studio's founder, **Constantinos Doxiadis** (1913–1975), was a leading theoretician of *Ekistics*, an interdisciplinary doctrine on human settlements, and already steered the development of several large-scale UN projects (Trajanovski 2021a, 11). Their initial groundwork in Skopje, co-conducted with Yugoslav partners during mid-1964, resulted in several projections of the future city development which was to "continue indefinitely to grow apace" (Senior 1970, 82–84). In parallel, the Polish government started working on an alternative plan for Skopje under the leadership of **Adolf Ciborowski** (1919–1987), the chief planner of post-war Warsaw. The Poles drew on their practical and methodological experiences with the war-torn Polish cities, especially Warsaw, and aimed at disseminating beyond the Polish borders their so-called optimization reconstruction model of combining rational investments with computational analysis. Ultimately, they came up with a more modest and economically realistic scenario for Skopje's future development. Their proposal resonated with the expectations of the local and the UN experts and thus a group of Polish experts affiliated with the Warsaw planning office got on the board of the Skopje reconstruction project, while Ciborowski was appointed its Project Manager.

The task division between Greek, Polish, Yugoslav, and Macedonian experts ended up with the social survey being allocated to the Polish Polservice and the Macedonian Institute of Town Planning and Architecture (ITCA)—Skopje. Albeit "hoping to be responsible" for the social survey, the Greeks were instead given the task of drafting the regional plan for the city.[6] The decision to couple the domestic with the Polish experts for the social surveying was further justified with ideological arguments, such as in the official claims that "contemporary achievements of the Western European urban sociology cannot contribute much" to the planning of Skopje (Tolic 2019, 58–59). From such a standpoint, the Polish sociologists were much more welcome. As mentioned before, as the Polish–Yugoslav relations normalized after 1956, the academic exchanges followed suit. However, the Polish sociological expertise was not as immune to *Western European urban sociology* as the local authorities might have expected. The leader of the Polish team of four which came to conduct the social survey in Skopje, **Zygmunt Pióro** (1916–1984), is a neat example of all the above mentioned. Assistant to Obrębski at the post-war Łódź University, Pióro spent a great amount of time scrutinizing migration, industrialization, and urbanization in Polish towns during the 1950s and 1960s.[7] He was especially versed in French and American urban sociology and even published in *Ekistics* in the early 1960s, the main journal promoting Doxiadis' theory. Moreover, his main scholarly project evolved around the idea of promoting the American notion of *social ecology* into an empirical research apparatus (more in Kryczka 1986), an approach that was echoed in the Skopje survey (Trajanovski 2021a, 16). Those optics might have been the reason behind their rejection of cooperation with Macedonian sociologists, despite the initial consultations.[8] The Poles hence ended up recruiting

---

[6] **Joel Halpern** (1929–2009), an American ethnographer and anthropologist, one of the forerunners of the second wave of family relations research in Yugoslavia mentioned in the first chapter, was considered to be part of the Greek research team due to his vast fieldwork experience in the country (Tolic 2019, 58–59).

[7] From a similar background was **Zbigniew Sufin** (1932–2023), the other Polish sociologist on the team of four, who was also on the board of the initial Polish project-team for developing the Skopje plan. He also had experience in social surveying in several Polish towns during the late 1950s and early 1960s.

[8] Some of the faculty of the PMF ended up cooperating with the ITCA and the UN, such as Mitko Panov, who authored a report about the history of Skopje. Stoilko Ivanovski proceeded with co-authoring a study about the functioning of the self-management system in the post-earthquake conditions, funded by the Ministry of Science and published in 1964 (Ivanovski et al. 1964).

and training a group of 10 Macedonian instructors themselves, as well as 70 interviewers.[9]

The co-heads announced the start of the pilot in late December 1964 and the proper survey for early January 1965. Facing different sorts of challenges along the way, the team managed to reach the assigned numbers of the area's sampled households with a few weeks' delay: 4006 households out of 48,541 in Skopje or 8.1 percent of the total population of 200,218 in November 1964. They also conducted 100 "extensive interviews" with locals, administrative, and factory workers, "direct uncontrolled observations of human behavior, and ecological interpretation" (Tomic et al. 1965, 4). Needless to say, the scale and scope of the study in Skopje were unparalleled. Albeit the main study goal was to obtain information about housing, living conditions, and family incomes as fodder for urban planning (and its legitimization, one can say), it was also designed to be a tool for assessing the locals' social activities and long-term expectations of their city for the first time in the urban history. The surveying, however, unveiled a set of social trust issues and ramifications of the population and reconstruction politics. The group behavior and the interethnic relations in the city thus assumed a far more important place in the final report than anticipated in the preparatory materials. The team, for instance, found a peculiar communal tendency to gravitate within the ethnocultural and religious neighborhoods, even if offered housing with better standards in different locations. As a response, and in line with the social-ecological reasoning, the team proposed reimagining the city center as a space of intercultural exchange, an idea which was reinstituted in the Japanese–Croat collaborative team plan for the city center of Skopje. However, few of the social study findings were included in the overview of the Skopje urban project, while the survey was set aside only to reappear in the 1990s (Trajanovski 2021a)—a point which will be discussed in the last chapter.

---

[9] The Macedonian instructors were chosen from the pool of ITCA's associates, while the interviewers were students from different faculties in Skopje. **Mimoza Nestorova-Tomik** (b. 1929), a Macedonian architect associated with the ITCA, appeared to be a fit for the co-head position for the social survey as she had attended an urban sociology course during her fellowship in the USA in the early 1960s and knew English. She also recalls the kindness and cooperativeness of the Poles, who supported her and provided her materials in urban sociology before the study (Trajanovski 2021a, 17).

The Institute for Sociological, Political and Juridical Research (1965)

The impetus for empirical sociological research in Macedonia was already traced back to the earliest such attempts in the 1950s and early 1960s, while the scopes and ambitions of those very attempts were also considered to be illustrations for the institutional and political hesitation about sociology at the beginning of the decade. As of the mid-1960s, however, one can note a certain shift in their deliberation of sociological research, a sort of growing up to the "need" (Lukić 1959) for such a knowledge in the local context. The main reason for convening the syndical plenum in Skopje in 1966 is very suggestive of the above point: all the parties stated that despite the pressing needs, the implementation of (mostly social) scientific results in the work of labor organizations did not take the "desired dimensions" during the previous years (Republički sovet 1966, 10; a similar argument in Kulturen život 1968). The formation of the first sociological institute in Macedonia in 1965 was thus expected to untangle the above situation by providing the rightful *dimension* of sociological research and training.

Similar to the case of the Economic Institute, the ISPPI was also established with a decision of the Skopje University Council, confirmed by the then-Macedonian government on 5 February 1965. It took several months for the ISPPI to appoint its first associates, who "resettled" from other academic institutions in the country (Josifovski and Kepeska 1978, 93), and start functioning as an independent research institution and an intermediary body of the Skopje University, providing social scientific training and expertise to its other units (Mihajlovski 1991; Verigik 1991; Jakimovski et al. 2010; Borota Popovska et al. 2015). Its first director was **Aleksandar Hristov** (1914–2000), a professor of law at Skopje University and an expert in legal history and the history of the Macedonian revolutionary struggle. His profile and appointment are immensely suggestive, if not symptomatic, of the early ISPPI agenda, an aspect which will be discussed in the next section, but not atypical *per se*: the other sociological research institutes in Yugoslavia had employees of different academic backgrounds as well, having in mind the lack of sociological training for most of the post-war period. Hence, in a similar vein, the first generation of ISPPI employees had academic backgrounds in philosophy (3), social sciences (6), natural sciences (2), and sociology (3). Unlike the other institutes, however, in Skopje, the number of employees younger than 35 was almost the same (5) as the ones aged from 35 to 55 (6), while there was only one employee older than 55. At the Yugoslav level, those numbers were much more in favor of the older generations (Bogdanović et al. 1990, 31).

The initial scope of the work of the ISPPI was determined by its mission statement. It reads:

[The ISPPI aims to] scientifically study sociological and political-juridical phenomena in the country, to encourage and organize the study of sociological and political-juridical scientific issues, as well as those of societal development;

- to develop and advance research methods in social sciences;
- to work on the improvement of scientific personnel and to train young scientists in the field of sociological and political-juridical sciences;
- to provide material and other conditions for studying and researching;
- to organize various forms of work with professional staff, in order to train them for independent scientific work;
- to organize the collection of documents for the practical teaching and teaching exercises at the faculties and social sciences of Skopje University;
- to provide teaching of all degrees in social sciences for all faculties of the Skopje University;
- to organize the presentation of problems in the field of sociological and political-juridical sciences in the form of consultations, discussions, and other suitable venues;
- to provide and immediately communicate the results of its scientific research work;
- to issue publications;
- to develop versatile necessary cooperation with the relevant institutions, organizations, and individuals dealing with the study of sociological and political-juridical sciences in the country and abroad. (Jakimovski et al. 2010, 5)

Against the background of its guiding document, the institutional profile of the ISPPI was further defined in the coming several years. First and foremost, Hristov, himself with a legal background, justified the idea of linking sociological and political with juridical research under one roof (unlike in the other Yugoslav centers) with the nature of the main research object itself: all three scientific approaches were seen as necessary for grasping the nuances of the workers' regimes, their labor conditions, and self-management in general (Republički sovet 1966, 43–44).

Although the ISPPI had a pool of employees sharing an interest in empirical research and a solid budget (Georgievski and Gurovska 2003, 108), it lacked the cadres and experience to operate it in its early years. The results of its first empirical research project, for instance, commissioned by the Macedonian Youth Council in 1966 to obtain data about the youth social organization, were rather exploratory, "in line with the real capacities of the researchers" (Josifovski and Kepeska 1978, 94). As a response, as of 1967, the ISPPI secured the services of 22 new employees and appointed a new director, Slavko Milosavlevski, who stayed at this post until April 1969. It also started providing postgraduate training in social sciences, an aspect which will be discussed in more detail in the next chapter, and initiated contacts with other Macedonian and Yugoslav institutions. Everything seemed set for more rigorous research. And, indeed, up until 1970, the ISPPI associates carried on several research projects on different topics predominantly related to the history and the practice of the SKM, together with the Faculty of Law, but also pertaining to the normative aspects of the labor organizations and the electoral system in the country. In the late 1960s and early 1970s, the Institute expanded its research scope to cover audience surveys about TV Skopje, demographics, and sociology of the family, rural sociology, and youth delinquency (Jakimovski et al. 2010, 57–59). An anecdote from the late 1960s hints at the institutional ambitions despite its relatively short history and limited expertise and personnel: during walkthroughs of foreign guests at the ISPPI facilities, it was not uncommon for the host to present the workplaces of the ISPPI associates as offices of whole research departments. The final phase of its institutional profiling occurred in the mid-1970s when the ISPPI started publishing a scientific bulletin—*Godišnik na ISPPI* (Annual of the ISPPI)—and commenced conducting annual public opinion polls in Macedonia. Both the *Annuals* and the public polls will be discussed in more detail in the next chapter.

Assuming a Label

The above review of sociological research in 1960s Macedonia suggests that two research themes prevailed: the rural areas, with the interethnic relations in the state as an inevitable yet weak addendum. The associates of the PMF and the Economic Institute, for instance, researched the Macedonian periphery in the early 1960s prioritizing the prospects of rural development in the initial phases before moving to the side effects of the rapid modernization, industrialization, and rural-to-urban migration in the mid-1960s. The interethnic relations in those studies were presented in an undertone, while sociological research proposals on this particular subject failed, by default, to see the light of day.[10] However, the team of social surveyors in Skopje, together with their leverage stemming from the post-earthquake reconstruction agenda, showed that the interethnic dynamism deserves more sociological attention. This episode is thus illustrative as it reflects the shift in the treatment of sociology in Macedonia by experts and non-experts likewise. Therefore, the late 1960s and early 1970s saw a different set of deliberations about sociology. In this particular context and time period, the dominant mode of strategizing about sociological research was in its autonomization against other scientific discourses. More importantly, the Macedonian sociologists used power positions to argue in favor of the disciplinary boundaries, while the political field was not considered a threat. I do view this period as a particular closure of the process of institutionalizing Macedonian sociology in the 1960s by bringing up a sociological "label" (Voříšek 2008, 90) in the national context, which helped reconfigure the perceptions of the scope of sociology and its goals. In the next chapter, I will discuss how the institutionalization continued in the course of the 1970s, albeit in a different political environment and with a different object of autonomization.

One of the first sociological exchanges in the 1960s is embedded in the emergence of the widely understood rural sociology in Yugoslavia. This is best illustrated with the inauguration of the *Sociologija sela* (Sociology of the village) journal in Zagreb in 1963 which immediately assumed the role of an eclectic all-Yugoslav platform for publishing research results about "all the aspects of the rural society" including, *inter alia*, migration, industrialization, and urbanization, but also, up until that point, the less popular subjects of family and kinship institutions, religious organizations, and intercultural relations (Milinković 1980, 153; also see Petrovic et al. 1996; Petak et al. 2002).[11] Ultimately, the journal, the circle around it, and the

[10] Most illustrative is the case of Sinadinovski, anew, who pitched a research project about the political participation and integration of the Macedonian Albanians in the early 1960s, which was to be conducted by a team of 10 researchers and 30 interviewers of INI, whose director was Hristov at that point, "since there [was] no sociological institute in Skopje" (Sinadinovski 1988, 279–304).

[11] The reinvigorated research agenda also allowed for a reconsideration of Cvijić's work from a "sociological standpoint" (Kostić 1963, 13–14) as its methodological precursor, as well as a come-back of some scholars who had done corresponding research in the past, such as Erlich (e.g., Erlich 1964).

network of organizations working in this branch contributed to the reimagining of Yugoslavia as a "sociological laboratory" attractive for Western rural sociologists. For instance, one of the earliest such surveys of the Yugoslav villages was coordinated by the European Sociological Center in Paris (Borela 1967, 143).

The initial Macedonian takes on rural sociology slid toward the gender and interethnic relations in the state. As of the mid-1960s, a Faculty of Philosophy in Skopje research group, on the pretext of kinship relations research, started exploring the multicultural, multiethnic, and multicon-fessional borderland region of Polog in Northwestern Macedonia. The first fieldwork was coordinated by Blaga Petroska and took place in 1964 and 1965. Dissatisfied with the 1961 population census results, the team (of associates of the Faculty) gathered demographic data from the local municipalities and courts and prepared questionnaires for 153 rural and 256 urban families.[12] The survey, much like in Erlich's case from the late 1930s—whose influence is visible throughout the study yet not directly quoted—to a great extent depended on the local schoolteachers' willing-ness to cooperate. Therefore, only 62 questionnaires were returned to the researchers in 1965; however, as stated in the final report, they were suf-ficiently representative of all the 45 villages in the region (Petroska 1967, 63–66). In the final report, in an Engelsian spirit, Petroska differentiated several types of families between the two main poles of the least developed *patriarchal* family type and the most developed *administrative* family type. Her main contribution pertains to the gender relations in all the fam-ily types living in Polog: she claimed that none of them can be deemed *modern* in meeting the principles of "consistent and complete" gender equality. The "perseverance of the male authority in the family *by default* translates into an unequal position of the woman," maintained Petroska (1967, 116). Similar to Erlich, she also found the non-economic factors, such as *cultural* and *historical legacies*, equally important for the tenacity of the patriarchal authority. Hence, Petroska saw the Muslim (Turkish and Albanian) families as less developed than the others (Macedonian and Serbian) due to their economic deprivation and culture, but also made sure that the (political) *progressive forces* would eventually foster social

---

[12] As a result of the 1953 Yugoslav-Turkish *Gentlemen's Agreement*, a mass emigration of non-Slavic and Slavic Muslim populations from southern Yugoslavia and especially Macedonia to Turkey took place. Nearly 140,000 people emigrated in the course of the 1950s (more in Pezo 2018).

change in the region. This conclusion, albeit not clearly stated, resonated with the 1960s affirmative action politics.

Soon after the publication of the above study Petroska undertook another one related to the sociology of family, this time focusing on the zadrugas in Macedonia. The final report suggests a sense of urgency as a guiding research principle, as it was highlighted that this might be the very last examination of the soon-to-be-extinct family type in the country. Petroska, again, coordinated the research in 1968 and 1969, this time with the help of a group of her students who gathered materials from the local municipalities but also spoke with the local clergymen and Islamic religious leaders, and handed over questionnaires to the locals in their houses or at the bazaars or during other public events. The research subject required an additional sort of methodological finesse, as per the report, so the students were trained and expected to gather supplementary data using a "more subtle method than the survey" such as participant observation (Petroska 1973, 123). The outcome: they discovered the existence of 27 zadrugas all over the country, with the Macedonian ones being almost extinct, while the Muslim ones were more resilient to changes. As for the particular dynamism within the zadrugas and their immediate environments, Petroska observed as correlational the general decline of the number of zadrugas' members with the decline of the authority of zadrugas' heads.[13]

However, those research efforts were deemed "anecdotal" or "partial" by the two rural sociologists associated with the ISPPI, **Ilija Josifovski** and his student **Stefan Kostovski**, from a position of collaborators of a Yugoslav cross-national survey including Macedonia as a research area, and the ISPPI, as a research partner. Their study was a collaborative Zagreb–Ljubljana–Belgrade–Skopje endeavor sponsored by the federal Fund for Scientific Research and had a goal of sociological profiling of the Yugoslav villages as a means of grasping the social laws of their transformation. Drawing upon Weber and Western rural sociological scholarship, the project coordinators developed a model of two ideal-typical poles about villages that changed the least (*traditional village*) and the most (*transformed village*), and several subtypes and transformative patterns (Šuvar

---

[13] Trifunoski continued investigating the Macedonian zadrugas in the early 1970s, publishing a paper on this topic in Belgrade's journal *Etnološki pregled* (in Taševa 1997, 65).

et al. 1970).[14] The Macedonian researchers, equipped with the know-how and the cross-national research methodology, also turned to Polog as a Macedonian case study: they analyzed 89 households in 131 villages and came to several conclusions pertaining to social stratification and mobility (Josifovski 1973, 1974; Josifovski and Markovik 1973). Despite the focus on the transitory family types as vehicles of change in the rural societies, the researchers could not escape the issues of the religious structure and interethnic and interconfessional relations in Polog. Kostovski, for instance, came to a similar conclusion as Petroska in perceiving religion as a barrier to modernization (Kostovski 1972), while Josifovski, in his 1974 monograph, noted an ethnic aspect of the rural-to-urban migrations in Polog with the ethnic Macedonian villages tending to depopulate, opposite to the Albanian ones (Josifovski 1974).

The case of Slavko Milosavlevski's career and publications from the late 1960s are also illustrative of the process of sociological labeling in Macedonia. Milosavlevski was a local politician in Tetovo before finishing postgraduate programs in social sciences in Belgrade and Torino. He returned to Skopje in 1962, just in time for the "liberal" takeover of power followed by his career's take-off in the mid-1960s: he became a sociology professor at the Faculty of Law in Skopje and a director of the ISPPI, but also a member of SKJ's Central (1964) and Executive Committees (1966) and its Presidency (1969), alongside the high-profile functions in the SKM. He authored several books in the course of this period, as well, calling for a better democraticization of the state and the Party. Drawing upon the works of his Belgrade professors, Milosavlevski's major theoretical intervention pertained to the reconsideration of the classic Marxist understanding of the formal character of democratic mechanisms and institutions. His writings from this period hence discussed public opinion, political participation, elections, and interest and self-interest, among others, as means of maintaining the "delicate" socialist democracy (e.g., Milosavlevski 1968a, b, 1971).[15] Milosavlevski also called for an "absolute

---

[14] Such theoretical "eclecticisms" are in line with the observation of Halpern and Hammel about the leeways of the Yugoslav sociology of the 1960s (1969, 24).

[15] Milosavlevski and the sociological circle at the Faculty of Law in Skopje found some of the ideas about workers' democracy and self-management of **Mito Hadži Vasilev-Jasmin** (1922–1968) as a local precursor for their positions (Milosavlevski and Nedkov 1968). Hadži Vasilev-Jasmin was a high-profile Macedonian post-war communist, journalist, historian, and politician, and a member of the SKM's Presidency and its section for ideology.

equality" of all the "nations and nationalities" in and beyond Yugoslavia, a position derived from his understanding of political participation as well as national identities and nation-building (1968b, 199–202). In the context of the 1960s, his thesis about the nation as the *most important issue of democracy* resonated both with the Yugoslav debates about the national question and the regional tensions pertaining to the conflicting national imaginaries. His take on the national interests as a question of normative parity was somewhat different than the prevailing Yugoslav deliberations about nationalism as a reactionary ideology and contradictory to the socialist project. Ergo, he did not publish in the special sections of *Filozofija* (1967) or *Praxis* (1971) dedicated to the topic of nationalism amid the Croat Spring, despite the fact that his work was generally well received and translated in Yugoslavia in a timely manner.[16]

The last series of exchanges was the most straightforward result of the above context of the Bulgarian-Yugoslav/Macedonian relations. The series of bilateral ups and downs in the 1960s led Crvenkovski to propose a reconciliatory formula based upon a "Marxist approach" to history and historiography: the reluctance to attribute national qualifications to the pre-capitalist past would in effect lessen the tension about the "pure" and "falsified" history and hence allow for a breakthrough in the neighboring relations (Crvenkovski 1998, 69–89). The political incentive translated into two intellectual projects that proposed two different but complementary views on Macedonian history and ethnogenesis. The first one was the 1966 book by Dragan Taškovski titled *Raǵanjeto na makedonskata nacija* (The Birth of the Macedonian Nation—I use the second edition published in 1967), which was understood as a text that stood against doctrinal Macedonian historiography in terms of methodology and interpretation.[17] The Macedonian historiography was primarily centered upon the work of the INI, the only scientific institution entitled to conduct historical

[16] Milosavlevski's *Revolution and Democracy* (1968) was translated into Serbo-Croatian in 1969 and Slovene in 1970. He supposedly rejected the position of a director of Belgrade's Institute of Social Sciences in the late 1960s (Georgievski 2014).

[17] Taškovski, as a director of the SKM's training center, was aware of the minutes of the Yugoslav-Bulgarian meetings about the Macedonian nation. His archival fund contains such minutes starting from 1970. In MASA Archive "Haralampie Polenakoviḱ" in Skopje, Dragan Taškovski Fund, *Stenografska beleška od razgovorite pomeǵu delegaciite na SFRJ i NR Bugarija, održani vo Sofija na den 9, 10. XI 1970*. Interestingly enough, Taškovski's earlier historiographic work about the medieval past was hinted at by the Bulgarian delegation as problematic in the late 1960s (Crvenkovski 1998, 65–91).

research in socialist Macedonia, whose associates were by and large positivists and aimed at gathering data as fodder for the Macedonian national historiographic position (for an overview, see Trebst 1997). Its consensus about the ethnogenesis of the Macedonian people pertained to the eleventh century, which in turn stood in opposition to the Bulgarian official position about the formation of the separate Macedonian identity only after the Second World War.

Taškovski saw the reasons behind the "delayed birth" of the Macedonian nation in certain non-economic developments in the nineteenth and twentieth centuries (Taškovski 1967, 18; also see Taškovski 1974). In line with Yugoslav and Macedonian Marxist scholarship, he agreed that the breakthrough of capitalism in the region provided the critical infrastructure for the emergence of the national consciousness. However, contrary to the dominant historiographic narrative on Macedonian nation-building, he claimed that the halt in the development of the national program was a matter of arrested intellectual mobilization, rather than the economic deprivation of the Macedonian bourgeoisie: the Macedonian intellectuals were easily coopted to work for the neighboring agendas due to the lack of the medieval statehood tradition of the Macedonian nation. This proposal can also be read in the key of the dominant Marxist Yugoslav scholarship, such as Kardelj and his paradigmatic take on the Slovene nation-building (brief overview in Rogel 1984), which posited the medieval statehoods as "backbones" in the national developments. Taškovski thus looked at the ways of coopting the Macedonian intelligentsia, on the one hand, while on the other hand, he also embarked upon tracing its earliest forms of historical legitimization of the Macedonian nation-building project. Hence, although "empty-handed" in terms of medieval statehood tradition, he observed the local intellectual interests in the "antediluvian colossi" [mk. *prepotopski kolosi*] of Alexander the Great and Phillip II as an agential strategy that highlights the corresponding patterns of the delayed Macedonian and the other national mobilizations in the region.[18] Taškovski initially received critical reviews from Macedonian historians who deemed his "sociological approach" insufficiently based on archival data (e.g., Džambazovski 1967). Despite the initial criticism,

---

[18] A thesis corresponding to Hroch's *non-simultaneity of phase B*, that it the success of the national agitation (Hroch 2019). For a more detailed overview of the antiquization narrative of the Macedonian ethnogenesis, see Vangeli (2011) and Majewski (2013).

Taškovski's approach to the delayed national agitation was picked up by several late modern and contemporary historians in the 1970s. The other criticism of Taškovski's work pertained to his sidelining of the armed struggle in Macedonian nation-building. This topic was soon picked up by his colleague Aleksandar T. Hristov, the first director of the ISPPI and a former director of the INI, who also authored a book on the Macedonian ethnogenesis—titled *Sozdavanjeto na makedonskata država 1893–1945* (The Creation of the Macedonian State 1893–1945) and published in Skopje and Belgrade in 1971—based on his doctoral thesis defended in Belgrade in the mid-1950s. Similar to Taškovski, Hristov also considered the nation as a dynamic category that obtains its specific attributes at different points in time. His 1971 book postulates that one should not "dwell deep into the past for evidence" about the Macedonian particularity, since the MRO's "de facto" governing structures and experiences from the late nineteenth century are convincing enough to explain striving for Macedonian statehood (1971, 1–10). Hristov developed this thesis in the coming years as part of the ISPPI department on the Macedonian nation, which will be discussed in brief in the next chapter. Here, it is important to note that he differentiated two periods in the "continual struggle" for autonomous institutions: the first one in the mid-nineteenth century, or the first calls for clerical and educational autonomy, and the second one from the formation of the MRO in 1893 up until 1913, with the formation of independent political organizations (Hristov 1982, 9–10). In the early 1970s, Hristov's work was also perceived as "not exclusively historiographic" by Macedonian historians; however, his "state-legal treatment of the complex phenomena" on the national liberation of the Macedonian peoples was considered to be *more useful* and *serious* (e.g., Veljanovski 1973).

Along with the changes of the liberal communists and the shift in their agenda in the early 1970s came the revisiting of the newly proposed ethnogenesis narrative in Macedonian scholarship. A neat example is the 1972 article published in the INI's *Glasnik*—titled "On the ethnogenesis of the Macedonian people"—which traced the "process of the creation of the Macedonian people" back to the pre-Slavic sixth and seventh centuries and finished up in the second half of the tenth century with the formation of the "Macedonian feudal state" (Panov 1972, 77; also see Panov 1999, 9–18 and Antoljak 1972). In addition, the notion of ethnogenesis became more employed in the context of the debate about Macedonian Muslims which, as mentioned in the previous chapter, had its prehistory in some political solutions and several studies from the 1960s. As of the early 1970s, Palikruševa-Nazim's thesis was by and large opposed both by experts and leaders of the local community of Macedonian Muslims, who now mobilized to prove their allegiance to the Macedonian nation and belonging to the Macedonian ethnicity (e.g., Limanoski 1984). Her thesis was nonetheless picked up by sociologists, such as Sinadinovski, who, drawing upon the Marxist dynamic understanding of ethnicity, claimed that the "historical argument" about the Islamization of the Macedonian Slavs is oversimplistic and falls short of explaining the nuances of the community (e.g., Sinadinovski and Gruevski 1976).

REFERENCES

Adži-Mitreski, Kočo, et al. 1960. *Metodologija za analiza na rabotenjeto na industriskite pretprijatija*. Skopje: Ekonomski institut.
Antoljak, Stjepan. 1972. "Makedonija" i "Makedoncite" vo sredniot vek (prilog kon etnogenezata na makedonskiot narod). *Glasnik na INI* 16 (1): 111–133.
Bešlin, Milivoj. 2021. "Faded Scratches in Marble": Federal b/ordering of socialist Yugoslavia. In *Boundaries and Borders in the Post-Yugoslav Space: A European Experience*, ed. Nenad Stefanov and Srdjan Radović, 27–50. Berlin and Boston: De Gruyter.
Bogdanović, Marija, et al. 1990. *Sociologija u Jugoslaviji: Institucionalni razvoj*. Beograd: Institut za sociološka istraživanja Filozofskog fakulteta u Beogradu.
Bojanovski, Dime. 1954. Čifličkite odnosi vo Makedonija okolu 1903 godina. *Godišen zbornik na Pravno-ekonomskiot fakultet vo Skopje* 1: 468–471.
Bojanovski, Dime, Kiril Džonov, and Ana Pemovska. 1955. *Razvitokot na zemjodelstvoto vo Makedonija*. Skopje: Ekonomski institut.
Bojanovski-Dize, Dime. 1974. *Prilog za izučuvanje na opštestveno-ekonomskite odnosi vo Makedonija XV-XVI vek*. Skopje: Makedonska kniga.
Borela, Rada. 1967. Internacionalna anketa o našem ruralnom društvu. *Zbornik radova Sociološkog instituta* 1: 143–145.
Borota Popovska, Mirjana, et al., eds. 2015. *50 godini Institut za sociološki i političko-pravni istražuvanja: 1965-2015*. Skopje: Institut za sociološki i političko-pravni istražuvanja.
Bošale, Nikola. 1962. Stambene zajednice kao predmet prostornog planiranja: Osvrt na Simpozijum urbanista Jugoslavije. *Sociologija* 4 (3–4): 216–217.
Bošale, Nikola, et al. 1987. *Sostojbi i ocenki na sostojbite vo oblasta na naučnoistražuvačkite dejnosti vo SRM i globalnite nasoki na nivniot razvoj*. Skopje: Ekonomski institut and ISPPI.
Bucholc, Marta. 2016. *Sociology in Poland: To Be Continued?* Basingstoke: Palgrave Macmillan.

Čokrevski, Tomislav. 1973. Možnosta za marksističko zasnovanje na sociologijata na partijata. In *Marksizmot denes,* ed. Desanka Miljovska et al., 253–260. Skopje: Društvo za filozofija i sociologija na SRM.

Čokrevski, Tomislav, Nikola Bošale, and Slavko Milosavlevski. 1965. *Komunistite i graǵanite za demokratskite odnosi vo Sojuzot na komunistite.* Skopje: CK na SKM.

Crvenkovski, Krste. 1989. *Vo odbrana na makedonskata kauza.* Ohrid: Nikola Kosteski i avtorite.

———. 1998. *Na branikot na makedonskata samobitnost.* Skopje: INI.

Denitch, Bogdan. 1971. Sociology in Eastern Europe: Trends and Prospects. *Slavic Review* 30 (2): 317–339.

Džambazovski, Kliment. 1967. Dragan Taškovski, Raǵanjeto na makedonskata nacija, NIP Nova Makedonija Skopje 1967 godina. *Glasnik na INI* 11 (3): 245–256.

Erlich, Vera St. 1964. Porodični odnosi prije prodora individualizma. *Sociologija sela* 5–6: 37–47.

Georgievski, Petre. 2012. *Sociologijata kako kritika na opštestvenata, obrazovnata i kulturnata promena.* Skopje: Matica makedonska.

———. 2014. A Brief Reflection on the Life and the Professional Journey in the Field of Sociology of Professor Slavko Milosavlevski. *Sociološka revija* 15 (2): 7–24.

Georgievski, Petre, and Mileva Gurovska. 2003. Macedonian Sociology in the 1990s: Between the Old Conceptions and New Challenges. In *Sociology in Central and Eastern Europe: Transformation at the Dawn of a New Millenium,* eds. Mike Forrest Keen and Janusz L. Mucha, 107–116. London: Praeger.

Gigov, Strahil. 1973. *Seḱavanja.* Skopje: Naša kniga.

Ginić, Ivanka. 1964. Merenje nivoa urbanizacije u svetlu skorašnjih popisnih podataka. *Stanovništvo* 4: 427–456.

Hristov, Aleksandar T. 1971. *Stvaranje makedonske države 1893-1945.* Beograd: Savremena administracija.

———. 1982. *Prilozi za istorijata na makedonskata politička misla.* Skopje: NIO Studentski zbor Skopje.

Hroch, Miroslav. 2019. Asynchronicity of National Movements. *Studies on National Movements* 4: 1–15.

Ilić, Miloš. 1960. Neki rezultati i iskustva ankete prema studiskom projektu "Socijalna struktura i pokretljivost radničke klase Jugoslavije". *Sociologija* 2 (2): 137–147.

Ivanovski, Stoilko. 1966. *Sociološki istražuvanja: Rabotni i životni uslovi na železničarite od Makedonija.* Skopje: ŽTP.

Ivanovski, Stoilko, et al. 1964. *Funkcioniranjeto na samoupravniot sistem vo uslovite sozdadeni so zemjotresot.* Skopje: Ministerstvo za nauka.

Jakimovski, Jorde, et al. 2010. *45 godini Institut za sociološki i političko-pravni istražuvanja – Skopje.* Skopje: Univerzitet "Sv. Kiril i Metodij" Skopje.

Janevski, Zoran, ed. 2022. *70 godini Ekonomski institute – Skopje*. Skopje: Ekonomski institute.

Jordanovski, Stojan. 1962. *Sociologija so osnovi na politička ekonomija*. Skopje: Gimnazija Cvetan Dimov.

Josifovski, Ilija. 1973. Mešovita domaćinstva kao nosioci promena u selima Pologa. *Sociologija i prostor* 39: 54–68.

———. 1974. *Makedonskoto, albanskoto i turskoto naselenie na selo vo Polog: Sociološka studija*. Skopje: Institut za sociološki i političko-pravni istražuvanja.

Josifovski, Ilija, and Jovanka Kepevska. 1978. Empirijska sociološka istraživanja u SR Makedoniji. *Revija za sociologiju* 8 (3–4): 93–99.

Josifovski, Ilija, and Petar J. Markoviḱ. 1973. *Demografskiot razvoj i proizvodstveno-ekonomskite karakteristiki na individualnite zemjodelski stopanstva na selo vo Polog*. Skopje: Institut za sociološki i političko-pravni istražuvanja.

Kartalov, Risto. 1982. Agrarnite odnosi i agrarnata struktura vo Makedonija od krajot na XIX do prvata polovina na XX vek. *Istorija* 18 (1–2): 79–96.

Kilias, Jarosław. 2017. *Goście za Wschodu: Socjologia polska lat sześćdziesiątych XX wieku a nauka światowa*. Kraków: Nomos.

Kostić, Cvetko. 1963. Razvitak i predmet sociologije sela. *Sociologija sela* 1 (1): 5–24.

Kostovski, Stefan M. 1972. *Religijata kaj selskoto naselenie vo Dolni Polog*. Skopje: ISPPI.

Kryczka, Piotr. 1986. The Issues of Urban Sociology in Poland. *The Polish Sociological Bulletin* 73–74: 13–25.

Kulturen život. 1968. Stopanskite organizacii i naučno-istražuvačkata dejnost. *Kulturen život* 13 (3): 3–4.

Lazić, Mladen. 2011. Sociology in Yugoslavia. Correlation Dynamics Between Critical and Integrative Social Theory in Liberal Socialism. In *Sociology and Ethnography in East-Central and South-East Europe*, ed. Ulf Brunnbauer, Claudia Kraft, and Martin Schulze Wessel, 87–106. München: Oldenbourg Verlag.

Le Normand, Brigitte. 2008. The Modernist City Reconsidered: Changing Attitudes of Social Scientists and Urban Designers in 1960s Yugoslavia. *Tokovi istorije* 3–4: 141–159.

Limanoski, Nijazi, ed. 1984. *Makedonci muslimani*. Skopje: Kulturno-naučni manifestacii na Makedoncite muslimani od SR Makedonija.

Lubaš, Marčin. 2021. *Raznoverci: Međureligiskiot soživot na selo vo Zapadna Makedonija*. Skopje: Makedonsko studentsko etnološko društvo.

Lukič, Radomir. 1959. Društveni uslovi razvoja sociologije u Jugoslaviji. *Sociologija* 1 (2–3): 97–113.

Majewski, Piotr. 2013. *(Re)konstrukcje narodu: Odwieczna Macedonia powstaje w XXI wieku*. Warszawa: SWPS.

Marinov, Čavdar. 2020. *Makedonskoto prašanje od 1944 do denes: Komunizmot i nacionalizmot na Balkanot*. Skopje: Fondacija Otvoreno opštestvo – Makedonija.

Mihajlovski, Stojmen. 1991. Dvaeset i pet godini rabota, razvitok i afirmacija na Institutot za sociološki i političko-pravni istražuvanja vo Skopje. *Godišnik na ISPPI* 13 (1): 7–57.

Milinković, Bosiljka. 1980. Istraživanja sela i poljoprivrede u Jugoslaviji. *Sociologija sela* 18 (69–70): 149–161.

Milosavlevski, Slavko. 1968a. *Demokratija i politička akcija.* Skopje: Nova Makedonija.

———. 1968b. *Revolucija i demokratija: Ogledi od političkata sociologija.* Skopje: Kultura.

———. 1971. *Revolucija i antirevolucija: Pokušaj kritike političkog sistema socijalizma.* Beograd: Revija.

Milosavlevski, Slavko, and Milan Nedkov. 1968. Političkata teorija vo deloto na Mito Hadži Vasilev-Jasmin. *Pogledi* 5 (6): 16–19.

Milosavlevski, Slavko, Tomislav Čokrevski, and Stoilko Ivanovski. 1964. *Participacijata na neposrednite proizvoditeli vo opštestveno-političkiot život na komunata.* Skopje: Glaven odbor na SSRNM.

Mladenovski, Ǵorǵe. 1997. Blaga Petroska – portret za istorijata na makedonskata sociologija. *Sociološka revija* 3 (1–2): I–VIII.

Mumford, Eric. 1992. CIAM Urbanism After the Athens Charter. *Planning Perspectives* 7: 391–417.

Padgett, Jack F. 1973. Philosophy and Social Planning in Yugoslavia. *Social Theory and Practice* 2 (4): 439–458.

Panov, Mitko. 1958. Ulogata na geografijata i nejzinata praktična primena vo urbanističkoto planiranje. *Godišen zbornik na Prirodno-matematički oddel* 11: 119–132.

———. 1969. Nekoi metodološki elementi vo proučuvanjeto na geografskata sredina. *Geografski razgledi* 7: 3–17.

Panov, Branko. 1972. Za etnogenezata na makedonskiot narod. *Glasnik na INI* 16 (3): 77–90.

Panov, Mitko. 1976a. *Geografija na SR Makedonija: Prirodni i socio-geografski karakteristiki.* Skopje: Prosvetno delo.

———. 1976b. Proces urbanizacije u kontekstu demografske structure stanovništva u SR Makedoniji. *Geografski glasnik* 38: 201–208.

———. 1978. Prostorni aspekti mreže seoskih naselja. *Sociologija sela* 61–62: 3–10.

Panov, Branko. 1999. *Makedonija niz istorijata.* Skopje: Menora.

Petak, Antun, Vlado Puljiz, and Maja Štambuk. 2002. Časopis Sociologija sela, razvoj sela i poljoprivrede, razvoj ruralne sociologije. *Sociologija sela* 40 (3–4): 227–251.

Petroska, Blaga. 1967. Oblici na semejstvoto vo Polog. *Godišen zbornik na Filozofskiot fakultet* 19: 62–128.

———. 1973. Struktura, privređivanje i starešina porodične zadruge (Rezultati empiriskog istraživanja). *Sociologija i prostor* 40–42: 120–130.

Petrovic, Edit, Ruzica Petrovic, and Andrei Simic. 1996. Family Research and Theory in Yugoslavia. *Marriage & Family Review* 22 (3–4): 259–286.

Pezo, Edvin. 2018. Emigration and Policy in Yugoslavia: Dynamics and Constrains within the Process of Muslim Emigration to Turkey during the 1950s. *European History Quarterly* 48 (2): 283–313.

Popoviḱ, Mihailo V. 1963. *Osnovi na sociologijata za III klas gimnazija*. Skopje: Prosvetno delo.

Radičeski, Neven. 2013. *Liberalizmot vo Makedonija (1966-1974)*. Skopje: Makedonika litera.

Ramet, Pedro. 1984. *Nationalism and Federalism in Yugoslavia, 1963–1983*. Bloomington and London: Indiana University Press.

Republički sovet. 1966. *Naučno-istražuvačkata aktivnost vo rabotnite organizacii i iskustvata od nivnoto povrzuvanje so naučnite institucii*. Skopje: Republički sovet na SSJ za Makedonija.

Rogel, Carole. 1984. A Marxist Looks at the Sixteenth Century: Edvard Kardelj's View of the Slovene Reformation. *Slovene Studies* 6 (1–2): 49–55.

Rusinow, Dennison. 1977. *The Yugoslav Experiment 1948–1974*. Berkley and Los Angeles: University of California Press.

Satterwhite, James. 1992. *Varieties of Marxist Humanism: Philosophical Revision in Postwar Eastern Europe*. Pittsburgh: University of Pittsburg Press.

Senior, Derek. 1970. *Skopje Resurgent: The Story of a United Nations Special Fund Town Planning Project*. New York: United Nations.

Sher, Gerson S. 1977. *Praxis: Marxist Criticism and Dissent in Socialist Yugoslavia*. Bloomington and London: Indiana University Press.

Sinadinovski, Jakim. 1959. Prvi pokušaji empiriskih istraživanja radničkog samoupravljanja. *Sociologija* 1 (1): 141–152.

———. 1960. Prvi posleratni udžbenik sociologije u Poljskoj. *Sociologija* 2 (3–4): 112–117.

———. 1961a. Neke strukturalne promene poljske radničke klase u svetlosti empirijskih istraživanja. *Sociologija* 3 (1): 129–141.

———. 1961b. Sociološka istraživanja participacije i integracije šiptarske nacionalne manjine u Makedoniji. *Sociologija* 3 (2): 120–131.

———. 1962a. Filozofska antropologija ili filozofija čoveka. *Filozofija: Jugoslovenski časopis za filozofiju* 3: 111–118.

———. 1962b. Stavovi i odnosi neposrednih proizvođača u procesu formiranja radnih zajednica. *Sociologija* 4 (3–4): 158–176.

———. 1964. *Funkcionisanje sistema samoupravljanja u svetlosti rezultata istraživanja ponašanja i stavova 10% članova kolektiva u izuzetnim okolnostima života i rada nakon zemjotresa u Skoplju*. Skopje: PMF.

———. 1968. Odnosot na visokokvalifikuvanite metalski rabotnici od tri različni starosni generacii na nekoi belgradski pretprijatija sprema problematikata na proizvodstvoto, vnatrešnata raspredelba i samoupravuvanjeto. *Godišen zbornik na Prirodno-matematičkiot fakultet* 16 (4): 277–317.

———. 1970. Raspredelbata, bezrabotnosta i socijalnata nesigurnost kaj nas. *Godišen zbornik na Prirodno-matematičkiot fakultet* 18 (6): 179–213.

———. 1971. Nekoi karakteristiki na povoeniot proces na deagrarizacijata i industrijalizacijta na SR Makedonija. *Geografski razgledi* 7–8: 37–59.

———. 1974. Psihosocijalnata i političkata atmosfera vo Gostivarsko vo 1941 godina. *Istorija* 10 (1): 140–149.

———. 1985. Formiranjeto na partizanskiot odred "Jane Sandanski" i negovite aktivnosti vo zimskite i proletnite meseci 1943/1944 godina vo Karaorman i Debarca. Istorija.

———. 1988. *Nacionalnoto prašanje i meǵunacionalnite odnosi kaj nas*. Skopje: Studentski zbor.

Sinadinovski, Jakim, and Zoge Gruevski. 1976. *Trite mavrovski sela*. Skopje: Zaednica na naučnite dejnosti.

Sinadinovski, Jakim, and Stoilko Ivanovski. 1963. Akcioni program sociološkog istraživanja u porušenom Skopju. *Sociologija* 5 (1–2): 63–78.

Sinadonovski, Jakim, Stoilko Ivanovski, and Mitko Panov. 1969. *Titovveleškite sela: Socio-ekonomski ispituvanja*. Skopje: Republički fond za finansiranje na naučnoispituvačkata rabota and Sobranie na opštinata vo Titov Veles. *Istorija* 21 (2): 207-219.

Skovajsa, Marek, and Jan Balon. 2017. *Sociology in the Czech Republic: Between East and West*. Basingstoke: Palgrave Macmillan.

Spasič, Ivana, Jelena Pešič and Marija Babovič. 2022. *Sociology in Serbia: A Fragile Discipline*. Basingstoke: Palgrave Macmillan.

Spaskovska, Ljubica. 2020. Constructing the 'City of International Solidarity': Non-aligned In00ternationalism, the United Nations and Visions of Development, Modernism and Solidarity, 1955–1975. *Journal of World History* 31 (1): 137–163.

Supek, Rudi. 1959. Jugoslavenska sociologija i program SKJ. *Sociologija* 2–3: 3–14.

Šuvar, Stipe, et al. 1970. Tipologija ruralnih sredina u Jugoslaviji (studijski projekt). *Sociologija i prostor* 27–28: 47–67.

Taneski, Vladimir. 1962. *Sociologija: Sovremeno opštestvo*. Skopje: Skopski Univerzitet.

———. 1964. *Sociologija: Istoriski razvoj na opštestvenata misla*. Skopje: Skopski Univerzitet.

Taševa, Marija. 1997. *Etničkite grupi vo Makedonija: Istoriski kontekst*. Skopje: Filozofski fakultet.

Taškovski, Dragan. 1967. *Raǵanjeto na makedonskata nacija*. Skopje: NIP Nova Makedonija.

———. 1974. *Kon etnogenezata na makedonskiot narod*. Skopje: NIK Naša kniga Skopje.

Tolic, Ines. 2019. The Skopje Urban Plan Project and Doxiadis Associates. In *The Future as a Project: Doxiadis in Skopje*, ed. Kalliopi Amygdalou, Kostas Tsiambaos, and Christos-Georgios Kritikos, 38–49. Athens: Hellenic Institute of Architecture.

Tomic, Mimoza, et al. 1965. *Report on Social Survey: Prepared for the United Nations as Excecuting Agency for the United Nations Special Fund*. Skopje: Polservice and ITPA.

Tomović, Vladislav A. 1968. *Post-War Sociology in Yugoslavia*. Windsor: University of Windsor.

———. 1969. Historical Materialism or Sociology in Yugoslavia. *Canadian Slavonic Papers* 11 (2): 199–211.

Trajanovski, Naum. 2021a. Zbor imaat graǵanite: The First Sociological Study, the Polish Sociological Expert Aid to Macedonia in the Mid-1960s and the Post-Earthquake History of Interethnic Relations in Skopje. *Colloquia Humanistica* 9: 1–42.

———. 2021b. The City of Solidarity's Diverse Legacies: A Framework for Interpreting the Local Memory of the 1963 Skopje Earthquake and the Post-earthquake Urban Reconstruction. *Journal of Nationalism, Memory & Language Politics* 15 (1): 30–51.

Trebst, Stefan. 1997. *Bugarsko-jugoslovenskata kontroverza za Makedonija 1967-1982*. Skopje: INI.

Uzunov, Nikola. 1961. *Faktori i metodi na industrijalizacijata*. Skopje: Kultura.

———. 1975. *Empiriska analiza za vlijanieto na ekonomskite, socijalnite i demografskite faktori vrz migracijata od selo vo grad vo SR Makedonija*. Skopje: Ekonomski fakultet.

Vangeli, Anastas. 2011. *Antička segašnost: Osvrt kon grčko-makedonskiot spor za Aleksandrovoto nasledstvo*. Skopje: Templum.

Veljanovski, Nove. 1973. D-r Aleksandar Hristov, Sozdavanjeto na makedonskata država 1893-1945, Misla, Skopje, 1971, 404. *Glasnik na INI* 17 (1): 304–306.

Verigiḱ, Dušan M. 1991. Metodološkite postapki vo istražuvanjata vo Institutot za sociološki i političko-pravni istražuvanja – Skopje: period 1966-1990. *Godišnik na ISPPI* 13 (1): 59–72.

Voříšek, Michael. 2008. Antagonist, Type, or Deviation? A Comparative View on Sociology in Post-War Soviet Europe. *Revue d'Historie des Sciences Humaines* 18: 85–113.

———. 2012. *The Reform Generation: 1960s Czechoslovak sociology from a comparative perspective*. Kalich: Kalich Publishers.

Wawryszuk, Paweł. 2018. Normalization of Polish-Yugoslav Relations After Władysław Gomulka's Return to Power (1956–1958). *Istorija 20. veka* 36 (2): 139–154.

CHAPTER 4

The Voices of the Double-Periphery: The Crisis Years and the Inertia of Macedonian Sociology (1970s–1980s)

Abstract This chapter follows the development of Macedonian sociology during the 1970s and 1980s, tracing two major patterns. The first one pertained to the process of completion of the sociological institutionalization instigated in the 1960s. Against the backdrop of the downfall of sociology in the major Yugoslav academic centers in the early 1970s, the Macedonian sociologists faced a different domestic reception of their expertise in comparison to the late 1960s. As a response to the novel situation, they became engaged in a series of deliberations upon the roles of sociology and sociologists in the state and society going through a multifaceted and unsettling crisis. In several cases, constituting the second pattern, those reconsiderations resulted in initiatives aimed at demonstrating the autonomy of Macedonian sociology.

Keywords Sociology • Socialist Republic of Macedonia • Sociological profile • Institutionalization • Inertia

The social unrest during the Yugoslav late 1960s—from the Croat Spring to the student demonstrations and the Albanian protests in Kosovo and Western Macedonia—married with the economic recession that hit the country in the early 1970s, resulted in yet another substantial recalibration of the federal political course. In short, the root causes of the hardship were traced back to "national-separatism" and the "rotten liberalism, bureaucratism, and technocratism" of the elites, and a solution was seen in their retrenchment and change (Cohen 1979, 462–468). This credo translated into a "conservative counteroffensive" in socialist Macedonia (Crvenkovski and Milosavlevski 1996, 98), which brought the SKM group around **Lazar Koliševski** (1914–2000) back to power in 1972. The power play impacted the careers of the leading liberal communists: Crvenkovski was ousted in 1972, while Milosavlevski refused to self-criticize so he was removed both from the SKM and the Faculty of Law in Skopje by 1974. As a neat demonstration of the new party line, **Angel Čemerski** (1923–2003), the succeeding Secretary of the SKM after Crvenkovski, deemed the public criticism unwelcome (Politika 1975) and depicted the "many currents and understandings" within the SKJ and the SKM of the 1960s as "one of their major weaknesses" (Nikolić 1973). In one of the rare publicized criticisms of Milosavlevski, the new leadership singled out the fact that "he writes a lot" as his crucial wrongdoing (Georgievski 2014, 8).

The 1974 Yugoslav Constitution had a double function in this regard. On the one hand, it expanded the reach of self-management by increasing communal funds and inviting a vast set of socialist self-governing organizations to the decision-making process (Leonardson and Mirčev 1979). The revised political operationality now included the category of delegates as mediators between the SKJ (and the national Leagues of Communists) and the local organizations of associated labor and self-interest communities (Rusinow 1986). The delegate system thus stripped the competencies of the technocratic politicians, now considered to be the very source of the crisis.[1] Moreover, the 1970s saw a massive campaign for "deprofessionalization" of politics, instructing the delegates to perform their tasks "on a part-time or amateur basis" (Cohen 1982, 15).[2] In this very context, the cooption of cadres shifted from professional training—which was one of the prevailing ways of instrumentalizing sociology in the course of

---

[1] This also meant a halt of the practice of having sociologists in the party leadership, such as Milosavlevski in Macedonia, **Miroslav Pečujlić** (1929–2006) in Serbia, and **Stipe Šuvar** (1936–2004) in Croatia.

[2] In 1969 Macedonia, for instance, only two of the total number of 339 representatives in all the political bodies were industrial workers, while only one was an agricultural worker (Georgievski 1972b, 82). The changes boosted their participation as of the early 1970s; however, the general percentages were lower than the Yugoslav average and their numbers decreased until the mid-1980s (Popovski 1984).

the 1960s—to ideological instruction in classic and Yugoslav Marxism. For instance, a network of Marxist schools emerging in the 1970s aimed at preparing the new "socio-political workers" to be guardians of self-management (Cohen 1979, 469–470; 1983). Even more, the "transfer" of the Marxist education from the party to the universities and the other research centers—"under the pressure of the forces of certain time"— was now openly proclaimed a mistake which allowed for a mutation of "philosophical and sociological schools" into capitalist "eclecticism" and stripping it away from the self-managerial practice (Kardelj in Radenović 1981, 25). On the other hand, the 1974 Constitution adopted the 1960s "confederalizing" amendments "almost intact" (Rusinow 2007, 144), thus transferring much of the power to the republics as a means of keeping the national Leagues content. In turn, with the liberal factions cast aside, the reforms facilitated an even greater accumulation of power in the national Leagues than in the 1960s, now left with the complex delegate system as the only balancing mechanism (Rusinow 1977, 1986; Cohen 1982; Burg 1983).

The above developments impacted the thriving Yugoslav sociology of the 1960s. Five of the eight Belgrade professors who were scapegoated and dismissed after the student demonstrations were sociologists— charged for, much like the case of Socrates, exerting "a deleterious anti-socialist influence on the young generation" (Spasić et al. 2022, 52)—while *Praxis* ceased to exist in 1974. Sociology in the major Yugoslav centers was therefore "re-peripheralized" (Cosovschi in Spasić et al. 2022, 59), only to reemerge in the early 1980s as a possible remedy for the persistent crisis, embodied in the failures to suppress the Albanian unrest and stabilize the economy, capped with Tito's death in 1980. In Macedonia, the 1980s saw further deterioration of interethnic relations and living standards, which will be touched upon in more detail in the next chapter. One illustrative event for the 1980s sociological reemergence was the three-day conference in Portorož, Slovenia, in November 1983, which gathered, after some time, approximately 250 Yugoslav sociologists to discuss the "integrating and disintegrating" processes in Yugoslav society. The gathering provoked massive media interest which further disseminated the sociologists' urges for democratization of social and political life (e.g., Marinković 1983). It also encouraged a number of sociologists, social scientists, and philosophers to stand up during the 1980s and argue about the *crisis of Marxism* in its lack of providing suitable answers for the pressing issues. Drawing upon the corresponding Western Marxist criticism, the local incarnations of those exchanges allowed for a restart of the critical discourses and a reconfiguration of the Yugoslav sociological dialogue.

The two decades covered in this chapter are suggestive of two developmental patterns of Macedonian sociology during this period. Despite the general downfall of sociology in the larger Yugoslav centers, the Macedonian 1970s saw a gradual completion of the institutional arrangements, already instigated during the previous decade. This was certainly not an atypical process. Against the background of the mid-1970s self-managerial reform of higher education and research in Yugoslavia, the start of the first bachelor study program in Skopje was tuned in with the similar developments at the other peripheral Yugoslav universities, such as the creation of sociological chairs in Prishtina (1973), Zadar (1974), Novi Sad (1976), and Nikšić (1977) (Duller 2018, 172). However, the reception of the work and activities of the Macedonian sociologists was not as enthusiastic as in the 1960s. This, in turn, pushed them into pursuing a series of initiatives aimed at displaying the sociological merits for the new era of Macedonian politics. In the next section, I cover the long deliberation over the seemingly practical issues of sociological expertise, profession, and profile in Macedonia in the course of the two late socialist decades. I then turn to the set of pioneering activities from the early and mid-1970s, such as the issuing of the first specialized sociological and the first critical journal, the launching of the first structured public survey, and the start of the beyond Yugoslav cross-national sociological exchanges of the late 1970s. The histories of all those initiatives demonstrate the strategic negotiations and eventual compromises of the Macedonian sociologists, determining their career trajectories and work in the course of the 1970s and 1980s.

THE QUESTION OF THE PROFILE

As already mentioned in the previous chapter, sociological courses were already offered at several faculties in Skopje during the 1960s. Among the social sciences and humanities, the Faculty of Law offered courses in general and political sociology to its first-year bachelor students, similar to the Faculty of Economics, which offered a course in sociology to its freshmen.[3] The Faculty of Philosophy offered a course in sociology to first-year students and one in the basics of the social sciences which mostly relied on sociological literature. An early 1970s comparative study of the sociological syllabi in Yugoslavia noted that the Faculty of Philosophy was ahead of Law and Economics in Skopje in terms of the quality of the course readings, with the latter two clinging to "outdated" literature (Cvjetičanin 1972, 109–110).[4] From 1973 to 1976, in line with the new political agenda, the Faculty of Philosophy started to offer a course in "Marxist sociology with self-management socialism" to all the other faculties, institutes, and graduate and postgraduate programs in Macedonia (Georgievski 1978, 100). The goal and the scope of this course and the redressed Marxist education in Macedonia were neatly outlined by the philosophy professor **Dimitar Dimitrov** (b.1937) for Zagreb's *Sociological Review* [scr. *Revija za sociologiju*] already in 1978: he argued that it failed to stimulate critical thinking, which in turn transformed Marxism into a mere "metaphysics" (Dimitrov 1978, 112).

Such was the general educational background (back and forth in time) behind the development of the two stand-alone sociological programs in socialist Macedonia. The first one dates back to the academic year 1967–1968, when the ISPPI inaugurated two postgraduate tracks in sociology: the first one in general sociology and the second one in political sociology. The two two-year study programs were initially projected to produce "scientific cadres" for the ongoing and prospective research of the Institute (Kambovski 1987, 10), in the different, for sociology, social and political contexts. They were envisioned as a combination of two tri-semestral (sociology and sociological methodology) and one bi-semestral course (history of sociological theories), plus courses in statistics and a

---

[3] As hinted at in the previous chapter, the economics students had a "hard time" with the study materials in sociology and their results were "more than modest" as per their instructor (in Taneski 1964, 5).

[4] It might be the case that the author of the study missed the 1971 sociology textbook authored by Milosavlevski, Josifovski, and Čokrevski, which was much informed by the Frankfurt School, and especially Marcuse's *negative thinking*, and thus differed from the previously written Macedonian textbooks (1971, 5–6). The immediate effects of the textbook might be found in the results of one student survey at the Faculty in 1973 which suggested that sociology was by far the most popular subject (Pelivanov 1973, 91). In the late 1960s and early 1970s, the sociology lectures by the Faculty of Law instructors were organized in the largest convention center in Skopje, *Univerzalna sala*, due to the high interest (Milosavlevski 1996, 62).

foreign language during the second year, complemented with an individual selection of one specialized sociology course which was to be studied for two semesters. The list of specializations predominantly matched the interests and the research projects of the ISPPI associates, but it also reflected the Institute's attentiveness to the newest developments in and beyond Yugoslavia. Therefore, the list included courses in sociology of culture, urban sociology, family sociology, and social pathology, as well as the Yugoslav delegate system and mass communications as of the mid-1970s.

The two programs were inaugurated just prior to the decision allowing free enrollment choice at Skopje University (except at the Medical Faculty), effective as of 1968. It did not help much in the first few years as the two programs enrolled a total number of 18 students in general and 15 in political sociology up to the academic year of 1972–1973. Only seven managed to complete the programs, three in general and four in political sociology. The management was, however, quick to recognize "certain weaknesses" pertaining to the initial format of the program in the early 1970s and sought a solution in "liberalizing the regime for student enrollment" in 1974. The second significant reform manifested as a shift from the individual study tracks and one-on-one consultations, which proved to be insufficiently motivating and fast-paced, into the more habitual *ex-cathedra* teaching scheme. The changes appeared to be neatly tailored as they boosted student enrollment as early as in the academic year of 1974–1975: 59 students in total, 34 in general, and 25 in political sociology (Godišnik na ISPPI 1976, 8).

The popularity of sociological education and the decreasing numbers of sociology students at other Yugoslav universities in the early 1970s were highlighted as the major triggers behind the idea of initiating a bachelor program in sociology in Skopje (Georgievski 1978, 101). After a brief deliberation, it was decided for the Faculty of Philosophy—and not the ISPPI—to host such a program, a decision that can be pinned down, again, to two main reasons. The first one resonated with the previous experience in conducting sociology courses by five already employed sociology instructors, who turned out to be the core of the Sociology Group after 1975: Miljovska, Petroska (who was the first chair), Georgievski, and the then-assistants **Marija Taševa** (b.1940) and **Ǵorǵe Mladenovski** (b.1947) (Minoski 2020, 297). The missing elements, such as a library and classrooms, were resolved after the formal establishment of the Sociology Chair [mk. *Katedra za sociologija*] by the Faculty of Philosophy in 1973, which was tasked with preparing the enrollment: arranging the syllabi, assigning the courses, and equipping the Chair with literature. Ergo, in 1974, only a year prior to the start of the enrollment, the Sociology Chair purchased 629 sociological books and journals (Georgievski 1978, 100).[5] The classroom issue was fixed by default in the course of the same year with the settling of the Faculty of Philosophy and the Faculty of Philology into one of the buildings of the new Skopje University campus, erected during the post-earthquake urban reconstruction of the city.

The second reason pertained to the legislative changes in the work of the scientific institutes and universities from the mid-1970s. They primarily aimed at introducing the self-managerial principles in higher education—and projected an improvement in the financing, discussed below—which in turn facilitated their cooperation in developing new research and teaching programs. For instance, the Faculty of Law and the ISPPI formed a Center for Social Sciences [mk. *Centar za opštestveni nauki*] based on a self-managerial association agreement in 1976 (Kambovski 1987, 8).[6] In addition, upon an early 1970s initiative of *Nova Makedonija* and a university committee led by Dančo Zografski, the Faculties of Law, Economics, Philosophy, and Philology joined forces to organize the first Macedonian graduate program in journalism which enrolled its first students in 1977 (Dokmanoviḱ 2007, 179–183). Against this background, the initiation of the bachelor program in sociology at the Faculty of Philosophy in Skopje tended to suggest its "same status" as the older and considered-to-be more traditional study groups in philosophy, pedagogy, and history, as well as the one in psychology, initiated only a year before the sociological one (Georgievski 1978, 101). The sociologists at the Faculty of Philosophy of Skopje also referred to the corresponding programs at the universities in Belgrade, Zagreb, Sarajevo, and Ljubljana, with emphasis on the first two, as blueprints for the development of the bachelor study program in Skopje (Georgievski 2012, 99–100). In this context, the first 82 sociology students (45 regular and 37 extramural) were welcomed in 1975 by the now-renamed NNSG in Sociology. The number of enrolled students increased in 1976 (309 in total), making it

---

[5] For a comparison, the National Library in Skopje was able to purchase a similar number of books (696) in 1981 (Kartalov 1985, 215).

[6] Despite the "formal elements" stipulated with this merger, there were no other implications in the work of the ISPPI (Mihajlovski 1991, 9).

the most popular program at the Faculty of Philosophy during that academic year, while the number of enrolled students remained high in 1977 (219) and 1978 (316).

The first several cohorts of sociology students from both the Faculty of Philosophy and the ISPPI brought along a series of issues related to their profile and employment. First and foremost, it appeared that there was a serious concern with the number of students advancing from one to another study year. For instance, out of the first generation of 82 enrolled students at the Sociology Group of the Faculty of Philosophy, 21 advanced to the second year, 12 to the third, and only eight to the final fourth year. The proportions repeated for the next generation of students (Georgievski 1978, 102–103). Georgievski, a sociologist of education himself, hinted at the quality of secondary education and the entry exam, calling for more profound and cross-national research on this phenomenon.[7] However, it soon became evident that the uncertainties about the educational profile and the graduates' prospects might be one of the major rationales behind the above developments. Two aspects appeared to be important in this regard. On the one hand, the late 1970s saw an increased tendency toward scientific specialization which was supported by a state educational reform. In this context, the Faculty of Philosophy and the NNSG in Sociology followed suit by introducing two study tracks as of 1977: one for graduate sociologists and another for graduate high school teachers in sociology and Marxism and self-management. This, however, appeared to be an "unsuccessful hybrid" model, not necessarily tailored to fix the immediate issues of the sociology program. In response, Georgievski proposed specializations in specialized sociologies, involving the students in sociological research (in cooperation with the ISPPI, but also with other Yugoslav programs and research centers), and a reconsideration of the Marxist education in the state, suggesting, for instance, inter-university courses in specialized sociology as a response to the specializing tendencies in science (Georgievski 1978, 104).

The second set of issues about the profile, on the other hand, occurred already with the first graduated cohort of sociology students in the early

---

[7] In his 2012 take on the history of the Sociology Group in Skopje, Georgievski adds the "way of studying" typical for the Yugoslav universities of the 1970s, that is, the usage of more and different sources as course materials and the stricter criteria for passing exams., as the most important factor for the low numbers of advancing students (Georgievski 2012, 99–101).

1980s (the first one in April 1980). Up until the end of 1984, 107 students graduated in sociology in Macedonia out of which 27 were unemployed, while according to Petroska's insights, not all of the sociology graduates held "relevant working positions" (Petroska 1985, 194). As an immediate response, the Sociology Group dropped its dual profiling in 1978 and reintroduced the general sociological track in 1980. It also added several new members to its teaching staff: **Amalija Jovanoviḱ** (b.1943), **Mileva Ǵurovska** (b. 1957), **Nelko Stojanoski** (b. 1946), **Hristo Kartalov** (1944–2017), **Jovan Korubin** (1948–2006), and **Ilija Aceski** (b. 1952) in the early 1980s, and **Zoran Matevski** (b. 1957) and **Ilo Trajkovski** (b. 1960) as of the mid-1980s (Georgievski 2012, 102–103; Trajkovski 2000; Minoski 2020, 299–300). The Group cooperated with **Dimitar Mirčev** (1942–2016), **Vlado Popovski** (b. 1941), **Lazar Nikodimovski**, and Stefan Kostovski, who were formally part of the Faculty of Philosophy's new Chair in Marxist and Humanistic Education, but also professors from other faculties of the Skopje University such as Sinadinovski (Kamberski 1986; Georgievski 2012, 102–103). It is important to note that the vast majority of the new employees of the Sociology Group, deemed the "second generation" of Macedonian sociologists (Trajkovski 2000), were graduates of the ISPPI programs. This "one-way fluctuation" (Kambovski 1987, 8) of cadres from the ISSPI to the Faculty of Philosophy was recognized as a critical issue for the work of the Institute in Skopje, the consequences of which will be discussed below.

Back to the unclear postgraduation prospects, the sociology instructors at Skopje University turned back to their specialized knowledge to suggest new career options for their graduates. The special section of the 1985 *Annual of the Faculty of Philosophy* best illustrates those attempts as it contains their answers pertaining to the reasons for the "very slow" societal acceptance of the sociological profession. One of those main reasons, as put by Petroska in her introductory text, was that the Macedonian citizens were unable to make a clear distinction between the work scopes of sociologists, social workers, and political scientists (Petroska 1985, 13). The long-term solution was hence considered to lie in a major reassessment of sociology as a profession [mk. *profesija*] indispensable to the self-managerial socialism. Therefore, some associates traced the sociological focus back to facilitating practical aspects of labor relations—such as in "labor rationalization" (Petroska 1985) and in the light of the automatization and technicization of work (Nikodimovski 1985; Ǵurovska 1985)—while others provided more theoretical observations about class, self-management, and sociology (Georgievski 1985; Kartalov 1985; Mladenovski 1985). The special section also contained articles that hinted at the particular research interests of the Macedonian sociologists. For instance, Taševa, drawing upon American industrial sociology scholarship, highlighted the unique role of sociologists in settling workplace conflicts and unemployment (Taševa-Pocevska 1985), Jovanoviḱ used sociological cases to argue in favor of the difference between the "formal and real [gender] equality" (Jovanoviḱ 1985, 238), Korubin discussed the potentials of information and communication sciences (Korubin 1985), and Stojanoski highlighted the sociological research on "sociopathology" (Stojanoski 1985).

The associates of the ISPPI were in a rather different position in the late 1970s, however. Unlike their colleagues in the Sociology Group, they did not engage in convincing about the need either of their profile or of their empirical sociological research (Josifovski and Kepevska 1978, 96).[8] Their main issue pertained to the above legal reforms which initially aimed at liberalizing scientific work, especially in terms of the institutional revenues which could be now divided among the employees (Bošale et al. 1987, 223).[9] It would not take long for the ISPPI associates to notice that, after the reforms, sociological research in Macedonia deteriorated into projects of lesser quality dependent upon the personal contacts with the authorities and tailored for their needs (Josifovski and Kepevska 1978, 96). In turn, sociological outputs were affirmative rather than critical, while the Institute associates developed a practice to reorient toward "globalist" topics in lieu of researching the pressing societal needs which were less likely to receive funding. As an illustration, up until 1978, the ISPPI conducted a set of rather descriptive takes on the new Constitution, the judiciary, and the political and electoral systems of socialist Macedonia. Furthermore, its major research focus at the turn of the 1970s and during the 1980s was put on proving the congruence of the delegate system on different social and political levels (e.g., Mihajlovski 1978; Hristov 1979; Mirčev 1979). The ISPPI coordinated several other research projects during this period. Starting from 1970, it led a longer cross-institutional examination of

[8] The full segment reads: "[w]e stand that there is no need to convince that our socialist self-managerial society require empirical sociological research. According to us, to hold an opposite view would mean a deviation from the basic Marxist and scientific-socialist positions in the field of social research" (Josifovski and Kepeska 1978, 96).

[9] The reform also aimed at stimulating a more efficient research flow. For instance, from 1967 to 1969, only 105 of the total number of 226 commissioned research projects were finalized (Lazaroski et al. 1971).

addictions and drug users in the state, involving criminologists, neuropsy-chiatrists, and representatives of the relevant industries, such as penologist and a "liberal" **Ljupčo Arnaudovski** (b. 1931). Albeit recreating the dominant "social pathology" paradigm of the day (Šurbanovski 1978), the research scope, interdisciplinarity, and communication of the findings with the wider public seem extraordinary. Several individual researchers published their extended projects' contributions as separate monographs, such as the case of Amalija Jovanovik's study of marriage as a carrier of social mobility in socialist Macedonia. Jovanovik thus filled the gap in the mid-1970s ISPPI research on social stratification, touched upon below, by unveiling its different gendered aspects and hinting at certain empirical data which contradicted the preliminary hypotheses. Religion, for instance, appeared to be very significant in the homogamies, more than the engage-ment in the Second World War resistance and liberation (Jovanovik 1981).

In parallel, the ISPPI ran a public opinion survey (the first annual issue was published in 1975), while it also started publishing its *Annual* in 1975. The survey reports and the *Annuals* best reflected the major strug-gles of the ISPPI associates, and they will be briefly discussed from this perspective below. All those activities made overwhelming the everyday ISPPI agenda during the 1970s. Hence, a vast number of its graduates and employees transferred to positions at Skopje University or other insti-tutions across the state, using the platforms of the ISPPI to publish their work, such as in the ISPPI's book series "Sociological studies" (e.g., Georgievski 1972a), or to cooperate on research projects. This was cer-tainly a reversed process compared to the early years of its functioning when it was the ISPPI that was recruiting experts from other institutions without a hitch. The transfers to the University were also unlike the career trajectories of the Macedonian academic historians who were more eager to relocate to the INI during the same period (more in Brown 2000).

The preparations for the "systematic surveying of public opinion" at the ISPPI were traced back to 1969 and the endorsement of the "sociol-ogy of the party" agenda, while the ISPPI conducted a pilot study in 1972 (Godišnik na ISPPI 1976; Popovski et al. 1977, 5). As already mentioned, they started publishing a regular public opinion survey in 1975 as part of their Center for Public Surveying, established during the very same year. The first few issues of the annual reports suggest the struggles to reconcile the surveying goals with the "negative view" of public opinion in the Marxist classics (and the immediate Macedonian political context, one might add). Drawing upon Yugoslav and Polish public opinion surveying experiences in socialist state contexts, as well as theoretical inspiration from the Frankfurt School, they came up with a rather modest response: public opinion was proposed as an indicator of potential social and political patterns of behavior, while a "pluralism of thoughts" was legitimized as a reflection of the different social groups' stances on common experiences (Dijalog 1973; Spasov in Popovski et al. 1977, 11; Kartalov et al. 1975). The first surveys of approximately 1200 informants were also exploratory in terms of surveying methodology and stratified sampling (Spasov 1977; Mirčev et al. 1978), as well as resolving some practical issues related to the lack of responses in rural areas. However, as of 1978, they included nonparametric statistics and gathered enough comparative material to be able to leave the theoretical considerations aside and engage with new topics such as media content reception and opinions on pressing political events, e.g., the ones in Kosovo or Poland of the early 1980s (Simovska et al. 1980; Spasov et al. 1982, 1983; an overview for the statistical methods in Verigik 1987).

The ISPPI public surveys of the 1970s and 1980s, as the only such publicly available endeavor in late socialist Macedonia, allow for a certain insight into the *patterns of behavior* of Macedonian citizens, but also the patterns of behavior of the authorities, that is, their political ideas, anticipations, and even consternation. The late 1970s surveys, for instance, suggested that the citizens were the least satisfied with the healthcare services. As of 1980, with the first in the series of comparative analyses, it became evident that there was a decreasing tendency in the percentages depicting the citizens' unfamiliarity with the SKM activities: from approximately 27 percent in 1976 to approximately 43 percent in 1979 (Simovska et al. 1980, 137–138). Even more striking is the breakdown into population segments as it suggests a clear gap between the experts and administrative workers—who appeared to be far more interested in the political events but also in joining the SKM—and the workers, who were more disinclined to follow the SKM activities. The gap widened in the course of the next few years, indicating that the vast majority of the SKM public were the SKM members themselves (e.g., Spasov et al. 1983).

As of the early 1980s, one can also note a certain shift toward probing political narratives in the annual public surveys. For instance, respondents were asked questions about the risks of an eventual return of the liberals in politics, the reasons for the economic crisis, and the meaning of the scapegoating slogan of the day, "ideological-political differentiation" (Spasov et al. 1982, 206–234), to all of which the informants showed little to no interest or understanding. Moreover, the ISPPI surveyors addressed the issue of political influence in surveying in the introduction to the 1986 edition, deeming it "legitimate" scientific enterprise, independent from political ingraining, which can be of benefit for the policymakers (Nedelkovski et al. 1986, 3–11). In practice, however, the issue appeared to be of another sort: as per the ISPPI associates, the authorities and the general public showed little to no attentiveness to the annual surveys (e.g., Jovanović 1981). In spite of that, however, the surveyors started appreciating the benefits of the political "indifference" as it allowed them to be "more autonomous, free, critical, and impartial" (Nedelkovski et al. 1986, 4). As time went by, it became apparent to the ISPPI surveyors that the political decision-makers conducted their own public opinion polls, which were not necessarily disclosed (e.g., Spasov et al. 1989).

The ISPPI's *Annual* is illustrative of the research interests of Macedonian sociologists, as well as their scientific ambitions in the course of the 1970s and 1980s. It contained several sections: the more standard ones of sociological sciences, political sciences (*politology* as of the early 1980s), and social pathology, as well as the irregular ones of social thought, history, and the Macedonian national question, which I will briefly touch upon below. The *Annual* had special sections dedicated to Marxist personages such as Gramsci (1976), Luxemburg (1977), and Tito, to whom the whole 1980 festschrift was dedicated in the wake of his death. The vast majority of the authors were Macedonians associated with both the ISPPI and the NNSG in Sociology at the Faculty of Philosophy in Skopje, while the first articles of non-Macedonian Yugoslav sociologists were published in 1981. The first two issues of the *Annual* exemplify the strong focus on rural sociology from theoretical (e.g., Kostovski 1975; Taševa-Pocevska 1975; Kartalov 1976) and methodological aspects (Bubevski 1975). What they had in common was the ISPPI research projects they were related to; hence different authors discussed different aspects of the findings in the texts for the *Annuals*. The journal was also used as an organ for announcing the future research of the ISPPI. For instance, the 1975 issue indicated the continuation of the "longitudinal systematic" empirical studies of "the migrations and the changes of the villages" in socialist Macedonia, focused on the mountain villages after 1975 (Kostovski 1975, 19–20). On that account, the journal is also illustrative of the shifts in the rural sociology perspectives in Macedonia. The 1978 issue provides insights into the research interest in the "rural culture" (Jovanovski 1978), while the 1981 issue contains the findings of the research project about the political participation in rural areas and local municipalities in socialist Macedonia (Mirčev 1981; Tufai 1981). Mirčev's research at the intersection of sociology and political sciences is nowadays considered to be the pioneering political science endeavor in Macedonia (e.g., Cekik 2015). It appeared against the backdrop of the prevailing interest in the functioning of the delegate system as mentioned above.

The special section on the Macedonian question was in direct relation to the department on the Macedonian nation within the ISPPI, established in the early 1970s. Its work is, again, illustrative of the shifting sociological optics about Macedonian nation-building in the aftermath of the liberal crackdown in socialist Macedonia. Namely, the major focus was now put on tracing the intellectual history of "Macedonian social thought" in different historical periods, starting from the seventh century. It was manifested in several individual efforts at the beginning, while in the mid-1970s, during Taškovski's presidency of the ISPPI, it transformed into a platform for a more structured collaborative research of Macedonian and Yugoslav scholars. The main project as of 1975 was coordinated by the Zagreb University and aimed at mapping the history of philosophy in Yugoslavia, including sociological and cultural thought, as "an ideological synthesis of our national existence at this place in the Balkans" (as per its proposal). Its theoretical and methodological framework, however, remained vague. Therefore, certain scholars, such as **Slavko Dimevski** (1924–1990), examined Macedonian social thought from the seventh to the eighteenth century (Dimevski 1981, 1989).[10] It also urged other scholars to seek interpretations about nations and nationalisms in non-Marxist authors (Simovski 1977) and adjust their historical analyses to the comparative research perspective, such as in the case of Hristov (1982).

The topic of the development of Macedonian social thought animated several other sociologists in the course of the 1980s, not necessarily affiliated with the ISPPI. For instance, **Nikola Bošale** (1929–2019), a sociologist and politician, a former associate of the SKM Center for Marxism, and a professor of sociology and tourism in Ohrid, published a longer sociological study about the trans-historical virtues of St Clement of Ohrid's

---

[10] Dimevski was a former deacon who proceeded both with his scholarly and clergical career becoming a historian of religion associated with the INI (1957–1962), TV Skopje (1967–1975), and the ISSPI and its Department on the Macedonian Nation (as of 1975), while in parallel taking upon the presbyter clergical title (1963) and leading the Macedonian Orthodox Church's educational and publishing activities.

humanism which was printed by the Ohrid Museum in 1983 (Bošale 1983). Milosavlevski, who was now "ostracized" in his native Vratnica in the vicinity of Skopje, independently published an "ethno-sociological" study of his village while preparing several studies of the sociology of the Macedonian national consciousness (e.g., Milosavlevski 1997; for context, see Taševa 2014). He published two such volumes and several political memoirs after the fall of the socialist regime in Macedonia.

The 1980s also saw an opening of the Macedonian Academy of Sciences and Arts to legal, economic, and natural sciences topics, after its initial work in the historical and linguistic fields since its establishment in 1967. As already mentioned, the MANU was formed at the peak of the liberal communist rule in Macedonia. Its major goals pertained to the affirmation of Macedonian science, culture, and arts amid the regional contestations of the Macedonian identity. Even Tito recognized this task, deeming the establishment of the Academy necessary for a holistic understanding of the economic, political, and cultural history of the Macedonian peoples, "a history which is often falsified" (Tito 1970; also see Tomovski et al. 1988, 14). MANU hence organized several gatherings about the pressing issues of the Macedonian society as of the early 1980s. Their topics of interest shifted from "ethnic traditions" in Yugoslavia in 1981, a conference that brought together participants from the USSR, Bulgaria, and the other East-Central European socialist states (Tomovski et al. 1989), to Yugoslav self-management (e.g., Dimitrov et al. 1982) and urbanization, urban politics, demographics, and economic growth in the mid-1980s (e.g., Bogoev 1985; Kolev and Georgiev 1986).[11] These activities built upon the Social Sciences Department of MANU [mk. *Oddelenie za opštestveni nauki*], whose first head was Miljovski. Miljovski also initiated and edited a book series of MANU about the economic history of Macedonia which aimed at publishing unpublished scripts or republishing early post-war analyses about different economic aspects of the interwar period. The

[11] In the mid-1980s, MANU started to engage other relevant institutions, such as the other faculties, state statistical offices, and governing institutions, in their projections about the mid- and long-term economic and demographic development of Macedonia. Some of them involved sociologists from different institutions, such as the 1983 gathering in Leunovo aimed at discussing the outcomes of the 1981 population census (Bogoev 1985). Those activities were predominantly coordinated by Miljovski and, after Miljovski's death, **Ksente Bogoev** (1919–2008), an economist and academician who held some of the highest political positions in Macedonia (1968–1977) before becoming the Head of the National Bank of Yugoslavia (1977–1981).

series, for instance, included Blagoev's review, first published in 1948, of the industries in Macedonia stretching back to the late nineteenth century (Blagoev 1979) and the 1960 study of Sidovski about the industrial development in the interwar period based on post-war statistical data and surveys of the Economic Institute and the Faculty of Law and Economics in Skopje (Sidovski 1980). Unlike in other regional states, however, such as in Bulgaria (see Genov 2002), MANU did not follow the Soviet model of establishing its own sociology institute. In the post-Yugoslav period, the Academy remained engaged in topics related to sociology and the intellectual, cultural, and political history of Macedonia, publishing, for instance, 28 volumes of the project "Istorijata na kulturata na počvata na Makedonija" (official translation: Cultural History of Macedonia), including a volume on the history of ideas without a sociological account (Stardelov et al. 2000).

In parallel to MANU's interest, there were other openings to sociology following the establishment of the new tertiary educational institutions in socialist Macedonia. For instance, the second Macedonian university, the University of "St Kliment Ohridski" in Bitola, established in 1979 and operating under this name since 1994, offered a sociology course as part of its Pedagogical Academy. Its first rector was **Stefan Gaber** (1919–1999), who changed his position at the ISPPI for the one in Bitola. There was an already functioning Macedonian Scientific Society in Bitola, established in 1960, with a social scientific section. A few years after the inauguration of the University in Bitola, in 1985, the Faculty of Economics in Prilep also introduced introductory courses in philosophy and sociology, whose first instructor was **Ljupčo Pečijareski** (b. 1954).

"DEPROVINCIALIZATION"

"The institutionalization of sociological studies put forward the need for the *deprovincialization* [of Macedonian sociology] or its establishment within the Yugoslav sociology of the 1970s and the wider European frames as of the 1980s" (Georgievski 2012, 108). Thus, Petre Georgievski summarized the two last socialist decades of Macedonian sociology. The specter of deprovincialization illuminates the strategic negotiations and eventual compromises that Macedonian sociologists undertook during this period. They are even more evident (than in the above discussed mostly intra-institutional developments) when reviewing professional activities, networking, and engagement beyond their associated institutions. The different strategies of the relatively small-scale Macedonian sociological community hence materialized in various formats, oftentimes powered by the very same set of actors. Most importantly for this period, they unfolded in a series of networking events in Macedonia and several initiatives aimed at building bonds with other sociological communities. As such, they are also suggestive of the hybrid positionings of Macedonian sociologists between the oftentimes competing platforms and sociological standpoints.

The first of the struggles pertained to the institutional profile of the national association of sociologists. As mentioned in the previous chapter, the Macedonian Association of Philosophy and Sociology was initiated in 1962 as part of the JUS network. The Sociological Section of the Macedonian Association had 25 members in 1969, out of which 18 worked at Skopje University or the ISPPI. The very formation of the national Association was a result of the enthusiasm of individuals amid the previous decade's pronounced sociological institutionalization. Macedonian sociologists had such a platform in the 1960s, while those in Vojvodina, for instance, which were more than 100, did not manage to establish one in the course of the 1970s (even though the 1974 Constitution granted Vojvodina a *de facto* republican status). Despite the Association, the Macedonian sociologists failed to keep to the JUS's agenda of sociological "consultations" in the late 1960s. The consultations, in this jargon, were the sociological gatherings in different formats with a single goal of discussing an assigned topic. This, in turn, provoked a "heated debate" among the Macedonian Association members in 1970, resulting in the first calls for a disbanding of the philosophical, sociological, and politological sections of the national association (Bogdanović et al. 1990, 162–163). The Association eventually gained traction in organizing national sociological consultations in the 1970s before separating from the philosophers and political scientists in 1984.[12] Still, the heavy focus on national affairs sidelined their interest and participation in the major sociological exchanges of the 1970s both in and beyond Yugoslavia,

---

[12] This might be connected with the only all-Yugoslav sociological gathering organized in Macedonia in the course of the 1980s, that is, the 1984 one on the topic of "sociology and economy" organized by the sociologists at the Faculty of Philosophy in Skopje (Minoski 2020, 312).

such as the International Sociological Association's World Congresses of Sociology in Varna (1970), Toronto (1974), and Uppsala (1978).[13]

The Macedonian sociologists found other common ground with the humanists and the other social scientists in Macedonia. The two "social questions" journals, *Pogledi* (as of 1964) and *Dijalog* (as of 1972), provide great examples of the nuances of those very coalitions.[14] The first one, *Pogledi*, was initiated at the peak of the liberal communists' rule in Macedonia as an agenda-setting intellectual outlet, issued by the party publisher *Komunist* and edited by the SKM instructors in Marxism and sociology. Hence, in the late 1960s, it was common for Milosavlevski, Nedkov, and other Yugoslav liberal communist politicians and sociologists to publish scholarly articles in the annual (and often biannual) *Pogledi*. The journal remained somewhat critical in the early 1970s, allowing for sociologists and philosophers to argue in favor of a critical Marxism against a mere Marxology (e.g., Stardelov 1972, 929). The second journal, *Dijalog*, is no less engaging. Launched by the Macedonian Students' Association and edited by a group of emerging intellectuals—headed by Vlado Popovski, a legal scholar and a disciple of the liberal circle at the Faculty of Law in Skopje, interested in history and sociology and cooperating with the ISPPI and the Faculty of Philosophy at that point—it was published only twice before it was banned.[15] *Dijalog* was a product of the same political milieu at the turn of the 1970s; however, it had a more ambitious editorial agenda which was apparent already from the cover

---

[13] It was not uncommon for the Yugoslavs to attend those Congresses. For instance, the Yugoslav delegation of 14 sociologists from Belgrade, Zagreb, and Ljubljana traveled to Toronto, while two Slovene sociologists presented the findings of the cross-national, Slovene-Macedonian comparative research on social stratification and mobility (in Chall et al. 1975, 298).

[14] Worth mentioning, as well, is the journal *Social Politics* [mk. *Socijalna politika*], issued as of 1973 by the University college for social workers in Skopje, which published on the topics of, *inter alia*, youth delinquency and demography and frequently published the works of sociologists, such as Sinadinovski, Josifovski, and Georgievski, as well as Miljovski. Another important journal was *Cultural Life* [mk. *Kulturen život*], with the subtitle *Culture, Art, and Social Questions*, published by the Cultural-Educational Association of Macedonia.

[15] The journal proceeded to be published as of 1992, which will be covered in the next chapter. The introductory text of the 1992 issue is clear in its depiction of the "anti-liberal coup" as the major rationale for the halt of the journal in the early 1970s.

page.[16] More elaborately, its board embraced the *marginality*, *inferiority*, and *provinciality* of the Macedonian economy, politics, and culture as postulates for reconsidering the state's position within and beyond the Federation. The suggested formula was against "imitative institutionalism" (Popovski 1972, 11) and in favor of specializations in targeted fields, optimization of human resources, and a *dialogue* with the newest social and political trends. This positioning, in turn, entitled the authors of *Dijalog* to call for better educational, youth, and cultural politics. As an illustration, the first issue finished with a text criticizing the lack of scientific literature in Macedonian, both Marxist and non-Marxist (Temkov and Muhik 1972), while the second issue discussed the pitfalls of reform in higher education (e.g., Denkovski 1973).

The first issues of *Dijalog* hence read as a peripheral attempt to find its own voice, not necessarily related to integrating to the larger centers of Yugoslav sociology. In doing so, it also reads as a more critical outlet than *Pogledi*, even though it was not uncommon for the very same authors to simultaneously publish in both of them. For instance, ISPPI's Stefan Kostovski chose *Dijalog* over *Pogledi* to present his empirically informed thesis about a sociological reconsideration of religion as a social feature that impacts on present "national relations," a standpoint diverging from the Marxian one (Kostovski 1972). **Boris Nonevski** (1948–2021), another Macedonian sociologist who graduated in Belgrade, worked at the ISPPI in the early 1970s, and edited the SKJ's Central Committee organ *Socijalizam* in the late 1970s, also chose *Dijalog* to argue in favor of a holistic understanding of culture (Nonevski 1973). In addition, *Dijalog* brought the first translations of Western philosophical and anthropological scholarship in Macedonian, such as the authors around the journal *Social Research*. Those articles were much in line with Zagreb's faction of Praxis creative Marxism and its emphasis on anthropology and humanism in addressing the critical issues of alienation and emancipation (e.g., Parsons 1966). As neatly observed by Hodges, the strong inclination toward the early Marxian writings in the Yugoslav Marxist theory of the 1970s appeared to be flexible enough to "balance" between the different intra-Yugoslav provenances, such as the more "dogmatic" Macedonian

---

[16] Starting from the very title, meaning *Dialogue* in Macedonian, compared to the more patronizing *Viewpoints* (*Pogledi*). The subtitle of *Pogledi* was a *Journal for social questions*, while that of *Dijalog* was a *Journal for social questions and critique*.

one and the more "revisionist" Slovenian one (Hodges 1977, 59).[17] It also provided the structuring intellectual thread in Macedonia of the 1970s and early 1980s, penetrating much of the older and newer struc- tures of social scientific life. The delicate contrast between the different stakeholders in the national context is hence best illustrated with the very treatment of this topic.[18]

In 1972 only two critical events took place, both of them illustrative of the above point. The first one was a scientific conference on the occasion of the 90th anniversary of the death of Marx, organized by the Macedonian Association of Philosophy and Sociology in Ohrid in November 1972. It mostly gathered senior philosophers (e.g., Josifovski) and sociologists (e.g., Miljovska and Taškovski, the latter a president of the Association at that point), the Yugoslav orthodox Marxist veterans Nedeljković, Goričar, and Šešić, as well as two East German and a Polish representative, and several aspiring scholars (e.g., Georgievski and Muhiḱ). Setting the ground for the discussion, the introductory text of Jonče Josifovski aimed at exposing the dangers of the recent *anthropologizing* of Marx (Josifovski 1972). The proceedings of the Ohrid meeting were published in a sepa- rate volume (Miljovska et al. 1972) and in a special issue of *Pogledi* (1972). The other event was the instituting of the "school for young Marxists" in late 1972, which had its first edition in December 1973 in Oteševo, another lake venue in Macedonia. The School was initiated by the circle behind *Dijalog* in cooperation with the national Youth and Student Organizations, the ISSPI and the Skopje University, and the Association of Philosophers and Sociologists.[19] The first edition focused on key Marxist notions and, unlike the above gathering, was able to host only one guest from the nearby city of Niš. The proceedings, co-edited by Georgievski, showcase the conveners' strategic turn to researchers from other national institutions in their quest for establishing a critical dialogue about pressing issues involving, *inter alia*, Marxism in urban planning, ecosophy, and art (see Georgievski et al. 1974).

---

[17] Zaninovich observes a corresponding pattern, deeming it the "specter of young Marx" in the Yugoslav Marxism (Zaninovich 1969, 308–312)

[18] The 1974 Macedonian textbook on Marxist philosophy provides an interesting example as it gathered three authors with somewhat different positions about the theory of reflection vis-à-vis the praxist epistemology (see Josifovski et al. 1974).

[19] It was named "Stiv Naumov – Mite Bogoevski" after the two Macedonian students and Partisan fighters who lost their lives in the Second World War.

The banning of *Dijalog* and the gradual transformation of the School into a more apologetic enterprise is yet another indication that the line of the *seniors* prevailed over that of the *juniors* in Macedonia, hence mimicking the outcomes of the SKM saga at the turn of the 1970s.[20] The Macedonian sociologists and philosophers were thus expected to readjust their positions, while their inter-Yugoslav exchanges were minimized in order to reduce the flow of critical ideas. Therefore, only Čokrevski was able to publish his paper presented in Portorož in the special issue of *Sociologija*, while just a few of the younger intellectuals, such as Muhik and **Ljubomir Cuculovski** (b. 1948), who started their careers at the ISPPI before moving to the philosophy group at the Faculty of Philosophy, participated in critical all-Yugoslav sociological and philosophical debates during the 1980s (e.g., Đurić 1983).[21] In turn, and similar to the federal context, this avoidance of critical engagement led to a general "downplay" of "sensitive topics" in the professional periodicals (Devic 1998, 399; for context, see Donev 2008). The 1983 commemoration of the 100th anniversary of the death of Marx again well illustrates the new treatment of Marxism in Macedonia. The round anniversary brought about a five-day-long scientific conference in Skopje under the title "Marx and our contemporaneity" whose proceedings were published in a special issue of the Faculty of Philosophy's *Annual* (more about the event in Petkovska 1983). The general tone of the published presentations is rather apodictic, concurring with the thesis that much of the erstwhile pressing issues in politics and science could be fathomed by reverting to the classic, cure-all Marxian writings. Hence, the volume contains texts on the Marxian contributions to the study of mathematics, Byzantology, ancient philosophy, world literature, and French culture, among others.

The above event/publication is also indicative of two other interesting features. Firstly, it confirms that the role of a leading Marxist intellectual

---

[20] The critical agenda was somewhat picked up by the journal *Treta Programa* (Third Program), issued by Radio Skopje in the course of the 1980s.

[21] In another instance, Milosavlevski recalls an episode from 1982, when he was invited to participate in an event titled "Socialism and Liberalism" in Belgrade. He claims that he received a phone call from the state security service asking him to reconsider his participation, even though he did not plan to comment on the ongoing issues and instead prepared a presentation on the different political camps of the interwar VMRO (Milosavlevski 2004, 12–13). Milosavlevski managed to publish only two articles in two Belgrade-based journals after his ouster and premature retirement in his mid-40s in 1974.

in 1980s Macedonia was assumed by **Aleksandar Grličkov** (1923–1989), a professor of economics who moved to Belgrade in 1965, where he taught international economic relations and eventually became a part of the SKJ's Presidium in 1974. Grličkov emerged as one of the major Yugoslav authorities on the international communist movement in the 1970s, calling for better cooperation between the socialist and social-democrat parties in and beyond Europe (e.g., Grličkov 1978). As an illustration, he was one of the two Macedonians *in toto* to publish such a take in the three-volume compilation titled *Marksizmot i samoupravuvanjeto* (Marxism and Self-Management) which aimed at becoming the new programmatic canon of Yugoslav Marxism as of the late 1970s (Radenovik 1981). He held a more doctrinaire understanding of Marxism in the 1980s, however, arguing in favor of its universality and against "those who devalue Marxian theoretical thought" (Grličkov 1983, 14). This line of argumentation primarily targeted sociological calls for a reconsidered Marxist epistemology as a remedy for the ongoing crises. Grličkov thus localized much of the 1980s Yugoslav derogatory campaign against the sociologists as *crisologists* (Spasić et al. 2022, 58–60). Secondly, it hints at some of the discursive ways of realigning with this old-new ideological stand. For instance, suggestive enough was the case of **Georgi Stardelov** (1930–2021), a professor of philosophy and aesthetics at the Faculty of Philosophy in Skopje and a director of the ISPPI from 1971 to 1973, who opted for a critical Marxism in the 1970s (e.g., Stardelov 1972) before assuming a critical stance toward the erstwhile "Marxist theory of crisis"— which he considered to be "in crisis itself"—and articulating a thesis about the inherency of multiple and contingent crises in socialism as capitalist legacies (Stardelov 1983, 49; also see Stardelov 1986).

Likewise in the mid-1960s episode of the Skopje social survey, the remedy for the ostensible isolation of the Macedonian sociology of the 1970s came in the form of yet another Polish–Macedonian sociological cooperation platform.[22] This time, the cooperation appeared to be the series of Kraków-Skopje sociological meetings launched in 1979; and making through the post-socialism, albeit in different formats. Prior to the formal

---

[22] One of the earliest such platforms was the interwar Skopje-based "Circle of the Polish-Yugoslav League" [scr. *Kolo Poljsko-Jugoslovenske lige*] led by the historian Aleksije Jelačić, mentioned in the first chapter. The Circle published a history of Poland in Serbian in 1933, authored by Jelačić as part of his series of histories of Slavic nations (Jelačić 1933). The book was endorsed by the famed Polish historian Oscar Halecki.

proposal for an institutional cooperation, Sinadinovski, a Polish speaker himself, paid a visit to Kraków in the mid-1970s and returned captivated by the history and the institutional development of Krakovian sociology and its research prospects (Sinadinovski 1976; Kwaśniewicz in Niezgoda 1979). The partnership between the two universities was formalized thanks to the chairs of the sociological departments in both the cities, that is Georgievski in Skopje and **Władysław Kwaśniewicz** (1926–2004) in Kraków, while **Marian Niezgoda** (b. 1943) from the Jagiellonian University's Institute of Sociology soon emerged to be the *spiritus movens* behind the initiative (Niezgoda 1979, 5–6; Georgievski 2012, 109). Everything was thus set for the first event to take place in Kraków, in early December 1979, hosting several sociologists associated with the Faculty of Philosophy in Skopje. The choice of the first topic—industrialization and urbanization—best resonates with the initial organizational reasoning behind the seminars: they should reflect the shared social and sociological research experiences from the two national contexts. Although not very aware of the particularities of the other societies, the first event was deemed fruitful as the formal and informal conversations allowed for an exchange of basic information, while it finished up with a set of proposals for joint research in the future (Niezgoda 1979, 113–116). The 1980s biannual consortiums followed suit in covering the topics of social structure (in 1981 in Skopje 1981; see Georgievski and Korubin 1983), self-management (in 1983 in Kraków; see Szumakowicz 1983), and rural sociology (in 1985 in Skopje; see Kartalov and Stojanoski 1988).

The cross-national meetings during the 1980s appeared to be rewarding for the two sociological communities, although in slightly different manners. For the Macedonians, it was an instant resolution of the *deprovincialization* complex (e.g., in Georgievski 2012). Polish sociology was now perceived as esteemed and well situated, even westward-looking, albeit state socialist. They soon became aware of the Western interest in the Polish sociological findings as insights into the looming crisis of the 1980s socialist Europe (for the Krakovian context, see Bryda and Pawnik 2009). Still, there were enough commonalities to be addressed and a history of cross-national cooperation to be built upon. One such case was the 1964 initiative for launching an annual Polish-Yugoslav philosophical and sociological conference (Trajanovski 2021, 15–16), but also the more immediate partnership of the linguistics departments in Skopje and Kraków. A team of Polish sociologists from Wrocław visited the ISPPI in the late 1980s, as well; however, this cooperation failed to establish continuity.[23] For the Krakovians, on the other hand, the brief excursions to Yugoslav Macedonia during the troubled times at home were a well-received distraction: they enjoyed the cordial hospitality of the Macedonian sociologists, the sociological perspectives stemming from the different demographic, cultural, and political realities, as well as the cultural offerings of Macedonia (e.g., Frysztacki 2009, 30). After the vocal Yugoslav (predominantly Praxis) sociologists' objections to the persecution of the Warsaw professors following the March 1968 events, Skopje University appeared to be an ideal fit for such a rebound: far from the above turmoil, which eventually shifted the Polish interest of Yugoslav Marxism into its orthodox variations during the 1970s (Bielińska-Kowalewska 2012), yet close enough for obtaining first-hand insights of the Yugoslav sociopolitical realities and sociological perspectives.

The presentations at the closed Skopje-Kraków seminars were printed as proceedings in the languages of the hosting institutions (the 1979 and 1983 editions were published in Polish, and the 1981 and 1985 in Macedonian; the 1990 Skopje edition of the seminar on the topic of societal crisis was not published). As of 2004, the proceedings were published in English (Georgievski et al. 2004; Niezgoda 2004; Niezgoda et al. 2009). The different developmental trajectories of both the sociological institutes and their hosting states shaped the post-socialist editions of the sociological seminar series, which is a tendency well visible in the published volumes. For instance, in the post-socialist editions, it is evident that there are no more attempts at comparisons. However, the partnership evolved in the new millennium to include other European sociological institutes (e.g., Bacher et al. 2011) and to host Polish researchers in Macedonia (e.g., Lubaš 2021). Most recently, the sociological cooperation between Skopje and Kraków evolved beyond the two institutes since another two institutions, now from Kraków and Bitola—both of them specialized in pedagogics—issued a cross-national edited volume about the modern educational challenges (Szyszka et al. 2015).

---

[23] The reason for the visit pertained to the Macedonian refugees from the Greek Civil War (1946–1949) to Poland, some of them repatriated in socialist Macedonia. A group of Polish ethnographers and sociologists from Lower and Upper Silesia started to develop interest in the non-Polish ethnic communities settled in the so-called Regained Lands after the Second World War, that is, the state's Western Borderlands, as of the 1960s (e.g., Hofman-Liandzis and Pudło 1963). The cooperation with the ISPPI was halted due to the start of the Yugoslav Wars, while only sporadic review articles managed to be published in the ISPPI's Annual in the 1980s (e.g., Pudlo 1987).

REFERENCES

Bacher, Johann, et al., eds. 2011. *Selected Research Papers in Social Change, Education, Labour Market, and Criminology*. Linz: Trauner Verlag.

Bielińska-Kowalewska, Katarzyna. 2012. Kako je poljski revizionizam *mimoišao* tzv. praxis-filozofiju: Recepcija jugoslovenske filozofije u Poljskoj tokom 60-ih i početkom 70-ih u kontekstu sudbine poljskog revizionizma i njegove karakteristike. In *Praxis: Društvena kritika i humanistički socijalizam*, ed. Dragomir Olujić Oluja and Krunoslav Stojaković, 269–292. Beograd: Rosa Luxemburg Stiftung.

Blagoev, Borislav. 1979. *Monografski materijali za raǵanjeto i razvitokot na industrijata vo Makedonija*. Skopje: MANU.

Bogdanović, Marija et al. 1990. *Sociologija u Jugoslaviji: Institucionalni razvoj*. Beograd: Institut za sociološka istraživanja Filozofskog fakulteta u Beogradu.

Bogoev, Ksente, ed. 1985. *Problemi na demografskiot razvoj vo SR Makedonija*. Skopje: MANU.

Bošale, Nikola. 1983. *Kliment Ohridski i školata na humanizmot*. Ohrid: Zavod za zaštita na spomenicite na kulturata i naroden muzej Ohrid.

Bošale, Nikola et al. 1987. *Sostojbi i ocenki na sostojbite vo oblasta na naučnoistražuvačkite dejnosti vo SRM i globalnite nasoki na nivniot razvoj*. Skopje: Ekonomski institut and ISPPI.

Brown, Keith. 2000. A Rising to Count on: Ilinden Between Politics and History in Post-Yugoslav Macedonia. In *The Macedonian Question: Culture, Historiography, Politics*, ed. Victor Roudometof, 143–172. New York: Columbia University Press.

Bryda, Grzegorz, and Wojciech Pawnik, eds. 2009. *Oblicza socjologii krakowskiej*. Vol. I. Kraków: Nomos.

Bubevski, Dušan. 1975. Nekoi misli za faktorite na migraciite na naselenieto i rabotnata sila vo SR Makedonija. *Godišnik na ISPPI* 1 (1): 65–76.

Burg, Stephen. 1983. *Conflict and Cohesion in Socialist Yugoslavia: Political Decision Making Since 1966*. Princeton: Princeton University Press.

Cekik, Aneta. 2015. Political Science in Macedonia. In *Political Science in Europe at the Beginning of the 21st Century*, ed. Barbara Krauz-Mozer et al., 287–305. Kraków: Wydawnictwo Uniwersytetu Jagiellońskiego.

Chall, Leo P., et al., eds. 1975. Abstracts of Papers Presented at the VIIIth World Congress of the International Sociological Association. *Sociological Abstracts* 47: 241–316.

Cohen, Lenard J. 1979. Partisans, Professionals, and Proleterians: Elite Change in Yugoslavia, 1952–78. *Canadian Slavonic Papers* 21 (4): 446–478.

———. 1982. Politics as an Avocation: Legislative Professionalisation and Participation in Yugoslavia. In *Communist Legislatures in Comparative Perspective*, ed. Daniel Nelson and Stephen White, 14–46. London: The Macmillan Press.

Cohen, Lenard. 1983. Regional Elites in Socialist Yugoslavia: Changing Patterns of Recruitment and Composition. In *Leadership Selection and Patron-Client Relations in the USSR and Yugoslavia*, ed. T.H. Rigby and Bohdan Harasymiw, 95–137. London and New York: Routledge.

Crvenkovski, Krste, and Slavko Milosavlevski. 1996. *Našiot pogled za vremeto na Koliševski*. Skopje: Misla.

Cvjetičanin, Veljko. 1972. Stanje nastave sociologije i formiranje marksističkog pogleda na svijet na fakultetima društvenih nauka te visokim i višim nastavničkim školama. *Revija za sociologiju* 2 (2–3): 107–113.

Denkovski, Denko. 1973. Dostapnosta na obrazovanieto na Univerzitetot "Kiril i Metodij" vo Skopje. *Dijalog* 2–3: 56–73.

Devic, Ana. 1998. Ethnonationalism, Politics, and the Intellectuals: The Case of Yugoslavia. *International Journal of Politics, Culture, and Society* 11 (3): 375–409.

Dijalog. 1973. Makedonskoto javno mislenje. *Dijalog* 2 (2–3): 165–186.

Dimevski, Slavko. 1981. *Makedonskite opštestveno-kulturni tekovi vo feudalizmot*. Skopje: ISPPI.

———. 1989. *Istorijata na makedonskata pravoslavna crkva*. Skopje: Makedonska kniga.

Dimitrov, Dimitar. 1978. Marksizmot kao nastavni predmet. *Revija za sociologiju* 7 (3–4): 110–113.

Dimitrov, Evgeni, Milan Nedkov, and Petre Georgievski, eds. 1982. *Samoupravuvanjeto kako zakonitost vo socijalističkiot razvoj na Jugoslavija*. Skopje: MANU.

Dokmanoviḱ, Mišo. 2007. Istoriskiot razvoj na Pravniot fakultet. In *Praven fakultet "Justinijan Prvi" – Istoriski razvoj 1951–2006*, eds. Vlado Popovski et al., 21–85. Skopje: Praven Fakultet "Justinijan Prvi".

Donev, Dejan. 2008. Pedeset godina neuvjetovanja mišljenja. *Filozofska istraživanja* 3: 539–545.

Duller, Matthias. 2018. Yugoslav Sociology: Political Autonomy under a Single-Party Regime. In *Social Sciences in the "Other Europe" since 1945*, ed. Adela Hîncu and Victor Karady, 159–184. Budapest and New York: Central European University Press.

Đurić, Rajko. 1983. Sa naučnog skupa "Marks i savremenost" u Novom Sadu: Za kritičku teoriju socijalizma. *Politika*, December 12.

Frysztacki, Krzysztof. 2009. Między Polską a Macedonią: dwa światy, jedna socjologia. In *Sprostać zmianom: Szkice o powinnościach współczesnej socjologii*, ed. Krystyna Slany and Zygmunt Seręga, 29–33. Kraków: Nomos.

Genov, Nikolai. 2002. Sociology – Bulgaria. In *Three Social Science Disciplines in Central and Eastern Europe: Handbook on Economics, Political Science and Sociology (1989–2001)*, ed. Max Kaase et al., 386–404. Berlin: Informationszentrum Sozialwissenschaften.

Georgievski, Petre. 1972a. *Socijalnoto poteklo i životnata orientacija na srednoškolskata mladina: Analiza na empirisko istražuvanje vo srednite učilišta vo Skopje*. Skopje: ISPPI.

———. 1972b. Socijalnoto diferenciranje i nacionalnoto izrazuvanje. *Dijalog* 1: 73–86.

———. 1978. Razvoj sociologije na Filozofskom fakultetu u Skopju. *Revija za sociologiju* 8 (3–4): 100–108.

———. 1985. Potrebata i značenjeto na sociološkite istražuvanja vo stopanstvoto. *Godišen zbornik na Filozofskiot fakultet* 38: 199–208.

———. 2012. *Sociologijata kako kritika na opštestvenata, obrazovnata i kulturnata promena*. Skopje: Matica makedonska.

———. 2014. A brief reflection on the life and the professional journey in the field of sociology of Professor Slavko Milosavlevski. *Sociološka revija* 15 (2): 7–24.

Georgievski, Petre, and Jovan Korubin, eds. 1983. *Socijalnata struktura na NR Polska i SFR Jugoslavija, SR Makedonija: Zbornik na referati od vtoriot Skopsko-Krakovski sociološki seminar*. Skopje: Filozofski fakultet na Univerzitetot Kiril i Metodij vo Skopje.

Georgievski, Petre, Kiril Temkov, and Sveto Škarik. 1974. *Marksizmot i socijalizmot: Prva kniga na Školata na mladi marksisti "Stiv Naumov – Mite Bogoevski"*. Skopje: Studentski zbor.

Georgievski, Petre, Jovan Korubin, and Georgi Mladenovski, eds. 2004. *European Integration: Polish and Macedonian Experience. VIII Skopje-Cracow Sociology Seminar, 25 Years of Cooperation (1979–2004)*. Skopje: Faculty of Philosophy.

Godišnik na ISPPI. 1976. Deset godini od postoenjeto na Institutot za sociološki i političko-pravni istražuvanja vo Skopje. *Godišnik na ISPPI* 2 (1): 5–10.

Grličkov, Aleksandar. 1978. *Evropa vo očite na komunistite*. Skopje: Komunist.

———. 1983. Marks i marksizmot denes. *Godišen zbornik na Filozofskiot fakultet* 35: 13–28.

Ǵurovska, Mileva. 1985. Za potrebata od sociološko proučuvanje na rabotnata sredina vo uslovi na naučno-tehničkiot progress. *Godišen zbornik na Filozofskiot fakultet* 38: 249–253.

Hristov, Aleksandar T. 1982. *Prilozi za istorijata na makedonskata politička misla*. Skopje: NIO Studentski zbor Skopje.

Hodges, Donald C. 1977. Yugoslav Marxism and Methods of Social Accounting. In *Marxism, Revolution, and Peace*, ed. Howard L. Parsons and John Somerville, 53–65. Amsterdam: B.R. Grüner B.V.

Hofman-Liandzis, Krystyna, and Kazimierz Pudło. 1963. Z badań nad kulturą ludową emigrantów greckich na Dolnym Śląsku.

Hristov, Aleksandar. 1979. *Upravata vo delegatskiot sistem*. Skopje: ISPPI.

Jelačić, Aleksije. 1933. *Istorija Poljske*. Skoplje: Kolo Poljsko-Jugoslovenske Lige.

Josifovski, Jonče. 1972. Aktuelnosta na marksizmot. *Pogledi* 9 (7–8): 803–817.

Josifovski, Ilija, et al. 1974. *Osnovi na marksistička filozofija*. Skopje: UKIM.

Josifovski, Ilija, and Jovanka Kepevska. 1978. Empirijska sociološka istraživanja u SR Makedoniji. *Revija za sociologiju* 8 (3–4): 93–99.

Jovanović, Dragan. 1981. Da li se povečavaju socjalne razlike? Šta pokazuju rezultati ankete skopskog Instituta za sociološka i političko-pravna istraživanja. *NIN*, November 19.

Jovanoviḱ, Amalija. 1981. *Bračnata podvižnost vo SR Makedonija*. Skopje: ISPPI.

———. 1985. Nekoi sociološki sogleduvanja za položbata na ženata vo nekoi rabotni organizacii na združen trud. *Godišen zbornik na Filozofskiot fakultet* 38: 233–238.

Jovanovski, Jordan. 1978. Nekoi aspekti od kulturata na živeenje na selo vo SR Makedonija. *Godišnik na ISPPI* 4 (1): 167–181.

Kamberski, Kiro. 1986. 40 godini na Filozofskiot fakultet vo Skopje. *Godišen zbornik na Filozofskiot fakultet* 39: 5–12.

Kambovski, Vlado. 1987. 20 godini rabota i razvitok na Institutot za sociološki i političko-pravni istražuvanja. *Godišnik na ISPPI* 10–11 (1): 5–228.

Kartalov, Risto. 1976. Strukturni promeni na individualnite zemjodelski stopanstva vo SR Makedonija. *Godišnik na ISPPI* 2 (1): 83–98.

———. 1985. Sociološki aspekti na vrednuvanjeto na proizvodniot i tvorečkiot (umstveniot i fizičkiot) trud. *Godišen zbornik na Filozofskiot fakultet* 38: 209–216.

Kartalov, Risto, and Nelko Stojanoski. 1988. *Opštestveno-ekonomskite i kulturnite promeni na seloto vo NR Polska i SFRJ – SR Makedonija: Zbornik na referati od četvrtiot Skopsko-Krakovski sociološki seminar*. Skopje: Filozofski fakultet na Univerzitetot Kiril i Metodij vo Skopje.

Kartalov, Risto, et al. 1975. *Javnoto mislenje vo SR Makedonija – 1974*. Skopje: ISPPI.

Kolev, Blagoja, and Angel Georgiev. 1986. *Urbanizacijata i stopanskiot razvitok na SR Makedonija*. Skopje: MANU.

Korubin, Jovan. 1985. Procesite na informiranje vo združeniot trud i ulogata na sociologot. *Godišen zbornik na Filozofskiot fakultet* 38: 239–242.

Kostovski, Stefan. 1972. Nekoi zabeležuvanja za odnosot nacija – religija. *Dijalog* 1 (1): 142–150.

———. 1975. Sociologija na seloto. *Godišnik na ISPPI* 1 (1): 13–20.

Lazaroski, Jakov, Spase Makarovski, and Dimitar Mirčev. 1971. *Idejnite struenja vo reformata na Univerzitetot*. Skopje: Univerzitetska konferencija na SKM.

Leonardson, Gene S., and Dimitar Mirčev. 1979. A Structure for Participatory Democracy in the Local Community: The Yugoslav Constitution of 1974. *Comparative Politics* 11 (2): 183–203.

Lubaš, Marčin. 2021. *Raznoverci: Meģureligiskiot soživot na selo vo Zapadna Makedonija*. Skopje: Makedonsko studentsko etnološko društvo.

Marinković, Gojko. 1983. Nauka ili krizologija. *Danas*: 43–45.

Mihajlovski, Stojmen. 1978. *Položbata i ulogata na Sojuzot na komunistite vo delegatskiot sistem.* Skopje: ISPPI.

———. 1991. Dvaeset i pet godini rabota, razvitok i afirmacija na Institutot za sociološki i političko-pravni istražuvanja vo Skopje. *Godišnik na ISPPI* 13 (1): 7–57.

Miljovska, Desanka, et al., eds. 1972. *Marksizmot denes.* Skopje: Društvo za filozofija i sociologija na SR Makedonija.

Milosavlevski, Slavko. 1996. *Dvete lica na sobitijata.* Skopje: Zumpres.

———. 1997. *Sociologija na makedonskata nacionalna svest II.* Ljuboten: IP Ljuboten.

———. 2004. *Makedonski kontroverzi 1990-2003.* Skopje: Nova Makedonija.

Milosavlevski, Slavko, Ilija Josifovski, and Tomislav Čokrevski. 1971. *Sociologija.* Skopje: Kultura.

Minoski, Konstantin. 2020. Institutot za sociologija. In *Filozofski fakultet 1920-2020: Eden vek visoko obrazovanie, eden vek državotvornost,* ed. Ratko Duev, 297–316. Skopje: Univerzitet "Sv. Kiril i Metodij" – Skopje.

Mirčev, Dimitar. 1979. *Delegatskiot sistem na samoupravnata mesna zaednica.* Skopje: Praven fakultet.

———. 1981. Opštestveno-prostornata organizacija i razvitokot na opštinite vo SRM: Kon rezultatite na edno empirisko istražuvanje. *Godišnik na ISPPI* 7 (1): 187–202.

Mirčev, Dimitar, et al. 1978. *Javnoto mislenje vo SR Makedonija 1978: Izveštaj od anketno istražuvanje.* Skopje: ISPPI.

Mladenovski, Ǵorǵe. 1985. Samoupravuvanjeto i samoupravnite odnosi kako predmet na sociološkite istražuvanja. *Godišen zbornik na Filozofskiot fakultet* 38: 229–231.

Nedelkovski, Živko, et al. 1986. *Javnoto mislenje vo SR Makedonija: Izveštaj od anketno ispituvanje broj 12/86.* Skopje: ISPPI.

Niezgoda, Marian, ed. 1979. *Procesy uprzemysłowienia i urbanizacji w społeczeństwie socjalistycznym: Materiały I seminarium Krakowsko-Skopijskiego.* Kraków: Wydawnictwo Uniwersytetu Jagiellońskiego.

———, ed. 2004. *The Consequences of Great Transformation: Transactions of VII Kraków-Skopje Sociological Seminar.* Kraków: Wydawnictwo Uniwersytetu Jagiellońskiego.

Niezgoda, Marian, Maria Świątkiewicz-Mośny, and Aleksandra Wagner, eds. 2009. *Culture in Transition – Transition in Culture.* Kraków: Wydawnictwo Uniwersytetu Jagiellońskiego.

Nikodimovski, Lazar. 1985. Mestoto i ulogata na sociologijata vo samoupravnozdruženiot trud. *Godišen zbornik na Filozofskiot fakultet* 38: 217–221.

Nikolić, Dragan. 1973. Neophodna reafirmacija demokratskog centralizma: Iz izlaganja predsjednika CK SK Makedonije Angela Čemerskog političkom aktivu u Kavadarcima. *Borba,* September 8.

Nonevski, Boris. 1973. Za kulturata – obid za pojmovno definiranje. *Dijalog* 2–3: 128–138.

Parsons, Howard L. 1966. Humanistic Philosophy in Contemporary Poland and Yugoslavia. *American Institute for Marxist Studies's Occasional Papers* 4.

Pelivanov, Todor. 1973. Studentot na Pravniot fakultet vo Skopje. *Dijalog* 2–3: 87–96.

Petkovska, Antoanela. 1983. Diskusijata na naučniot sobir "Marks i našata sovremenost". *Godišen zbornik na Filozofskiot fakultet* 35: 13–28.

Petroska, Blaga. 1985. Sociologija i profesijata sociolog vo našeto opštestvo. *Godišen zbornik na Filozofskiot fakultet* 38: 191–198.

Politika. 1975. Moramo biti protiv svake kritike koja razara: Izlaganje Angela Čemerskog na savetovanju u CK SK Makedonije. *Politika*, March 19.

Popovski, Vlado. 1972. Našata opštestvena preobrazba (Smislata na eden angažman). *Dijalog* 1: 7–22.

———. 1984. Socio-profesionalniot sostav na delegatskite sobranija vo SR Makedonija. *Godišen zbornik na Filozofskiot fakultet* 37: 265–284.

Popovski, Vlado, et al. 1977. *Ispituvanje na javnoto mislenje vo SR Makedonija: Rezultati od anketnoto ispituvanje.* Skopje: ISPPI.

Pudlo, Kažimjež. 1987. Političkite begalci od Grcija vo Polska vo godinite 1948-1985 (Pregled na problematikata). *Godišnik na ISPPI* 10–11 (1): 129–142.

Radenoviḱ, Predrag, ed. 1981. *Marksizmot i samoupravuvanjeto.* Vol. I. Skopje: Makedonska kniga – Kultura – Naša kniga – Komunist.

Rusinow, Dennison. 1977. *The Yugoslav Experiment 1948–1974.* Berkley and Los Angeles: University of California Press.

———. 1986. Yugoslavia. In *Leadership and Succession in the Soviet Union, Eastern Europe and China,* ed. Martin McCauley and Stephen Carter, 174–193. London: The Macmillan Press.

———. 2007. Reopening of the "National Question" in the 1960s. In *State Collapse in South-Eastern Europe: New Perspectives on Yugoslavia's Disintegration,* ed. Lenard J. Cohen and Jasna Dragović-Soso, 131–148. West Lafayette: Purdue University Press.

Sidovski, Kosta. 1980. *Razvitokot na industrijata na teritorijata na denešna SR Makedonija vo periodot meǵu dvete svetski vojni (1918-1941).* Skopje: MANU.

Simovska, Lidija, et al. 1980. *Javnoto mislenje vo SR Makedonija 1979: Izveštaj od anketno istražuvanje.* Skopje: ISPPI.

Simovski, Dušan. 1977. Okolu poimot nacija. *Godišnik na ISPPI* 3 (1): 203–228.

Sinadinovski, Jakim. 1976. Sovremenite opštestveni istražuvanja na Jagelonskiot univerzitet vo Krakov. *Godišen zbornik na Geografskiot fakultet* 22 (10): 91–100.

Spasić, Ivana, Jelena Pešić, and Marija Babović. 2022. *Sociology in Serbia: A Fragile Discipline.* Basingstoke: Palgrave Macmillan.

Spasov, Ǵorǵi. 1977. Javnoto mislenje i političkiot život. *Godišnik na ISPPI* 3 (1): 229–238.

Spasov, Ǵorǵi, et al. 1982. *Javnoto mislenje vo SR Makedonija 1981 godina: Istražuvački izveštaj*. Skopje: ISPPI.

———. 1983. *Javnoto mislenje vo SR Makedonija: Izveštaj od anketno ispituvanje broj 10/82*. Skopje: ISPPI.

———. 1989. *Javnoto mislenje vo SRM: Izveštaj od anketno ispituvanje broj 13/88*. Skopje: ISPPI.

Stardelov, Georgi et al. (eds.). 2000. *Istorijata na ideite na počvata na Makedonija*. Skopje: MANU.

Stardelov, Georgi. 1983. Marksističkata teorija na krizata denes. *Godišen zbornik na Filozofskiot fakultet* 35: 49–64.

———. 1986. Segašninata i idninata. *Godišen zbornik na Filozofskiot fakultet* 39: 45–48.

Stardelov, Ǵorǵi. 1972. Marksizmot i inteligencijata. *Pogledi* 8 (6–7): 929–935.

Stojanoski, Nelko. 1985. Nekoi devijantni pojavi na združeniot trud kako predmet na sociološka analiza. *Godišen zbornik na Filozofskiot fakultet* 38: 243–247.

Šurbanovski, Naum, ed. 1978. *Drogata vo Makedonija*. Skopje: ISPPI.

Szumakowicz, Andrzej, ed. 1983. *Samorządność i społeczeństwo socjalistyczne: Materiały III Krakowsko-Skopijskiego seminarium socjologicznego*. Wydawnictwo Uniwersytetu Jagiellońskiego.

Szyszka, Michał, et al. 2015. *Modern Social and Educational Challenges and Phenomena: Polish and Macedonian Perspectives*. Cracow: Pedagogical University of Cracow.

Taneski, Vladimir. 1964. *Sociologija: Istoriski razvoj na opštestvenata misla*. Skopje: Skopski Univerzitet.

Taševa, Marija. 2014. Slavko Milosavlevski's sociology of Macedonian national consciousness. *Sociološka revija* 15 (2): 25–49.

Taševa-Pocevska, Marija. 1975. Tipološkiot metod vo sociologijata na seloto. *Godišnik na ISPPI* 1 (1): 41–48.

———. 1985. Sociologijata vo funkcija na efikasnoto rabotenje vo stopanstvoto. *Godišen zbornik na Filozofskiot fakultet* 38: 223–227.

Temkov, Kiril, and Ferid Muhiḱ. 1972. Izdavanjeto na filozofska literatura kaj nas. *Dijalog* 1: 169–172.

Tito, Josip Broz. 1970. Pristapna beseda. In *Svečen sobir na MANU pri predavanjeto na diploma na počesen člen na Pretsedatelot na SFRJ Josip Broz Tito*, 17–28. Skopje: MANU.

Tomovski, Krum, et al., eds. 1988. *20 godini Makedonska Akademija na Naukite i Umetnostite 1967-1987*. Skopje: MANU.

———., eds. 1989. *Etničkite tradicii i sovremenosta: Meǵunaroden naučen sobir, Ohrid 14-15 septemvri 1981 g.* Skopje: MANU.

Trajkovski, Ilo. 2000. *Sociologija: Što e i kako se praktikuva?* Skopje and Melbourne: Matica makedonska.

Trajanovski, Naum. 2021. Zbor imaat graǵanite: The First Sociological Study, the Polish Sociological Expert Aid to Macedonia in the Mid-1960s and the Post-Earthquake History of Interethnic Relations in Skopje. *Colloquia Humanistica* 9: 1–42.

Tufai, Muzafer. 1981. Komparativna analiza na procesot na urbanizacijata na selskite i gradskite opštini vo SR Makedonija. *Godišnik na ISPPI* 7 (1): 227–250.

Verigik, Dušan. 1987. Koristenjeto na statističkite izvori na informacii vo naučnite istražuvanja. *Godišnik na ISPPI* 10–11 (1): 359–373.

Zaninovich, George M. 1969. The Yugoslav Variation of Marx. In *Contemporary Yugoslavia: Twenty Years of Socialist Experiment*, ed. Wayne S. Vucinich, 285–314. Los Angeles and London: University of California Press.

CHAPTER 5

A New Beginning, Anew: Macedonian Sociology in a New Era (1990s–2020s)

Abstract The last of the chapters following the trajectory of Macedonian sociology discusses the sociological adjustments to the most recent socio-political developments in the state. As of 1991, the Republic of Macedonia entered a turbulent era of domestic and regional challenges to its independence and sovereignty. Among them, the institutionalization of the delicate interethnic equilibrium emerged as one of the major political themes, structuring the political process in the three post-Yugoslav decades. The interethnic tensions had a brief violent escalation in the 2001 armed struggle between the state security forces and ethnic Albanian radicals. I discuss this period by providing an intellectual panorama of the major sociological activities as of the early 1990s. I also focus on the series of exchanges about the state's multiethnic prospects to present some of the dominant trajectories of producing and instrumentalizing sociological knowledge in post-Yugoslav Macedonia.

Keywords Republic of Macedonia • Sociology • Interethnic relations • Multiculturalism

The 1980s saw a further decline of the Yugoslav economy: the crisis drained all the energy supplies, industry worked with losses, and the banks were unable to maintain liquidity. In late socialist Macedonia, in turn, unemployment skyrocketed, salaries were approximately 30 percent lower than the Yugoslav average, and the first series of strikes occurred already in the early 1980s (Woodward 1995; Hudson 2003). All those events started to shake the trust in the leadership crisis management capacities. Federal funds were already inoperative and the growing political tensions suggested nothing but difficult days ahead. In response, in line with their Serbian counterparts, the Macedonian ruling clique started to depict the Albanian protests in Kosovo and Western Macedonia as a major security threat, thus deflecting the crisis by weaponizing the interethnic relations in the state. The rise of the numbers of the Albanian population as per the 1981 census and religious education in Albanian, for instance, were seen through the lens of "Albanian irredentism" and met with a massive campaign against Albanization, Islamization, and the alleged project of Greater Albania (Trajanovski 2021a, 23; also see Brunnbauer 2004).

The situation escalated in the mid-1980s to include the demolishing of walls surrounding Muslim households in several Macedonian cities, a ban on personal names suggesting Albanian nationalism, and a social support reform *de facto* tailored to exclude Albanian families in Macedonia (for context, see Neofotistos 2004), again, similar to the Serbian responses to the events in Kosovo which eventually boosted Serbian nationalism into the war (an overview in Pichler et al. 2021). The more economic standards declined, the more the "Albanian complex" in Macedonia was coming to the fore. In 1987, for instance, faced with soaring inflation of 190 percent and an unprecedented number of strikes, the Macedonian authorities still claimed Albanian nationalism as "the major danger at the moment" (Saveski 1987). In the name of "opportunism and inconsistencies" in the fight against the *major danger*, the SKM changed over 5000 state officials in 1988 and suspended a critical article of the 1974 Constitution in 1989, thus redefining the republican constitution by stripping away the mentions of Albanian and Turkish minorities. The societal responses to the scapegoating followed suit; for instance, an ISPPI poll from the late 1980s suggested that 90 percent of ethnic Macedonians not only supported the measures undertaken against Albanian nationalism, but perceived them as insufficient (Kočan 1988).

Against this background, in November 1989, parallel to the fall of the Berlin Wall and the turmoil in then-neighboring Romania, the SKM newly elected (younger) leadership introduced a *Glasnost*-like set of structural reforms in the state. In turn, they authorized pluralism, initially within the SKM and at a state level as of early 1990, democratic elections—which took place on 11 November 1990—and an independence referendum that was voted with acclamation by the Macedonian Parliament in August 1991, soon after the start of the military activities in Yugoslavia. The successful plebiscite—with more than 95 percent of the voters voting for an independent and sovereign Macedonia on 8 September 1991—aligned with the international community's presence in the state as well as the agency and political capital of the first President Kiro Gligorov, paved the way for an agreement over a peaceful withdrawal of the Serbian-dominated Yugoslav army from the territory of Macedonia, concluded in 1992. The Republic of Macedonia hence managed to embark on its democratic consolidation by avoiding the Yugoslav Wars of the 1990s, coupling political reforms with ethnocentrism. The regime change thereby unfolded as a top-down, elite-driven endeavor, nowadays dubbed the "Macedonian political spring" (Mirčev 2014).

Although the Albanian politicians boycotted the Constitution voting in 1991, while a vast majority of the Macedonian Albanians refused to participate in the referendum and the first post-Yugoslav population census in Macedonia, a multiethnic coalition was nonetheless formed in 1992. This helped legitimize the first democratically elected government in Macedonian history, being, as well, the first multiethnic cabinet in post-communist Europe (Stokes 1993, 252; also see Dimova 2008). In spite of the sporadic violent escalations during the 1990s, the socialist legacy of political representation of the minority groups appeared to suffice in relaxing the interethnic tensions.[1] Still, the slow-paced reforms, univocal media scene, and lack of investments during the social democratic government, married with the reinvigorated contestations from the neighboring states—over the name Macedonia with Greece, the Macedonian language and history with Bulgaria, the church with Serbia, and, up until 1998, the rights of the ethnic Albanians in Macedonia with Albania—seriously shook the ontological security of the Macedonian citizens (e.g., Karanfilova-Panovska 2001). Peace prevailed as the state managed to become a member of the UN in 1993 (under the provisional name Former Yugoslav Republic of Macedonia) and began its formal process of rapprochement with the European Union in 2000.

---

[1] One of Milosavlevski's last intellectual projects was the publishing of the socialist legal and political solutions related to the "Albanian question" in Macedonia, suggesting that the mid-1990s attempts at reforming minority rights in the state should take into consideration the progressive socialist politics over this very issue (Milosavlevski and Tomovski 1997, 5–9).

In 2001, however, soon after the first democratic change of government in Macedonia and the end of the Kosovo War, the interethnic tensions in Macedonia escalated to the verge of a full-blown civil war. The armed exchanges between a group of ethnic Albanian radicals and the Macedonian state security forces started in late January in the vicinity of Tetovo and spread to several areas populated by Albanians by August 2001.[2] The armed exchanges took the Macedonian society and political elites by surprise, including the two largest Albanian parties in the parliament. The latter eventually started to coordinate their objectives with the radicals, which contributed to legitimizing their fight as a struggle for human rights against their initial claims for territorial division of the Macedonian state. This boosted the peace negotiations brokered by the international community, which eventually resulted in the Ohrid Framework Agreement [mk. *Ohridski ramkoven dogovor*, ORD], signed on 13 August 2001.[3] Fundamentally, the ORD paved the way for redefining the state institutional arrangement by introducing a set of minority rights and a soft power-sharing system. Its ultimate goal was to create autonomy for the ethnic communities by devolving the power to local level and providing the municipalities a better financial capacity and a voice in security issues (e.g., Bieber 2008).

Despite being praised as a successful model for resolving minority rights issues, the ORD facilitated a peculiar citizenship regime of fulfilling one's rights and participating in the public sphere solely as a member of an ethnic or a religious community (Spaskovska 2012). This framework amplified ethnocentric discourses and policies, thus recreating the ethnic and religious divisions in other domains. The divisions are nowadays maintained with the various formal and informal commemorative activities related to 2001 which nurture the two mutually exclusive narratives of what had happened in 2001 and thus set the tone for the dominant ways of evoking the interethnic relations in the public discourse (Trajanovski 2022; Trajanovski and Georgieva 2023). In addition, the ORD was predominantly endorsed by the Albanian political camp in the early post-2001

---

[2] As per the 2002 population census, 64.2 percent of the Macedonian population identified as Macedonian, 25.2 percent as Albanian, 3.9 percent as Turkish, and 2.7 percent as Roma. In terms of religion, 64.7 percent identified as Orthodox Christian and 33.3 percent as Muslim.

[3] The several months of hostilities ended in more than 200 casualties and more than 170,000 refugees and internally displaced persons, two-thirds of them from ethnic Macedonain backgrounds.

years, while a vast majority of the Macedonian public intellectuals perceived its stipulations as humiliating and unsatisfactory for the ethnic Macedonians who were pushed to extend minority rights against the threat of civil war. This resentment, among other factors, materialized in the vote for the right-wing coalition led by VMRO-DPMNE in 2006, the party which was in power during the conflict and lost the first post-conflict elections in 2002.

The second VMRO-DPMNE cabinet (2006–2017) was formed upon the premise of a generation change in the party, now championing technocracy and social conservativism instead of nationalism. However, it soon slid toward electoral autocracy and illiberalism; the symbolic trigger is usually traced back to the first major international challenge of the state, that is, the 2008 Greek veto over Macedonia's full NATO membership (Trajanovski 2020). What followed was a sweeping policy shift in culture, history, and memory epitomized in the "Skopje 2014 project"—an umbrella term covering the approximately 130 memorial objects erected in the capital city of Skopje as of the late 2000s, envisioned to vest the urban landscape with ethnonational and European identity. The project and this politics in general ended up shattering not only the bilateral relations with Greece and Bulgaria, which now halted the Macedonian EU and NATO integrations in tandem, but also the domestic interethnic relations. After the major wiretapping scandal in 2015—involving high-level VMRO-DPMNE officials who were accused of illegally listening to over 20,000 calls (a brief summary in Maleska 2019)—an anti-governmental coalition of civil and political activists initiated a series of protests, targeting "Skopje 2014" as an embodiment of the regime, which led to snap elections in 2016. After the elections, the oppositional social democrats of SDSM managed to form a majority in 2017 and unblock the bilateral tensions by signing agreements with Bulgaria (2017) and Greece (2018). The latter changed the state name to North Macedonia and allowed it to join NATO in early 2020. Macedonian–Bulgarian relations deteriorated as of 2020, bringing up another set of Bulgarian blockades on the Macedonian path to the EU, which were eventually lifted in mid-2022.

The New Map

The two leading Macedonian sociological institutions, that is, the ISPPI and the now-renamed Institute of Sociology at the Faculty of Philosophy in Skopje, found themselves in limbo at the beginning of the 1990s. The raging Yugoslav Wars cut off not only the traditional ties with their Yugoslav counterparts but also the more recently established networks, such as the one with the Krakovian sociologists. On the other hand, it pushed them to seek other openings and networks: the most obvious choice was the International Sociological Association, which recognized Macedonia under its new constitutional name in 1993 and hosted Macedonian sociologists (Taševa), for the first time, at its Council meeting in Sweden during the same year (Sociološka revija 1995, 244–246). The decline of economic activity in the state due to the structural transformations and the Greek trade embargo on Macedonia in 1994–1995 impacted the state financing of academic life as well. For instance, the number of research projects conducted by the ISPPI in the course of the early 1990s dropped to only a few, mostly related to the 1990 state elections, while the 1992 issue of the ISPPI Annual was not published at all. However, the leverage of peace in Macedonia amid the hostilities in Yugoslavia, coupled with the democratic consolidation and the introduction of free market mechanisms, allowed for a set of interesting sociological developments in the early 1990s. They were all based upon the social capital of late socialism, now being able to be supported by both state and private enterprises. More importantly, two Macedonian journals emerged as *public sociology* platforms aiming to bring together the national sociologists and their Yugoslav and European colleagues in discussing sociological notions as a means of communicating anti-war discourses. They can also be read as a *post-factum* intellectual modeling of the regime change in Macedonia from the late 1980s and early 1990s, which was unarguably a top-down process immune from public impact (Maleska 1992; also see Mirčev 1991; Devic 1997). Among the most notable, here, are the debates about civil society, discussed below in this section, that informed an important segment of the sociological activities in the course of the 1990s.

The first case is the ambitious relaunching of *Dijalog* by the state-sponsored "Studentski zbor" publishing house with two issues in 1992, now run by a group of associates of the ISPPI. The new editorial board *de facto* rehabilitated Milosavlevski, who contributed to almost every one of its editions, and other Yugoslav liberal communists who were among the most outspoken opponents of the nationalist politics and warmongering in the region.[4] The first few issues of *Dijalog* thus had a goal of publicizing sociological interpretations for the novel political ambience, drawing upon different scholarly provenances and even their late socialist sociological research. For instance, ISPPI's **Emilija Simoska** (b. 1956), a sociologist of politics and a Minister of Education and Science from 1994 to 1996, built upon two ISPPI studies from 1989 to illustrate the "authoritarian consciousness" of the Macedonian youth during late socialism (Simoska 1992). This argument evolved into a more developed research agenda about the actions and mechanisms underpinning the political culture and myths in the state, the results of which were published in the coming years (e.g., Simoska et al. 2001; Hristova 2011; Indževska and Simoska 2012).[5] *Dijalog* ceased to exist in 1997 without a transparent explanation; however, it was relaunched anew in 2002 in a different format which will be touched upon below in this section. The second case is the quarterly *Balkan Forum: An International Journal of Politics, Economics and Culture*, first published in 1993 by *Nova Makedonija* in Skopje (in English, unlike *Dijalog* which was published in Macedonian). Its publishing was supported by several Macedonian companies and an annual subscription scheme in USD. The journal editor-in-chief was **Risto Lazarov** (b. 1949), a Macedonian writer, journalist, and the last director of *Tanjug*, the Yugoslav state news agency, while it had several sociologists and political scientists on its board such as Simoska and Mirčev. The journal linked theoretical texts about nationalism and human rights (e.g., see Yacoub 1993) with *littérature engagée* by Macedonian, regional, and European authors (e.g., Enzensberger, Miłosz).

The third case is related to the journal *Margina*, whose first issue was published in 1994. *Margina* was the first multidisciplinary journal to "problematize all the present values" of the transitory Macedonian society (Margina 1994, 4–5). Albeit not a typical sociological journal *per se*, the board of younger humanists associated with the independent publisher "Templum" translated critical philosophical and sociological texts and engaged, for the first time in Macedonia and involving Macedonian authors, with topics such as the open society and AI. The leverage of *Margina* came from its financing

---

[4] Despite his ouster, Milosavlevski remained somewhat close with this group while he reactivated much of these contacts with the restarting of his political career in 1990, first as a chairman of a minor social-democratic party and then as an ambassador of the Republic of Macedonia in Belgrade (e.g., Milosavlevski 2006).

[5] The sociological materials pertaining to the Yugoslav youth produced during the 80s were recently analysed in the monograph *The Last Yugoslav Generation* (Spaskovska 2017).

which was covered by the newly opened branch of the Open Society Foundation in Macedonia, operating under several names ever since. The Foundation was pivotal for the establishment of the first private media houses in Macedonia, as well as the first private outlets of the national minorities (Milčin 2018; for context, see Stubbs 2013; Mitrevski 2019). Besides *Margina* and the sponsoring of other academic and popular journals, its activities relevant for the Macedonian sociology extended to its cooperation with the ISPPI (e.g., Indževska and Simoska 2012) and its commissioning of several reports about the status of social scientific research and policing at the turn of the 2000s (e.g., Milčin et al. 2013). It also helped with the publication of sociological books, such as in the case of the Milosavlevski monograph on political history and the sociological analysis of the regime changes in Eastern and Southeastern Europe printed in 1993 (Milosavlevski 1993).

The late 1990s and early 2000s also saw the establishment of the first Macedonian think-tanks which developed sociological research, among them the Institute for Democracy "Societas Civilis" (1999), the Institute for Social and Humanistic Research "Euro-Balkan" (1999), and the Center for European Strategies "Eurothink" (2002). Other funding agencies and donors started to sponsor sociological research in this period. One such example is the national branches of the German political foundations Friedrich-Ebert-Stiftung (FES) and Konrad-Adenauer-Stiftung (KAS). FES, for instance, sponsored an ISPPI research project and a series of conferences on social exclusion, deprivation, and poverty (Jakimovski 2003), as well as the first-ever Bulgarian–Macedonian collaborative sociological project in 1998 pertaining to social stratification (Fotev and Jakimovski 1998). Previously, there were several individual contacts between Macedonian and Bulgarian sociologists. KAS supported the building of the website of the Macedonian Association of Sociologists, while it issues a scientific journal on "political-social topics" since 2003, titled *Political Though* [mk. *Politička misla*], which occasionally publishes sociological articles (e.g., Damjanovski 2021).

Against the backdrop of the political reforms of the early 1990s, the paradigmatic shift in Macedonian sociology was announced with Ilo Trajkovski's 1991 text on the role of sociology in the new political environment: a scientific discourse about societal development in lieu of a crisis, thus turning from the state to civil society as the "only authentic sociological domain" (Trajkovski 1991, 188). The civil society topic was already instigated in mid-1980s Yugoslavia (starting in Slovenia) as a discursive tool calling for cultural and social reforms and human rights (Devic

1998). However, it was a non-topic in Macedonia in the early 1980s due to the elitist vision of the reform process, championed by the socialist elite turned into social democrats after 1991 (e.g., Maleska 1992). The proto-pluralist initiatives in the Macedonian late socialist context were predominantly cultural (e.g., Daskalovski 1999), while the rare attempts at instigating critical debates about the state prospects failed to effect any significant changes (e.g. Devic 1997, 138).[6] In this context, Trajkovski's text initiated an exchange about the notion/translation of *societas civilis* in post-socialist Macedonia (e.g., Ivanov 1992; an overview in Trajkovski 1997). Soon the idea of promoting civil society education was picked up by the Institute of Sociology in Skopje as a means of societal adaptation to the new political reality and providing work placements for the sociology graduates. Civil society education in early post-socialist Macedonia was gaining traction, bearing in mind the emergence of informal educational platforms and the interest of foreign donors in this field (Trajkovski 2003). Thereby, in 1997, a group of sociology instructors from the Institute of Sociology, led by Trajkovski, in cooperation with the Ministry of Education and Physical Culture, prepared a proposal for introducing "civil educa-tion" as a subject in primary and secondary schools in the Republic of Macedonia, which led to the first pilot program in 1998 (Trajkovski 2003; Minoski and Petkovska 2017). However, its formal approval overlapped with the first-ever governmental change in Macedonia resulting in a set of alterations to the initial proposal; for instance, now non-sociologists were able to teach this subject. This, in turn, made the initial team behind the proposal a bit reluctant about its implementation. Most recently, there were several public criticisms pertaining to the "outdated content" of the civil education textbook (e.g., Jordanovska 2014), while the ways of improving the course are still debated (e.g., Ajrulai et al. 2020).

The two most significant events from 2001, that is, the armed conflict and the signing of the Stabilization and Association Agreement with the EU as one of the first post-Yugoslav states, informed, as well, the socio-logical dynamics in the state. As for the first point, the conflict and the ORD accelerated the project for establishing a higher education institu-tion in Albanian in Macedonia. Education in Albanian has been a heated issue since the 1980s, as hinted above. In 1994, an Albanian university was

---

[6] Noteworthy are the attempts at establishing a platform for discussing the state prospects by a group of university professors in Skopje (more in Dimova 2011) as well as the state-sponsored weekly *Mlad borec* (Young soldier) and its critical editorial politics in the late 1980s.

opened in Tetovo which was deemed illegal by the government, while the tensions at its opening ceremony resulted in a fatal incident (Bacevic 2014, 129). After 2001, as part of the ORD provisions, a university offering programs in Albanian, Macedonian, and English was established with foreign funding in Tetovo in November 2001 (the South-East European University, SEEU), while the University of Tetovo was inaugurated in 2004. The SEEU has a Faculty of Contemporary Social Sciences with several instructors with sociological backgrounds—such as **Jonuz Abdullai** (b. 1955), **Etem Aziri** (b. 1956), **Hasan Jashari** (b. 1956), and **Ali Pajaziti** (b. 1972)—and publishes a multidisciplinary peer-reviewed journal as of 2001, titled *SEEU Review*. The University of Tetovo nowadays offer a graduate program in sociology and issues several journals, such as *Philosophica* (since 2014), which publishes, among others, sociological analyses in English. Among the earliest sociology and philosophy instructors at the University of Tetovo was **Flora Sela Kastrati** (1961–2018), a poet, translator, politician, and scholar with a doctoral degree from the ISPPI who championed human rights and gender equality. Since the 1960s, only a few sociologists of non-Macedonian ethnic backgrounds have been associated with the ISPPI—such as **Muzafer Tufai** (b. 1936) and Aziri—while others publishing sociological analyses, such as **Fejzula Abdullai**, were affiliated, in his case, with social departments of local municipalities. On the other hand, the majority of the post-socialist line-ups of the elected editorial boards of the Macedonian Association of Sociologists were multiethnic.

The end of 2000 also saw the formation of the first European studies course in Macedonia, offered at the Faculty of Philosophy in Skopje and initially led by Mirčev and Kartalov.[7] The course was tuned in with the start of the Macedonian EU integration process and had an ambitious goal of becoming an interdisciplinary program exploring the "European

---

[7] Just a few years before, in 1997, the ISPPI inaugurated two postgraduate programs in communications and media. **Dona Kolar-Panov**, a new media expert who was an ISPPI associate at that point and the key person behind the establishment of the programs, authored the monograph *Video, War, and Diasporic Imagination* (Routledge, 1997) dealing with the VCR as a vehicle for the homeland-imported nationalist ideologies among the Croat and Macedonian communities in Australia. It was one of the first interdisciplinary social scientific studies published internationally by a Macedonian author.

paradigm" (Mirčev 2000, 201) beyond the EU institutions.[8] The EU integration momentum was also grasped to relaunch *Dijalog* as *Evrodijalog*, subtitled *A journal for European issues* and published by the Skopje-based Center for Regional Policy Research and Cooperation "Studiorum," and *New Balkan Politics*, which besides its print version had an online version, thus being one of the first online social scientific journals in Macedonia. The latter was edited by **Mirjana Maleska** (b. 1946), a professor in political sciences associated with the ISPPI, the Doctoral School of the Skopje University, and the SEEU. Its editorial team claimed legacy not only over *Dijalog*, but also *Pogledi* and *Balkan Forum*, whose cessation "for a number of different reasons" left the "people whose work is connected with social sciences in Macedonia [...] nowhere to publish" (Maleska 2001). Up until 2019, the majority of articles in *New Balkan Politics* were focused on sociological and political subjects, while the journal shifted from articles by foreign scholars to predominantly those with domestic authorship in the course of the 2010s. In 2003, it published, in English, a special section of texts on Bulgarian–Macedonian relations authored by Bulgarian sociologists and experts, thus blazing a new trail in the Macedonian social scientific periodicals.

Sociological courses started to be offered as part of different study programs in the late 1990s and early 2000s. In the late 1990s, the ISPPI co-organized several annual and international summer universities in Ohrid, in cooperation with Euro-Balkan (discussed below), which was designed as a platform for discussing the beyond national issues, such as the many aspects of the Balkan politics in its first few editions, ranging from its past, present, and future prospects. On a different note, sociology began to be taught at other academic centers in the state, including those in Kičevo and Štip. In 2003, the Faculty of Social Sciences turned American University of Europe emerged to be the largest private university in the state. It offers a sociology course as part of its Law and Political Science Faculty, based in Skopje. Nowadays, there are several other private universities in North Macedonia, such as the International Balkan University, which offer sociology courses as part of their graduate program.

---

[8] The EU integration was the topic of the international conference in Ohrid which took place in March 2006, co-organized by the IS, a group of francophone universities, and other regional institutes (Gurovska 2007).

Extracurricular sociological life in the state is mostly coordinated by the Macedonian Association of Sociologists with a series of activities ranging from organizing scholarly events to issuing a sociological journal (discussed below) and promoting sociology in primary schools, such as in its annual competitions for sociological knowledge for pupils. It also has a special group supporting sociology graduates in their job prospects. Most recently, the Association's main focus is on translating the work of the sociological classics, which builds upon the 1990s tendency toward rediscovering the work of non-Marxist sociology, such as the one of Weber and Durkheim, in the national context. In the mid-1990s, a sociological dictionary (1995) and a handbook in sociological theory (1998) were published by a team of sociologists associated with the Institute of Sociology led by Blaga Petroska. However, those endeavors were primarily closed to the nationally informed audiences (a more detailed overview in Georgievski 2011, 2012; Minoski and Petkovska 2017). In the past few years, for instance, the Association has printed translated works of Wright Mills (2019, 2020), Veblen (2021), Mead (2022), and Park (2023) in Macedonian. The forthcoming monograph on Norbert Elias, titled *Explaining Modern Social Reality: The Basic Concepts in Norbert Elias's Figurational Sociology* (2024), authored by **Kire Šarlamanov** (b. 1978) and **Jana Petreska** (b. 1993) and published by Central European University Press, continues this thread of reexamining the work of the classics, yet provides a certain novelty as it is one of the rare books in English authored by Macedonian sociologists based in the state (and a psychologist, in this case, as Petreska is a trained psychologist). Šarlamanov has recently published two other monographs in English with Springer, titled *Populism as Meta Ideology* (published in 2022) and *Habermas between Critical Theory and Liberalism* (published in 2024).

Several other sociological initiatives came as a response to another sort of academic opening, such as the publishing of several textbooks on the sociology of medicine by Kostovski and **Branislav Sarkanjac** (b. 1958) (1999, 2010), the latter being a professor of political philosophy whose major thesis will be discussed in more detail in the next section, and sociology of sport (Kepeska 2000; Anastasovski and Stojanoska 2010; Anastasovski 2018). The above initiatives were made possible due to the institutional support of the Chair in Humanistics [mk. *Katedra za humanistika*] at the Faculty of Philosophy in Skopje, an interdisciplinary and intermediary body of the Skopje University, established in 1978 with the goal of providing specialist courses in sociology to all interested faculty (Kepeska 2003).

In 1999, a group of feminist scholars, including sociologists, initiated gender studies in Macedonia as part of the International Center for European Culture "Euro-Balkan" which moved to be a graduate program at the Faculty of Philosophy in Skopje (Kolozova 2011), where it still functions in spite of the political obstructions in the mid-2010s. In 2007, the Research Center for Gender Studies in Skopje, which was part of Euro-Balkan as an autonomous project of the Macedonian Open Society branch, started issuing *Identities: Journal for Politics, Gender and Culture*. Since its inception, *Identities* has become the major national platform for engaging with issues related to the interrelation of identities in politics and cultures, inviting a vast set of foreign authors to the discussion. As of 2011, the two initiators and editors of the journal moved it to the newly formed Institute of Social Sciences and Humanities—Skopje, alongside the book series titled Theories of Identities associated with the journal. The Institute organizes a seminar series as of 2014 in collaboration with the Rosa-Luxemburg-Stiftung, titled "School for Politics and Critique" and tackling topics such as left politics, gender, technology, and the climate emergency.

Sociological analyses are also published in other scientific journals, such as in the Institute of Macedonian Literature's *Spektar* and *Kontekst*. The first one frequently publishes sociolinguistic analyses and texts dealing with identities in literature, history, culture, and politics, while the second one engages with interdisciplinary research of culture, including political, historical, and sociological perspectives (e.g., Georgievska-Jakovleva 2015; Opačik 2019). Topics related to sociology, social anthropology, and migrations are published by *Etnolog* and *EtnoAntropoZum* (EthnoAntropoZoom); the first one was issued by the Macedonian Ethnologists' Association from 1992 to 2005, while the latter one is issued by UKIM's Institute of Ethnology and Anthropology since 2001. Most recently, the relatively new journal *Sovremena filologija* (Journal of Contemporary Philology), issued by the UKIM's Faculty of Philology in Skopje, reapproached several sociologists and sociological concepts from a literature studies' perspectives. Several other publishers and institutes publish sociological analyses such as *Makedonika* (in Macedonian) and *Ditura* (in Albanian), while sociologists are frequently publishing in more popular outlets, such as *Puls* in the 90s and, most recently, the weekly *Fokus* (in Macedonian) and the monthly *Shenja* (in Albanian).

The most recent reports suggest that in the period from 1975 to 2020, a total number of 1304 students graduated in sociology from the Institute of Sociology in Skopje (Minoski 2020, 304). In 2011, the ISPPI and the Institute of Sociology joined forces to launch the doctoral program in sociology. This novelty, alongside the introduction of the European Credit Transfer System (ECTS) in the Macedonian educational system in 2017, not only restructured the sociological study program at the Skopje University but also shifted its focus toward European Union studies, which are now offered as one of the two specializations at a postgraduate level. Up until 2020, 229 students defended their MA degrees in Sociology and European Integration Studies, both offered by the Institute of Sociology, while 66 students obtained doctoral degrees in the above-mentioned program (Minoski 2020, 307). However, higher-level socio-logical education in Macedonia faces a set of older and newer challenges. The recurring set of challenges pertains to the lack of funding and work placements for sociology graduates. A series of studies of social scientific research and education in Macedonia from the late 2000s to the mid-2010s suggest that higher education politics in Macedonia shifted from being too centralized, with a strong emphasis on technical and technological disciplines in the 2000s, to reducing the total social scientific budget in the 2010s (Center for Research and Policy Making 2008; Milčin et al. 2013; Cekik et al. 2015). One of the most discussed recent issues is related to the integration of the ECTS system in Macedonian higher education and its reception by the students and the instructors (e.g., Pajaziti 2012; Aceski 2016).

THE MULTIPLE FACETS OF A MULTICULTURAL DEMOCRACY

The multicultural prospects of the post-Yugoslav Republic of Macedonia were among the major topics of interest of the Macedonian sociologists at the turn of the 1990s, as already suggested. Their arguments were mostly expressed in a popular scientific manner, much in line with the editorial agenda of the outlets in which they were able to publish this sort of research and reasoning (e.g., Trajkovski 1992; Ružin 1992). However, it soon became evident that the new political context allowed for a novel reimagining of the social role of the sociologists. The most pressing social issue related to interethnic relations and the state's multicultural prospects hence facilitated their taking on the role of public intellectual custodians of "cultural pluralism" in the Macedonian context. In turn, this also provided a new scientific common ground for the national sociological community; in the words of Taševa, "almost all" sociologists showed an interest in the topic of cultural pluralism in the early 1990s (1998, 7). In this section, therefore, I will try to show the dominant ways of arguing about the prospects of Macedonian multiculturalism in two separate phases, delineated by the 2001 armed conflict. During the first phase, which roughly covers the 1990s against the backdrop of the Yugoslav Wars, the major debate pertained to the questions of institutional isomorphism, that is, the need for and the extent of importing multicultural policies from other, mostly Western and liberal-democratic contexts. The second phase resonates with the conflict and its aftermath, epitomized in the "Skopje 2014." Both the conflict and the ethnocentric politics triggered a new set of reactions from many centers, based on different research ideas and goals.

The very first international conference of Skopje's Institute of Sociology was, suggestively enough, on the topic of "Cultural pluralism and societal integration." It was co-organized with the Association of Sociologists and hosted a number of foreign scholars in Ohrid in October 1994 (Korubin 1995a). A selection of the conference presentations was published in the new journal *Sociological Review* [mk. *Sociološka revija*] in its first issue in 1995; the journal was (and still is) published by the Association and its first editor was Jovan Korubin.[9] The first edition of the *Review* thus best illustrates the two different theoretical approaches to the subject matter. Korubin and Mladenovski, among other sociologists, grasped the event as a chance to self-reflect about the role of cultural identities and intellectuals in conflict. They both argued in favor of revalorization of one's own culture in identifying the bonding and disbonding features in a multicultural context (Mladenovski 1995; Korubin 1995b). Korubin proceeded along these lines in his major intellectual project of the 1990s pertaining to the normative potentials and scopes of the public intellectual exchanges (1999). The second pattern was trailed by Ferid Muhiḱ, now standing as the most popular Macedonian philosopher, who aimed at articulating an idiosyncratic Macedonian model of cultural pluralism defined by its tradi-

---

[9] The journal was initiated by the IS associates of the Macedonian Association of Sociologists, while the Faculty of Philosophy in Skopje has participated in the publication of the journal since 2007. As of 2011, the editorial board has undertaken several steps in making the journal more international, such as inviting foreign scholars to the editorial board, publishing articles in English, and opening up for foreign submissions (Trajkovski 2020).

tional set of mechanisms for pacifying conflicts, which can be only disturbed by the external legislative and ideological implants (Muhić 1995).

The somewhat common feature of this early debate about the vaguely defined prospects of the interethnic relations in the state resonates with what Marinov observes as the "multisemantics" of discursive multiculturalism (Marinov 2006, 38). The sociologists were attempting to be as precise as possible by invoking different scholarly traditions and multicultural policy experiences. This active quest for transfers of knowledge and good practices to the local context was also trialed by a group of psychologists at the Skopje University, led by **Olga Murdževa-Škarik** (b. 1944), who, equipped with foreign support, launched the Peace Laboratory [mk. *Laboratorija za mir*] at the Faculty of Philosophy in 1991. The Laboratory, which was renamed as the Balkan Peace Studies Center [mk. *Balkanski centar za mir*] in 1993, called for interdisciplinary research on the nonviolent conflict resolution and allowed for structured cooperation of psychologists and sociologists, among others (e.g., Mladenovski et al. 1999; for context, see Murdževa-Škarik 1994). The circle around the Center was also pivotal in relaunching the cooperation between local Macedonian and Albanian scholars in post-2001 Macedonia. A different, rather ethnocentric thinking pattern about the past and the present interethnic relations was noted as dominant, with rare exceptions, among academic Macedonian and Albanian historians during the 1990s (Dimova 2011; Miodyński 2022; Todorov in Trajanovski and Georgieva 2023).

Over the years, the second approach related to the "Macedonian model of multiculturalism" became conceptually more attractive against the background of the rising global resentment toward this term in the 1990s (for an overview of the global debate, see Balint and Lenard 2022). It eventually found its most ambitious local variation in an artistic/civil society project titled "Komşi_kapicik" from late 1990s Macedonia that was co-coordinated by Branislav Sarkanjac, another philosophy professor at the Skopje University. The project title referred to the Ottoman Turkish phrase for a small garden door connecting two neighboring estates in spite of the households' religious denominations or ethnic identities. Drawing upon this case, its authors argued against the uncritical receipt of foreign multicultural models, juxtaposing them with this and other past projections of local traditions of tolerance and histories of everyday peaceful coexistence (Sarkanjac 2000). Sarkanjac emerged as its main public proponent, consolidating it in a monograph published in 2001: here, drawing upon postcolonial theory and deconstruction, he called for a discursive and interpretative sovereignty over issues pertaining to identity, history-writing, and political design. The book became a national bestseller, by far surpassing the previous social scientific works (it had a third edition by 2009, in Sarkanjac 2009), and ended up shaping the political discourse as of the mid-2000s (discussed below).

The question of conceptual impositions sidelined the other challenges of Macedonian political and social multiculturalism, a danger which was even hinted at during the above project's final debate by a sociologist, Trajkovski, and a social anthropologist, **Goran Janev** (b. 1969) (Sarkanjac 2000, 105–147). It is worth noting, here, that the major sociological projects of the 1990s provided empirical evidence for some of the most pressing of those challenges. Aceski and **Naum Matilov**, for instance, went on to analyze the urban development of Skopje and concluded that the notion of "cultural pluralism" is virtually non-existent on a micro-scale (Aceski and Matilov 1997; Matilov 1994; Aceski 1996a, b).[10] A group of ISPPI associates researched the ethnic distance and the political culture in Macedonia, uncovering that there is no clear understanding and acceptance of the political system after a decade of its change (Malevska 1998; Simoska et al. 2001). Its recalibrated rural sociology agenda, led by the senior associate and a then-director **Jorde Jaḱimovski** (b. 1950), hinted at the "ethnocentrism" in values and behaviors among the two largest ethnic communities in the state (e.g., Jaḱimovski et al. 1995; Bubevski 1998).

Marija Taševa and her team at the Institute of Sociology also embarked on a large research project about the historical background and the contemporary state of interethnic relations in Macedonia. The historical account provided a new key for rereading the previously published literature on the interethnic relations in Macedonia—from Cvijić to Miljovska, Zografski, and Trifunoski—drawing upon the theories of group interaction and acculturation and what Taševa depicted as a "structural-dynamic" approach (Taševa 1997, 16–17). The analysis of the present-day situation was based on two surveys—of more than 570 respondents in Skopje in 1995 and more than 1100 from all around the state in 1997—and led her to argue that the interethnic gap in Macedonia predominantly resonates with the different religious identities (Taševa 1998). In response, the

---

[10] Aceski even used, for the first time in the Macedonian scholarship, the findings of the Skopje social survey from the mid-1960s in his overview of late socialist and early post-socialist urban development (Trajanovski 2021a).

Institute launched two projects about helping Albanian high school students to enroll in university programs (1997) and another one pertaining to the ethnic distance of the youth population in Macedonia (as of 1999). The undertone of the two projects, which were led by **Zoran Matevski** (b. 1957), **Antoanela Petkovska** (b. 1958), and **Konstantin Minoski** (b. 1964), was the ethnic distance.

The year 2001 was a juncture regarding the sociologically informed expert discourses about Macedonian multicultural prospects. As demonstrated by several sociological studies, the violent escalation worsened the perceptions and the quality of interethnic relations in the state (e.g., Georgievski 2006; Ringdal et al. 2007). This was also apparent for the younger generation of sociologists, such as Šarlamanov and **Aleksandar Jovanoski** (b. 1978), who came to similar conclusions applying the theories of symbolic interactionism and affective social distance and deriving their data from independently organized surveys (Šarlamanov and Jovanoski 2012, 2013). On the one hand, the ORD now shifted the debate toward the eventual pitfalls of the model of accommodating ethnic and religious diversities. The Open Society Foundation debate and its subsequent publication issued in 2005 best reflects the above point: it gathered a set of domestic scientific authorities to discuss the different aspects of the Macedonian multicultural model, now more carefully presented as a "model in making" (Dodovski 2005). On the other hand, contrary to the 1990s attempts at hypostatizing the local histories of tolerance, the critical discourse was now primarily focused on the contemporary tools for reaching political consensus.

The novel debate involved two camps, that is, one which saw the ORD, along with its downsides, as an opportunity for the state and another which rejected the ORD as an infringement of the liberal and civic state fundaments (for an overview of the second camp, see Vasilev 2013). The first camp, again, predominantly consisted of sociologists. For instance, **Petar Atanasov** (b. 1962), a political sociologist associated with the ISPPI, building upon his comparative take on the theories and practices of the global multicultural policies and the history of peace settlements related to the Yugoslav Wars, argued that the ORD-stipulated set of legal provisions allow for an advancement of democracy in an ethnically divided society (e.g., Atanasov 2003). A similar affirmative yet cautious approach to the ORD was taken by Ali Pajaziti, a sociology professor associated with the SEEU who emerged as the most prolific sociologist as of the 2000s, publishing approximately 15 monographs on the sociology of religion, political sociology, and public sociology in Albanian, Turkish, Macedonian, and English. He highlighted the inclusive model of human rights provided by the ORD in lieu of the "bluffing philosophy of coexistence" (Pajaziti in Dodovski 2005, 49) and backed his argument with different types of fieldwork in the state (e.g., Pajaziti 2013, 2020).

The announcement of the "Skopje 2014 project" in the late 2000s triggered another set of reactions from both domestic and foreign observers. The very first attempts to initiate a critical debate, such as those by the publisher "Templum" in the late 2000s, were met with a political rebuttal deeming the project a result of a popular demand antithetical to the elitist approaches to the city. In this very context, the first sociological reactions to the project forewarned about its fragmenting of the Macedonian society along ethnic and religious lines and aggravating the state's international image (e.g., Janev 2011; Pajaziti 2012). The critical discourses shifted to the project's more latent functions in time, for instance its mobilizing potentials, identity-related issues, and intrusion in the urban landscape (a detailed overview in Trajanovski 2020). The Institute for Social Sciences and Humanities came up with one of the first publicly available research surveys of citizens' opinions on the project in 2013, which revealed that they were rather unfavorable toward the historical narratives it promoted (Lechevska in Trajanovski 2020, 160). The Institute was scapegoated by the authorities after the publication of the findings and other such surveys were hence discouraged. The situation changed after the 2013 local elections, eventually leading to the publication of institutional evidence about the project. After the governmental change in 2017, a joint body of governmental and non-governmental actors depicted it not only as an "illustration" but also as "a product and an embodiment of the very concept of captured state" (in Trajanovski 2020, 163).

The most recent debate about the multicultural prospects of North Macedonia involves the two recent bilateral agreements as new pivotal references. Both the accords, as already suggested, were created in the name of unlocking the state's NATO and EU prospects, while, besides good neighborly relations, they also projected bilateral expert commissions on a parity basis that are to revisit issues related to problematic portrayals and enmity in history textbooks. The situation changed in 2020, when Bulgaria escalated the bilateral relations with North Macedonia over history- and memory-related issues resulting in several subsequent vetoes of the latter's kick-off of the accession negotiations with the EU. This, in turn, shifted the dominant public discourse over the bilateral reconciliation in North Macedonia: now the alleged concessions related to Macedonian history and identity which the SDSM government was ready to make for the sake of its EU membership were by and large depicted as coercive, stemming from an asymmetric and unfair pressure on the state. The reactions allowed for a re-securitization of the past and an emergence of a discourse that blends the above agreements, plus the ORD, into a singular narrative against foreign impositions. In a chapter I co-authored (to be published in 2024), we depicted the above restructuring of the public discourse in North Macedonia as a model case of intellectual responses in situations when they perceive their states to have inadequately responded to security threats posed to their titular nation's identity narrative. In those very situations, they rally around the lines of defense through "societal security seeking" or securitizing this narrative's foundational history-, memory-, and identity-related aspects (Trajanovski and Nikolovski 2024). The sociology instructors at the UKIM, for instance, albeit not being the most publicly visible protagonists of the above discursive front, participated in and organized several such academic initiatives in the course of recent years.

REFERENCES

Aceski, Ilija. 1996a. *Skopje – sociološka studija*. Skopje: Ekopress.
———. 1996b. *Skopje: Vizija i realnost*. Skopje: Filozofski fakultet.
———. 2016. *Univerzitetot na raspaḱe*. Skopje: Filozofski fakultet.
Aceski, Ilija, and Naum Matilov. 1997. *Razvojot na urbanite centri vo Republika Makedonija*. Skopje: ISPPI.
Ajrulai, Aiše, et al. 2020. *Realizacija na nastavata po graǵansko obrazovanie vo srednite učilišta: Izveštaj od sprovedenoto istražuvanje*. Skopje: Makedonski centar za graǵansko obrazovanie.
Anastasovski, Ivan. 2018. *Sociologija na fizičkoto obrazovanie i sportot*. Skopje: Fakultet za fizičko obrazovanie.
Anastasovski, Ivan, and Tatjana Stojanoska. 2010. *Nasilstvo, agresija i sport*. Skopje: Fakultet za fizička kultura.
Atanasov, Petar. 2003. *Multikutlturalizmot kako teoria, politika i praktika*. Skopje: Evro-Balkan.
Bacevic, Jana. 2014. *From Class to Identity: The Politics of Education Reform in Former Yugoslavia*. Budapest and New York: Central European University Press.
Balint, Peter, and Patti Tamara Lenard. 2022. *Debating Multiculturalism: Should There Be Minority Rights?* Oxford and New York: Oxford University Press.

Bieber, Florian. 2008. *Power-Sharing and the Implementation of the Ohrid Framework Agreement.* In *Power-Sharing and the Implementation of the Ohrid Framework Agreement*, ed. Stefan Dehnert and Rizvan Sulejmani, 7–40. Skopje: Friedrich-Ebert-Stiftung.

Brunnbauer, Ulf. 2004. Fertility, Families and Ethnic Conflict: Macedonians and Albanians in the Republic of Macedonia, 1944–2002. *Nationalism Papers* 32 (3): 565–598.

Bubevski, Dušan. 1998. *Strategija, politika i upravuvanje so razvojot na ruralnite sredini vo Republika Makedonija.* Skopje: ISPPI.

Cekik, Aneta, Klime Babunski, and Vesna Zabijakin-Chatleska. 2015. Report on the Evaluation of Research and Legal Conditions for the Establishment of a Social Science Data Archive in Macedonia. *South-Eastern European Data Services,* December 18.

Center for Research and Policy Making. 2008. *The Assessment of Research Capacities in Social Sciences in Macedonia.* Skopje: Center for Research and Policy Making.

Damjanovski, Ivan. 2021. Old Communities, New Controversies: The Community of Macedonian Speaking Muslims Between Ethnicity and Religion. *Politička misla* 19 (62): 23–46.

Daskalovski, Zhidas. 1999. Democratisation in Macedonia and Slovenia. *Journal for Labour and Social Affairs in Eastern Europe* 2 (3): 17–44.

Devic, Ana. 1997. Anti-War Initiatives and the Un-Making of Civic Identities in the Former Yugoslav Republics. *Journal of Historical Sociology* 10 (2): 127–156.

———. 1998. Ethnonationalism, Politics, and the Intellectuals: The Case of Yugoslavia. *International Journal of Politics, Culture, and Society* 11 (3): 375–409.

Dimova, Nevena. 2008. Identity of the Nation(s), Identity of the State: Politics and Ethnicity in the Republic of Macedonia, 1990–2000. *Ethnologia Balkanica* 12: 183–213.

———. 2011. Macedonian and Albanian Intellectuals and the National Idea(s) in Socialist Macedonia. *History of Communism in Europe* 2 (1): 227–255.

Dodovski, Ivan, ed. 2005. *Multikulturalizmot vo Makedonija: Model vo nastanuvanje.* Skopje: Fondacija Institut otvoreno opštestvo – Makedonija.

Fotev, Georgi, and Jorde Jakimovski. 1998. *Social Stratification in Bulgaria and the Republic of Macedonia.* Sofia and Skopje: Friedrich-Ebert-Stiftung.

Georgievska-Jakovleva, Loreta. 2015. Monumentalnost i identitet: Makedonskite kulturni politiki (2006–2016). *Kontekst* 15 (1): 7–30.

Georgievski, Petre. 2006. Etnička distanca u Makedoniji. In *Kulturni i etnički odnosi na Balkanu – Mogućnosti regionalne i evropske integracije*, ed. Ljubiša Mitrović, Dragoljub B. Đorđević, and Dragan Todorović, 177–197. Niš: Filozofski fakultet – Univerzitet u Nišu.

———. 2012. *Sociologijata kako kritika na opštestvenata, obrazovnata i kulturnata promena.* Skopje: Matica makedonska.

Georgievski, Petar, ed. 2011. *Sociologija i opštestvenite promeni: 30 godini studii po sociologija na Filozofskiot fakultet vo Skopje*. Skopje: Filozofski fakultet.

Ǵurovska, Mileva. 2007. Meǵunaroden seminar: Proširenata Evropa i nejzinite predizvici, so akcent vrz Zapadniot Balkan, Ohrid, 22-23 mart 2006 godina. *Sociološka revija* 15 (1–2): 140–144.

Hristova, Lidija. 2011. *Političkite identiteti vo Republika Makedonija*. Skopje: ISPPI.

Hudson, Kate. 2003. *Breaking the South Slav Dream: The Rise and Fall of Yugoslavia*. London: Pluto Press.

Indževska, Slavica, and Emilija Simoska. 2012. *Političkata kultura i identitetite*. Skopje: Fondacija Otvoreno opštestvo – Makedonija and ISPPI.

Ivanov, Ǵorǵe. 1992. Societas civilis: Novite protivrečnosti na edna stara rasprava. *Dijalog* 1: 133–144.

Jakimovski, Jorde, ed. 2003. *Socijalnata položba na naselenieto vo Republika Makedonija: Siromaštija, ekskluzija i participacija vo socijalniot život*. Skopje: ISPPI and Friedrich-Ebert-Stiftung.

Jaḱimovski, Jorde, Dušan Bubevski, and Naum Matilov. 1995. *Vlijanieto na industrijalizacijata vrz socijalnite procesi i promeni na selo vo Republika Makedonija*. Skopje: ISPPI.

Janev, Goran. 2011. What Happened to the Macedonian Salad? Ethnocracy in Macedonia. *Ethnologia Balkanica* 15: 33–44.

Jordanovska, Meri. 2014. Avtorot na sporniot učebnik po graǵansko: Vlasta sekogaš manipulira. *Prizma*, November 6.

Karanfilova-Panovska, Fani, ed. 2001. *Makedonija 1989–1999*. Skopje: Institut otvoreno opštestvo.

Kepeska, Jovanka. 2000. *Temi od sociologijata na sportot*. Skopje: UKIM.

———. 2003. 25-godišen jubilej na Katedrata za humanistički studii na Filozofskiot fakultet vo Skopje. *Godišen zbornik na Filozofskiot fakultet* 56: 501–507.

Kočan, Ismet. 1988. Rezultati najnovijeg ispitivanja javnog mnjenja u Makedoniji: Optimizam sa zadrškom. *Vecernje Novosti*, June 5.

Kolozova, Katerina. 2011. On the Status of Gender Studies in Macedonia Today. *Aspasia* 5 (1): 183–187.

Korubin, Jovan. 1995a. Kon prviot broj. *Sociološka revija* 1 (1): I–II.

———. 1995b. Tranzicijata, kulturniot pluralizam i intelektualcite. *Sociološka revija* 1 (1): 30–38.

———. 1999. *Zbogum intelektualci*. Skopje: Matica makedonska.

Kostovski, Stefan, and Branislav Sarkanjac. 1999. *Sociologija na medicinata*. Skopje: Filozofski fakultet.

Maleska, Mirjana. 1992. Makedonija 1989: Politički implikacii. *Dijalog* 1: 7–25.

———. 2001. Our Mission; Launching New Balkan Politics. *New Balkan Politics* 1.

———. 2019. North Macedonia. In *Thirty Years of Political Campaigning in Central and Eastern Europe*, ed. Otto Eibl and Miloš Gregor, 255–284. Basingstoke: Palgrave Macmillan.

Malevska, Mirjana. 1998. *Etničkiot konflikt i prilagoduvanjeto.* Skopje: Kultura.

Margina. 1994. Margina, elementi na samosvest (3). *Margina* 1 (4–5): 4–5.

Marinov, Tchavdar. 2006. Multiculturalism in the Balkans: Is It Necessary? The Use of the Term in the Context of the Balkans. *Identities: Journal for Politics, Gender, and Culture* 5 (2): 35–62.

Matilov, Naum. 1994. Promenite na semejnite odnosi vo urbanite sredini na Republika Makedonija od aspekt na strukturata na semejnite ulogi. *Dijalog* 8: 119–130.

Milčin, Vladimir. 2018. *25 godini posvetenost.* Skopje: Fondacija Otvoreno opštestvo – Makedonija.

Milčin, Vladimir, et al. 2013. *Istražuvanjata vo opštestvenite nauki vo Makedonija: Sostojbi, predizvici i preporaki za unapreduvanje na politikite.* Skopje: Fondacija Otvoreno opštestvo – Makedonija.

Milosavlevski, Slavko. 1993. *Istočna Evropa pomeǵu egalitarizmot i demokratijata.* Ljuboten: IP Ljuboten.

———. 2006. *Ambasadorski zapisi.* Ljuboten: IP Ljuboten.

Milosavlevski, Slavko, and Mirče Tomovski. 1997. *Albancite vo Republika Makedonija 1945-1995: Legislativa, politička dokumentacija, statistika.* Skopje: NIP Studentski zbor.

Minoski, Konstantin. 2020. *Institutot za sociologija. In: Filozofski fakultet 1920–2020: Eden vek visoko obrazovanie, eden vek državotvornost,* ed. Ratko Duev, 297–316. Skopje: Univerzitet "Sv. Kiril i Metodij" – Skopje.

Minoski, Konstantin, and Antoanela Petkovska. 2017. Sociology in Dialogue: Macedonian Sociology in-Between Surviving and Internalization. In *Forth ISA Council of National Association Conference.* Taipei, Taiwan: 8–11 May 2017.

Miodyński, Lech. 2022. Amnezja zaprojektowana. Albański kompleks, etnogenetyczny we współczesnej ocenie macedońskiego środowiska intelektualnego. *Kultura Słowian* 18: 39–52.

Mirčev, Dimitar. 1991. *Dramata na pluralizacijata: Politologija na krizata i sistemskite promeni.* Skopje: Komunist.

———. 2000. Zošto Evropa, zošto Evropski studii? *Godišen zbornik na Filozofskiot fakultet* 53: 193–204.

———. 2014. *Fermentacija na demokratijata i na nacijata: Site makedonski politički proleti 1943-1993.* Skopje: Silons.

Mitrevski, George. 2019. Publishing in Macedonia. In *Publishing in Yugoslavia's Successor States,* 187–210. New York and London: Routledge.

Mladenovski, Ǵorǵe. 1995. Kulturniot pluralizam i opštestvenata integracija. *Sociološka revija* 1 (1): 1–21.

Mladenovski, Ǵorǵe, et al. 1999. *Teorii na nenasilstvoto*. Skopje: Balkanski centar za mir.

Muhiḱ, Ferid. 1995. Kulturnata integracija i socijalniot pluralizam: Makedonskiot model. *Sociološka revija* 1 (1): 22–29.

Murdževa-Škariḱ, Olga. 1994. Akademsko proučuvanje na mirot. *Godišen zbornik na Filozofskiot fakultet* 47: 243–253.

Neofotistos, Vasiliki P. 2004. Beyond Stereotypes: Violence and the Porousness of Ethnic Boundaries in the Republic of Macedonia. *History and Anthropology* 15 (1): 1–36.

Opačiḱ, Ana. 2019. Kratka istorija na tri različni karnevali i nivnata sociološka funkcija. *Kontekst* 20 (1): 101–114.

Pajaziti, Ali. 2012. *Culturological Studies: Education, Politics, Identity*. Skopje: Dauti Foundation and Institute for Political and International Studies.

———. 2013. *Socio-Political Insights: Towards Debalkanization*. Saarbrücken: LAP Lambert Academic Publishing.

———. 2020. *Sociologika*. Skopje: Fokus Print.

Pichler, Robert, Hannes Grandits, and Ruža Fotiadis. 2021. Kosovo in the 1980s – Yugoslav Perspectives and Interpretations. *Comparative Southeast European Studies* 69 (2–3): 171–182.

Ringdal, Kristen, Albert Simkus, and Ola Listhaug. 2007. Disaggregating Public Opinion on the Ethnic Conflict in Macedonia. *International Journal of Sociology* 37 (3): 75–95.

Ružin, Nano. 1992. Soživot, kohabitacija, koegzistencija…? *Dijalog* 2: 131–138.

Sarkanjac, Branislav ed. 2000. *Komşi_kapicik: Kultura i politika (Umetnosta i deficitot na setilnosta)*. Skopje: 359° books.

———. 2009. *Po svoe: Makedonski katahrezis ili kako da se zboruva za Makedonija*. Skopje: Makavej.

Sarkanjac, Branislav, and Stefan Kostovski. 2010. *Sociologija na zdravjeto i bolesta*. Skopje: Filozofski fakultet.

Šarlamanov, Kire, and Aleksandar Jovanoski. 2012. The Multiculturalism in Republic of Macedonia, Observed Through the Perceptions for the Other Ethnic Groups: Framework of the Symbolic Interactionism. *International Journal of Humanities and Social Science* 2 (3): 64–70.

———. 2013. The Ethnic Relations in the Macedonian Society Measured Through the Concept of Affective Social Distance. *American International Journal of Social Science* 2 (3): 33–39.

Saveski, Zoran. 1987. Oportunizam – idealan saveznik. *Komunist*, November 2.

Simoska, Emilija. 1992. Političkata mitologija kako instrument na političkata socijalizacija. *Dijalog* 1: 87–93.

Simoska, Emilija, Nataša Gaber, and Klime Babunski. 2001. *Političkata kultura na graǵanite vo Republika Makedonija*. Skopje: ISPPI.

Sociološka revija. 1995. Informator. *Sociološka revija* 1 (1): 244–248.
Spaskovska, Ljubica. 2012. The Fractured 'We' and the Ethno-National 'I': the Macedonian Citizenship Framework. *Citizenship Studies* 16 (3–4): 383–396.
———. 2017. *The last Yugoslav generation: The rethinking of youth politics and cultures in late socialism.* Manchester: Manchester University Press.
Stokes, Gale. 1993. *The Walls Came Tumbling Down: The Collapse of Communism in Eastern Europe.* Oxford and New York: Oxford University Press.
Stubbs, Paul. 2013. Flex Actors and Philanthropy in (Post-)Conflict Arenas: Soros' Open Society Foundations in the Post-Yugoslav Space. *Croatian Political Science Review* 50 (5): 114–138.
Taševa, Marija. 1997. *Etničkite grupi vo Makedonija: Istoriski kontekst.* Skopje: Filozofski fakultet.
———. 1998. *Etničkite grupi vo Makedonija: Sovremeni sostojbi.* Skopje: Filozofski fakultet.
Trajanovski, Naum. 2020. "Skopje 2014" Reappraised: Debating a Memory Project in North Macedonia. In *Europeanisation and Memory Politics in the Western Balkans*, ed. Ana Milošević and Tamara Trošt, 151–176. Basingstoke: Palgrave Macmillan.
———. 2021a. *Zbor imaat graǵanite: The First Sociological Study, the Polish Sociological Expert Aid to Macedonia in the Mid-1960s and the Post-Earthquake History of Interethnic Relations in Skopje.* Colloquia Humanistica 9: 1–42.
———. 2022. *Remembering the 2001 Armed Conflict in Macedonia: Modes of Commemoration and Memorialization.* Belgrade: Humanitarian Law Center.
Trajanovski, Naum, and Lidija Georgieva. 2023. *Conflicting Remembrance: The Memory of the Macedonian 2001 in Context.* Skopje: Friedrich-Ebert-Stiftung.
Trajanovski, Naum, and Ivan Nikolovski. 2024. Making the Nation's Red Lines: The Role of Macedonian Intellectuals in Bulgaria-North Macedonia Dispute over History, Memory, and Identity. In *Disinformation in Memory Politics*, ed. Florin Abraham and Bartosz Dziewanowski-Stefańczyk. New York and London: Routledge.
Trajkovski, Ilo. 1991. Od krizološka kon postmoderna sociologija na krizata na "real-socijalizmot". *Godišen zbornik na Filozofskiot fakultet* 43–44: 179–191.
———. 1992. Teorii za etnopolitičkata mobilizacija. *Dijalog* 2: 95–110.
———. 1997. *Graǵansko sodružništvo: Metasociološka rekonstrukcija na makedonskoto priemanje na sovremeniot poim za societas civilis.* Skopje: Gocmar.
———. 2003. The Place and the Role of Civic Education in the Republic of Macedonia. *Journal of Social Science* 2.
———. 2020. Sociološka revija. In *Filozofski fakultet 1920-2020: Eden vek visoko obrazovanie, eden vek državotvornost*, ed. Ratko Duev, 201–203. Skopje: Univerzitet "Sv. Kiril i Metodij" – Skopje.
Vasilev, George. 2013. Multiculturalism in Post-Ohrid Macedonia: Some Philosophical Reflections. *East European Politics and Societies* 27 (4): 685–708.

Woodward, Susan L. 1995. *Socialist Unemployment: The Political Economy of Yugoslavia 1945–1990*. Princeton: Princeton University Press.

Yacoub, Joseph. 1993. Nations, Minorities, Communities and States. *Balkan Forum: An International Journal of Politics, Economics and Culture* 1 (5): 87–121.

CHAPTER 6

Conclusion

Abstract This chapter concludes the study by providing a summary of the historical account. It restates the major developments in the three periods of time, delineated by the different political settings, shifting national borders and frontiers, and questions pertaining to the recognition of the Macedonian state and nation. Despite clear political divisions, the study has shown that the flow of ideas, research topics, and methodologies in the context of Macedonia was porous, oftentimes transcending the ideological regime changes. The chapter ends with a very brief overview of the future of Macedonian sociology.

Keywords North Macedonia • Sociology • History of sociology • Macedonian sociology

The study covers the development of Macedonian sociology in three different political contexts, that is, prior to the establishment of the Macedonian state, after its formation as a federal unit of the state socialist Second Yugoslavia, and after the dissolution of Yugoslavia and the proclamation of the independent Republic of Macedonia. Against this background, I argued that the different political constellations shaped local social scientific developments, including sociology, associated with the territory of today's Republic of North Macedonia: they all set the coordinates of the research topics, means and logistics, and objectives. In brief,

© The Author(s), under exclusive license to Springer Nature Switzerland AG 2024
N. Trajanovski, *A History of Macedonian Sociology*, Sociology Transformed, https://doi.org/10.1007/978-3-031-48869-6_6

the first period was presented in light of the Serbianization agenda in Macedonia, while the major debate during this period was noted to be the one about the nuances of the ethnic belonging of the local Slavic population. After the war, the history of national sociology during state socialism unfolded in three subphases. During the early post-war period, with sociology forbidden in its pre-war form, the leading Marxist intellectuals instrumentalized the historical materialism to legitimize the existence of a Macedonian state and nation, thus providing for a somewhat atypical national sociological origination under state socialism. As of the 1960s and the series of social and political openings, sociology gained momentum as a chief critical enterprise, sliding toward a less privileged position in the early 1970s and the change of the political leadership in socialist Macedonia. Finally, the inauguration of the independent Republic of Macedonia, as well as the market reforms and the democratic transition, allowed for a new set of debates and activities pertaining to the role of sociology and sociological knowledge in the new, post-socialist era.

This historical account was used to map the ramified extensions in all the periods, tracing a set of continuities and discontinuities along the way. The first period hence contains several cases of intellectual opposition to the dominant state project, which, drawing upon alternative, for the immediate context, theories (e.g., collective action) and methodologies (e.g., functionalism), aimed at showcasing a different perspective of the local population, its everyday life, and sociopolitical goals. This period is also suggestive for the articulation of the first arguments pertaining to what would appear to be the dominant themes of the Macedonian sociology, that is, agrarian sociology, family structures, and interethnic contacts. The two post-war decades saw a reconfigured set of takes on those very topics, which were now adjusted to the new political project of the Macedonian state. What prevailed, moreover, was the dominant data gathering method of the interwar period, whose results were now read in a different national and ideological key. On the other hand, the early articulations of local agency, based, for instance, on the late Ottoman economic reforms, were sidelined as unfit since the new ideological architects sought to present this period in a more negative light, thus aiming to cement the argument about the arrested development of the national society at the turn of the nineteenth century. This line of thought was put forward as the answer to the pivotal Marxist question about the legitimacy of the state-building of a non-historical nation. Against this major intellectual struggle, the somewhat alternate projects in this period evolved from more critical ethnographies to explorations of Marxist-humanist links in the later period.

The 1960s brought a fresh understanding of the sociological potentials in the national context of socialist Macedonia, against the backdrop of the corresponding developmental patterns in and beyond Yugoslavia. Interestingly enough, the topics of the extended Balkan family of zadruga and the feudal system of chifliks in Macedonia reemerged as a major set of findings in spite of the initial research expectations put on the modernization, urbanization, and industrialization processes. In this very context, I argued that this and the other coterminous debates about the so-called ethnogenesis of the Macedonian nation provided the necessary scientific leverage for sociology in the national context. Those newly unlocked sociological potentials were short-lived, however, as they failed to break through the political changes of the 1970s. Although the sociological capital of the 1960s was enough to push for a completion of the sociological institutions as in the larger Yugoslav centers, such as a specialized journal and a graduate program in sociology, the Macedonian sociologists lost the scientific and disciplinary leverage of the 1960s. The sociological circle at the Faculty of Law was dissolved, for instance, while the ISPPI's work was far less critical throughout late socialism. Sociology was now expected to take less ambitious, even apologetic forms. Thereby, two particular patterns occurred in this period. A large portion of the Marxist instructors and academics, including the Macedonian sociologists, adapted to the new era by readjusting their positions. This was predominantly, even though not exclusively, the case with the first post-war generation. The erstwhile younger generation of sociologists (again, not exclusively) sought to find other outlets for articulating less dogmatic positions, which I argued to be the most exciting episode during this time period, spanning from cross-national networking on sociological premises to pioneering steps in publishing periodicals.

The 1980s ultimately made the active sociologists in Macedonian academia realize the entrepreneurial requirements of their profession. They started to look for possible outposts for their research and graduates themselves, while redesigning the program in parallel to best fit the pressing societal needs. In an incredible turn of events, the major result of the above quest came in a different political context. In parallel with the Yugoslav dissolution of the early 1990s, the peaceful start of the democratic reforms in Macedonia allowed for a set of possibilities for reinvesting the sociological knowledge and contacts. This, in turn, unfolded in several, arguably enough, successful initiatives—such as the institution of the civil education set forth by academic sociologists and the inauguration of anti-war journals aimed at popularizing social scientific knowledge—which ended up reimagining the role of the national sociologists in the immediate post-socialist decade. The new positionality allowed for an articulation of a set of constructive sociological insights and data into the questions about the Macedonian multicultural prospects. As I demonstrated in the last chapter, the majority of the Macedonian sociologists appeared to be more objective and insightful regarding the challenges pertaining to the ethnic identities and the interethnic relations in the state. This appeared to be the case in several critical instances in the course of recent decades, which in turn brought a reshuffling of several discursive coalitions on the above issue in the Macedonian public.

This text was written from the highest position on the abstraction ladder, which provided a fertile ground for overviewing patterns, developments, and shifts of the major concepts, actors, and institutions, but certainly left aside many and different interesting aspects of the history of Macedonian sociology. They might span from better approaches to micro-histories and biographical experiences of different sorts, to transnational exchanges and borrowings in different time periods. The grounded foci on a particular territory and the intellectual milieu which moved forward the idea about national particularity sidelined many other sociological themes, as noted in the introductory section, as well as the sociological production and activities of sociologists from North Macedonia active beyond the state borders. In times of a generation change of the academic sociology instructors—predominantly, but not exclusively, in Skopje—questions concerning the sociological profile for the new era are expected to reemerge in the short-term future of Macedonian sociology. Hence, it would be interesting to see how the new steering generations of sociologists in North Macedonia will tackle some of the more pressing (and inherited) issues, such as the state educational reforms needed yesterday rather than today, but also some of the emerging ones, such as the integration of Macedonian sociology in the dominant regional and international research networks. For such a small national sociological community, limited in cadres and funding, the only way out seems to lie in a constant improvement of the communication and collaboration between all the relevant state and non-state actors and organizations at home.

A Chronology of Major Events (Twentieth–Twenty-First Century)

Before the Second World War and the formation of the Macedonian state

Year	Society	Sociology
1903	Ilinden Uprising	Misirkov publishes *Za makedonckite raboti* (On the Macedonian matters) in Sofia
1906		Cvijić publishes *Posmatranja o etnografiji makedonskih Slovena* (Remarks on the Ethnography of the Macedonian Slavs) in Belgrade
1912–1913	First Balkan War, almost all Ottoman Empire's European territories overrun and partitioned	
1913	Second Balkan War, the territory of Macedonia divided into three	
1914	Start of the First World War with the Sarajevo assassination	
1918	End of First World Far; formation of the Kingdom of SHS	Cvijić publishes *La Péninsule Balkanique: Geographie Humaine*; Đordević publishes *Macedonia*
1920		Inauguration of the Faculty of Philosophy in Skopje as a branch of the Belgrade University

(continued)

© The Author(s), under exclusive license to Springer Nature Switzerland AG 2024
N. Trajanovski, *A History of Macedonian Sociology*, Sociology Transformed, https://doi.org/10.1007/978-3-031-48869-6

(continued)

Year	Society	Sociology
1921	Alexander I succeeds King Peter I; ban of the Communist Party	Inauguration of the Skopje Scientific Society
1923		Inauguration of the Macedonian Institute in Sofia
1924		Novaković publishes *Makedonija Makedoncima! Zemlja zemljoradnicima!* (Macedonia to the Macedonians, Land to the Peasants) in Čačak
1925		First issue of the *Annual* of the Skopje Scientific Society; Erdeljanović publishes *Makedonski Srbi* (Macedonian Serbs) in Belgrade
1928	Opposition withdraws from the Yugoslav parliament	Krušković publishes *Probleme sociologije* (Sociological Problems) in Skopje
1929	King Alexander I introduces the 6 January Dictatorship: Kingdom of SHS changed to Kingdom of Yugoslavia, South Serbia becomes Vardar Banovina	Nedeljković publishes *O psihičkom tipu Južnosrbijanaca* (*On the Psychic Type of the South Serbs*); inauguration of the Geographical-Ethnographical Student Society "Jovan Cvijić" in Skopje
1930		Slankamenac publishes *Pedagogika na univerzitetu* (University Pedagogics) and launches the sociology seminar in Skopje
1932		Obrębski arrives in Upper Poreče
1934	Assassination of King Alexander I in a Macedonian-Croat conspiracy	Ivanovski publishes *Zošto nie Makedoncite sme oddelna nacija* (Why We the Macedonians are a Separate Nation)
1935		First issue of *Makedonski vesti* in Sofia
1936		Arsov defends his doctoral thesis at the Sorbonne; last issue of *Makedonski vesti*
1937		First issue of *Luč* in Skopje; Erlich starts her survey about the changes of family life in Yugoslavia
1938		Last issue of *Luč*; Veselinov publishes *Natsionalno-porobeni narodi i natsionalni maltsinstva* (Nationally-Suppressed Peoples and National Minorities)
1939	Cvetković-Maček Agreement about the internal division of the Kingdom	

After the Second World War, Macedonian state as a federal unit of socialist Yugoslavia

1944 ASNOM (2 August); first issue of *Nova Makedonija* (29 October)	
1945 Codification of the Macedonian language	Nedeljković appointed a rector of the Belgrade University
1946 Start of the Greek Civil War (until 1949) Inauguration of the Skopje University; inauguration of the Faculty of Philosophy in Skopje	Taškovski appointed the first instructor of Marxism at the Faculty of Philosophy in Skopje; Trifunoski publishes several anthropogeographical studies
1948 Tito-Stalin split inauguration of the Institute of National History in Skopje	Nedeljković appointed an instructor of Marxism at the Faculty of Philosophy in Skopje; start of the research project *Aegean Macedonia in our history* (published in 1951)
1950 Inauguration of the Faculty of Economics in Skopje; inauguration of the Institute of Folklore "Marko Cepenkov"	Miljovska appointed an instructor of Marxism at the Faculty of Philosophy in Skopje
1951 Inauguration of the Faculty of Law and Economics in Skopje	
1952 KPM renamed SKM; inauguration of the Economic Institute in Skopje	Arsov appointed an instructor in international private law at the Faculty of Law and Economics in Skopje; closure of the Ethnological Group in Skopje
1953 The Yugoslav-Turkish *Gentlemen's Agreement* facilitates the emigration of approximately 140,000 Yugoslav citizens to Turkey	Bojanovski-Dize finishes his research about chifliks in Ottoman Macedonia
1954	Arsov dies in Skopje; Mićić appointed an instructor in Skopje; inauguration of the Yugoslav Sociological Association
1958 PMF separates from the Faculty of Philosophy in Skopje	A group of younger associates of the PMF (Sinadinovski, Panov) starts developing empirical sociological research ideas
1959	Inauguration of the *Kultura* book series
1961	Mićić publishes *Sovremenite građanski filozofi za marksizmot* (The Contemporary Bourgeois Philosophers about Marxism)
1962	Inauguration of the Macedonian Association of Philosophy and Sociology; Taneski and Jordanovski write some of the first sociology textbooks in Macedonian; Miljovska defends her doctoral thesis in Belgrade

(*continued*)

(continued)

1963	New Yugoslav Constitution further institutionalizing self-management and decentralization Crvenkovski assumes power in socialist Macedonia; Skopje earthquake (26 July); UN decision to support the post-earthquake urban reconstruction	Miljovska appointed a dean of the Faculty of Philosophy in Skopje
1964	KPJ Congress announces end of Yugoslavism; Milosavlevski appointed a member of SKJ's Central and Executive Committees (1966)	Start of the pilot for the Skopje social survey; the sociological circle at the Faculty of Law publishes first in the series of "sociology of the party" analyses; first issue of *Pogledi* (Viewpoints)
1965		Inauguration of the Institute for Sociological, Political, and Juridical Research in Skopje; Hristov appointed the first director of the ISPPI; completion of the Skopje social survey
1966	Ranković dethroned	Taškovski publishes *Raǵanjeto na makedonskata nacija* (The Birth of the Macedonian Nation), second edition in 1967
1967	Inauguration of the Macedonian Academy of Sciences and Arts; the Macedonian Orthodox Church proclaims autocephality	Petroska publishes her first sociological study; Zografski publishes his *Za makedonskoto prašanje* (On the Macedonian Question) Milosavlevski appointed a director of the ISPPI; the ISPPI introduces two postgraduate study programs
1968	Protest waves in Yugoslavia	Milosavlevski publishes *Revolucija i demokratija* (Revolution and Democracy)
1969		*Revolucija i demokratija* translated into Serbo-Croatian and Slovene (printed in 1970)
1971		Hristov publishes *Sozdavanjeto na makedonskata država* (The Creation of the Macedonian State) in Macedonian and Serbo-Croatian
1972	The conservative group of communists assumes power in Macedonia; Crvenkovski ousted	ISPPI launches its pilot research of the public opinion survey, its first considerations are traced back to 1969; first issue of *Dijalog* (Dialogue)
1973		Sociology Chair in Skopje; Marxist sociology offered at the Faculty of Philosophy in Skopje
1974	New federal constitution; Milosavlevski removed from the SKM and the Faculty of Law in Skopje	Josifovski publishes the Macedonian results of the all-Yugoslav rural sociology survey; Nedeljković becomes member of MANU

(*continued*)

(continued)

1975		Inauguration of the Sociology Group at the Faculty of Philosophy in Skopje; the ISPPI starts publishing an annual public opinion survey and a journal Inauguration of the Center for Social sciences in Skopje, co-coordinated by the ISPPI and the Faculty of Law
1977		The NNSG in Sociology introduces two study tracks
1978		Miljovska appointed a president of JUS
1979	Inauguration of the Bitola University	First Skopje-Kraków sociological seminar
1980	Tito dies aged 87	First cohort of sociology students graduates in Skopje; the NNSG reintroduces one study track
1983		A sociological conference in Portorož boosts Yugoslav sociology and sociologists
1984		Macedonian sociologists disjoin from the Association
1985		Special issue about the challenges of the sociological profession, published by the Faculty of Philosophy in Skopje; Faculty of Economics in Prilep starts offering sociology courses
1989	Start of the reform process in socialist Macedonia	

Independent Republic of Macedonia, North Macedonia as of 2018

1990	First democratic elections (November)	
1991	Independence referendum (September)	Trajkovski publishes his article on the new role of the sociology
1992	Peaceful withdrawal of the Yugoslav army from Macedonia; EC Arbitration Commission of the Peace Conference on Yugoslavia recommends recognition of Macedonia	Studentski zbor relaunches *Dijalog* with two issues in 1992; Milosavlevski reintroduced to the Macedonian public
1993	Macedonia becomes a member of the UN under the provisional name "the former Yugoslav Republic of Macedonia"	First issue of *Balkan Forum*; IS launches the project on the sociological aspects of the "ethnic coexistence" (1993–1998)

(*continued*)

(continued)

1994	Greek trade embargo of Macedonia	First issue of *Margina*; Albanian university opens in Tetovo amid contestations; Association of Sociologists organizes its first post-socialist gathering in Ohrid
1995		First issue of *Sociološka revija*; IS publishes a sociological dictionary
1998	First democratic change of government in Republic of Macedonia, VMRO-DPMNE forms government	Introduction of civil education as a subject in primary and secondary schools upon an earlier proposal of academic sociologists; IS publishes a handbook in sociological theory
1999		Korubin publishes *Zbogum intelektualci* (Farewell to Intellectuals)
2000	Macedonia begins the rapprochement with the European Union	Inauguration of the European studies course by the Faculty of Philosophy in Skopje
2001	Armed conflict in Macedonia, formally settled in August 2001	Inauguration of the South-East European University in Tetovo; first issues of *SEEU Review* and *New Balkan Politics*; Sarkanjac publishes *Makedonski katahresis* (Macedonian Catachresis)
2002	Parliamentary elections, SDSM forms government	Dijalog relaunched as *Evrodijalog*
2003	Inauguration of the Faculty of Social Sciences, now operating under the title American University of Europe-FON	Atanasov publishes *Multikutlturalizmot kako teoria, politika i praktika* (Multiculturalism as a theory, politics, and practice)
2005		A debate about the prospects of Macedonian multiculturalism as a "model in the making", sponsored by the national branch of the Open Society Foundation
2006	Parliamentary elections, VMRO-DPMNE forms government	
2007		First issue of *Identiteti* (Identities)
2008	Greece vetoes Macedonia's membership in NATO	
2011	"Skopje 2014 project" in full swing	First doctoral studies program in Macedonia, co-coordinated by the IS and the ISPPI
2013		The Institute for Social Sciences and Humanities - Skopje publishes the survey about "Skopje 2014"; Pajaziti publishes *Socio-Political Insights*
2014		First issue of *Philosophica*

(*continued*)

2016   Snap parliamentary elections after wiretapping scandal involving high-profile governmental officials, provoking protests

2017   SDSM forms government; signing of the treaty of friendship between Bulgaria and Macedonia

2018   Prespa Agreement with Greece; Macedonia agrees to change the name to North Macedonia

2020   North Macedonia becomes a full member of NATO; Bulgaria blocks the EU integrations over history and memory issues

2022   The Bulgarian veto is lifted, setting other sets of conditions for North Macedonia

Index[1]

[1] Note: Page numbers followed by 'n' refer to notes.

© The Author(s), under exclusive license to Springer Nature
Switzerland AG 2024
N. Trajanovski, *A History of Macedonian Sociology*, Sociology
Transformed, https://doi.org/10.1007/978-3-031-48869-6

GPSR Compliance

The European Union's (EU) General Product Safety Regulation (GPSR) is a set of rules that requires consumer products to be safe and our obligations to ensure this.

If you have any concerns about our products, you can contact us on ProductSafety@springernature.com

In case Publisher is established outside the EU, the EU authorized representative is:

Springer Nature Customer Service Center GmbH
Europaplatz 3
69115 Heidelberg, Germany

The manufacturer's authorised representative in the EU is Springer
Nature Customer Service Centre GmbH, Europaplatz 3, 69115 Heidelberg,
Germany. If you have any concerns regarding our products, please
contact ProductSafety@springernature.com

Printed and bound by CPI Group (UK) Ltd, Croydon, CR0 4YY
29/04/2026
02099471-0001